Limited Company Accounts (IAS)

Tutorial

NVQ Accounting Unit 11
AAT Diploma Pathway Unit 11

David Cox

Derek Street

osborne
BOOKS

Published by Osborne Books Limited
Unit 1B Everoak Estate
Bromyard Road
Worcester WR2 5HP
Tel 01905 748071
Email books@osbornebooks.co.uk
Website www.osbornebooks.co.uk

Cover and page design by Richard Holt

Printed by the Bath Press, Bath

British Library Cataloguing in Publication Data
A catalogue record for this book is available from the British Library

ISBN 1 872962 93 9

Contents

Acknowledgments

The authors wish to thank the following for their help with the editing and production of the book: Jean Cox, Michael Fardon, Michael Gilbert, Rosemarie Griffiths and Claire McCarthy. Particular thanks go to Roger Petheram of Worcester College of Technology and Chris Waterston of Leeds Metropolitan University for reading the text, commenting upon it, checking answers, and always being prepared to discuss any aspect of the book.

Thanks are also due to the Association of Accounting Technicians for their generous help and advice and permission to reproduce extracts from past examination questions and the Standards of Competence. Thanks also go to InBev SA and to the International Accounting Standards Board.

Authors

David Cox, the lead author of this text, is a Certified Accountant with more than twenty years' experience teaching accountancy students over a wide range of levels. Formerly with the Management and Professional Studies Department at Worcester College of Technology, he now lectures on a freelance basis and carries out educational consultancy work in accountancy studies. He is author and joint author of a number of textbooks in the areas of accounting, finance and banking.

Derek Street, who has compiled a number of the Student Activities, has had over fifteen years' experience of teaching accountancy students, including the AAT qualification at all three levels. His lecturing experience has been gained at Evesham College of FE, Gloucester College of Arts and Technology (GLOSCAT) and North East Worcestershire College.

Introduction

Limited Company Accounts (IAS) Tutorial has been written for students taking courses based on NVQ Level 4 Accounting and AAT Diploma Unit 11 'Drafting Financial Statements'.

Limited Company Accounts (IAS) Tutorial commences with the purpose of financial statements (including a study of key aspects of the *Framework for the Preparation and Presentation of Financial Statements*). It then develops the preparation and presentation of financial statements of limited companies – including the use of cash flow statements. The impact of international accounting standards on financial statements is considered in detail. The text includes the interpretation of accounts using accounting ratios, and the preparation of consolidated accounts for groups of companies.

An important development in 2002 was the issue by the European Union (EU) of a mandatory regulation requiring all EU companies listed on a regulated market (eg stock market) to prepare their consolidated accounts in accordance with international accounting standards from 1 January 2005. *Limited Company Accounts (IAS) Tutorial* studies international accounting standards (IAS) in detail as they are now required for Unit 11 and will be assessed by the Association of Accounting Technicians (AAT) from the June 2006 examination.

using the tutorial

Limited Company Accounts (IAS) Tutorial provides the student with the theoretical background to the subject while at the same time including plenty of opportunity to put theory into practice. The chapters of *Limited Company Accounts (IAS) Tutorial* contain:

- a clear text with worked examples and case studies
- a chapter summary and key terms to help with revision
- student activities – with answers at the end of the book

The tutorial text – with questions and answers – is therefore useful for classroom use and also for distance learning students.

the workbook and tutor pack

Limited Company Accounts (IAS) Workbook, the companion volume to this text, contains extended student activities and practice examination tasks. The answers to these tasks are included in a separate Tutor Pack.

If you would like a copy of any of our texts, please telephone Osborne Books Sales Office on 01905 748071 for details of how to order, or visit the Osborne online 24 hour shop on www.osbornebooks.co.uk where you can purchase the Workbook and obtain an order form for the Tutor Pack.

Web directory

There are a number of websites which will help to supplement your studies for Unit 11, *Drafting Financial Statements.*

information and accountancy news

www.accountancyage.com
- news and information service
- regular newsletter

www.accountingtechnician.co.uk
- website of AAT's magazine
- a Study Zone with articles written exclusively for the web
- question and answer Study Surgery

www.accountingweb.co.uk
- news and information
- includes a students' discussion forum

www.asb.org.uk
- the Accounting Standards Board
- gives details of UK accounting standards
- links to related sites

www.companieshouse.gov.uk
- gives information about forming and running companies
- provides details of how to obtain copies of company accounts and other statutory information

www.dti.gov.uk
- Department of Trade and Industry
- a large website with links to various sections of the Department

www.hmrc.gov.uk
- HM Revenue & Customs
- details of income taxes, corporation tax and VAT

www.iasb.org.uk
- the International Accounting Standards Board
- gives a summary of international accounting standards

www.iasplus.com
- gives details of international accounting standards
- news and information

www.opsi.gov.uk
- Office of Public Sector Information
- access to statutory instruments affecting the preparation of company accounts

accountancy associations

A selection of accountancy bodies and associations is given below, with their website addresses. As well as details of members' and students' services, they give information on assessment and examination schemes. Some sites also provide a news and information service.

www.aat.org.uk   –   The Association of Accounting Technicians

www.acca.org.uk   –   The Association of Chartered Certified Accountants

www.cimaglobal.com –   The Chartered Institute of Management Accountants

www.cipfa.org.uk   –   The Chartered Institute of Public Finance and Accountancy

www.icaew.co.uk   –   The Institute of Chartered Accountants in England and Wales

www.icas.org.uk   –   The Institute of Chartered Accountants of Scotland

firms of accountants

A selection of accountancy firms is given below. As well as advertising the firms and their services, a number of sites include technical information and notes on recent developments in accounting.

www.deloitte.com   – Deloitte

www.ey.com   – Ernst & Young

www.grant-thornton.co.uk   – Grant Thornton

www.kpmg.co.uk   – KPMG

www.pwcglobal.com   – PricewaterhouseCoopers

www.osbornebooks.co.uk – additional study material

The Osborne Books website www.osbornebooks.co.uk will be used to give information about changes and updating of the topics covered in this book.

Please note that if you have not studied the financial statements of sole traders and partnerships, or would like to revise them, explanatory material and questions may be downloaded from the Student Resources section of www.osbornebooks.co.uk

1 Purpose of financial statements

Unit 11 'Drafting Financial Statements' builds on earlier studies of financial accounting and comprises two elements:

- draft limited company financial statements
- interpret limited company financial statements

In this chapter we begin our studies by considering the

- general purpose of financial statements
- elements of financial statements
- accounting equation
- development of the regulatory framework of accounting
- Framework for the Preparation and Presentation of Financial Statements
- accounting concepts

Note

If you have not studied the financial statements of sole traders and partnerships, or would like to revise them, explanatory material and questions may be downloaded from the Student Resources section of www.osbornebooks.co.uk

PERFORMANCE CRITERIA COVERED

unit 11: DRAFTING FINANCIAL STATEMENTS

element 11.2

interpret limited company financial statements

A   identify the general purpose of financial statements used in limited companies

B   identify the elements of financial statements used in limited companies

INTRODUCTION TO *DRAFTING FINANCIAL STATEMENTS*

Unit 11, *Drafting Financial Statements,* is concerned solely with the financial statements of limited companies.The unit comprises two elements:

- Element 11.1 Draft limited company financial statements
- Element 11.2 Interpret limited company financial statements

For most students, this is the first time that you will have studied the accounts of limited companies. It is appropriate, therefore, to put limited companies in context. In previous studies you will have prepared the financial statements of sole traders and will then have moved on to the accounts of partnerships. The transition from sole trader to partnership financial statements is not too big a step with, instead of one person owning the business, two or more owners. The step from sole traders/partnerships to limited companies is rather greater as we deal with incorporated – ie formed into a corporation (company) – businesses, where the owners are members (shareholders) of the company. In addition, we have to become accustomed to new terminology: for example, fixed assets become non-current assets, stocks become inventories, debtors become receivables, and creditors become payables (there is a full list of the changed terms on page 35 in Chapter 2).

private sector organisations

Companies – together with sole traders and partnerships – are private sector (as compared with public sector organisations – such as local authorities, central government, the National Health Service – and other not-for-profit organisations – such as societies and charities). The following diagram illustrates the types of private sector organisations:

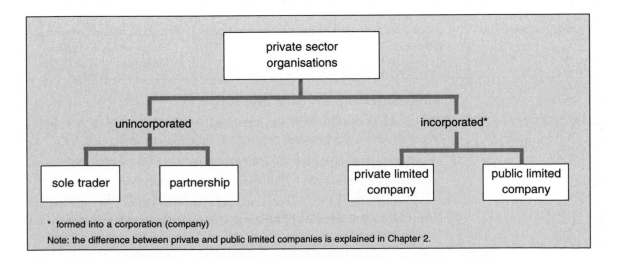

* formed into a corporation (company)

Note: the difference between private and public limited companies is explained in Chapter 2.

sole traders, partnerships and limited companies

Limited companies are more complex businesses to set up and to run. Chapter 2 explains the advantages of forming a company, the difference between private and public limited companies, and the types of shares issued. Chapter 3 covers limited company published accounts – which are available to shareholders and are filed at Companies House. The following table illustrates the key differences between sole traders, partnerships and limited companies:

	sole trader	*partnership*	*limited company*
ownership	• owned by the sole trader	• owned by the partners	• owned by the shareholders
legal status	• the sole trader is the business	• the partners are the business	• separate legal entity from its owners
members	• one	• between 2 and 20 (normal maximum)	• minimum of one shareholder; no maximum
liability	• unlimited liability, for debts of business	• partners normally liable for entire partnership debt	• shareholders can only lose their investment
legislation	• none	• Partnership Act 1890	• Companies Act 1985, 1989
regulation	• none	• written or oral partnership agreement	• Memorandum and Articles of Association
management	• owner takes all decisions	• all partners normally take an active part	• directors and authorised employees
financial statements	• private – not available to the public	• private – not available to the public	• must be filed at Companies House where available to the public

In particular, note from the table that:

- the Companies Act 1985, as amended by the Companies Act 1989, regulates the setting up and running of limited companies
- a company is a separate legal entity from its shareholder owners
- companies are managed by directors who are themselves shareholders
- companies – unlike sole traders and partnerships – must file their annual financial statements with Companies House, where they are available for public inspection

LIMITED COMPANIES

A walk or a drive around any medium-sized town will reveal evidence of a wide variety of businesses formed as limited companies – banks, shops, restaurants, hotels, bus and train operators, delivery firms. Many of their names will be well-known – HSBC Bank plc, Tesco PLC, Marks and Spencer plc, etc – and to be found in most towns and cities; others will be known only in their own area – Wyvern Wool Shop Limited, Don's DIY Limited, etc. The letters 'plc' stand for public limited company – this can be a large company whose shares might (but not always) be traded on the stock markets. The word 'limited' refers to a private limited company – often a smaller company than a plc, but whose shares are not quoted on the stock markets. In fact there are far more private limited companies than there are plcs. In Chapter 2, we will look further into the differences between the types of companies.

Virtually all limited companies can be described as being in the *private sector* where they are owned by shareholders who are looking for the company to make profits. A small number of limited companies are set up by not-for-profit organisations – such as societies and charities – to provide mutual services for their members and the community.

objectives of companies

For most limited companies the profit motive is commonly the most important objective. Profit is measured as the excess of income over expenses; sufficient profit needs to be generated each year to enable the owners (shareholders) to be paid dividends on their shares. Often there is a conflict within business between short-term profit and long-term profit: for example, a major investment in training will reduce this year's profit, but may well help to increase profit in future years. Once the profit motive has been satisfied, and particularly as a company increases in size, a range of other objectives is developed: examples include environmental issues – taking initiatives to improve the environment through becoming more energy efficient and reducing waste – and being a good employer – adding value to the output by providing better facilities and better training for the workforce.

FINANCIAL STATEMENTS AND THEIR PURPOSES

financial statements

The three main financial statements used by limited companies are:

- an **income statement** (which you will know already as a profit and loss account), to measure the financial performance of the company for a particular time period (the accounting period)
- a **balance sheet**, to provide a statement of the financial position of the company at a particular date
- a **cash flow statement**, to link profit with changes in assets and liabilities, and the effect on the cash of the company

Income statements and cash flow statements usually cover a twelve-month accounting period (but do not necessarily run to 31 December – the end of the calendar year); the balance sheet shows the financial position of the company at the end of the accounting period.

objective of financial statements

What is the objective of financial statements?

'The objective of financial statements is to provide information about the financial position, performance and changes in financial position of an entity that is useful to a wide range of users in making economic decisions'

This definition is taken from the *Framework for the Preparation and Presentation of Financial Statements* issued by the International Accounting Standards Board (see page 19).

Note the following from the definition:

- **financial position** – is reported through a balance sheet
- **financial performance** – is reported through an income statement
- **changes in financial position** – are reported through a cash flow statement
- **entity** – an organisation, such as a limited company, whose activities and resources are kept separate from those of the owner(s)
- **wide range of users** – financial statements are used by a number of interested parties (see below), from existing and potential shareholders through to lenders, employees and government agencies
- **economic decisions** – information from the financial statements is used to help in making decisions about investment or potential investment in the entity, eg to buy or sell a company's shares, to make a loan to the company, or to help in deciding whether to re-appoint or replace the management

users of financial statements

There is a wide variety of users – both internal and external – of financial statements of limited companies, as shown by the table on the next page. Study this table and then read the text that follows.

LIMITED COMPANY FINANCIAL STATEMENTS: INTERESTED PARTIES

Who is interested?	What are they interested in?	Why are they interested?
Existing and potential investors in a business	• Is the company making a profit? • Can the company pay its way? • What was the revenue (sales turnover) figure?	• To assess the performance of management • To see how much money can be paid in dividends • To see if the company will continue in the foreseeable future • To see if the company is expanding or declining
Lenders	• Has the company made a profit? • What amount is currently loaned? • What is the value of the assets?	• To check if the company will be able to pay finance costs and make loan repayments • To assess how far the lender is financing the company • To assess the value of security available to the lender
Suppliers	• Can the company pay its way? • What is the value of the assets?	• To decide whether to supply goods and services to the company • To assess if the company is able to pay its debts
Employees and trade unions	• Has the company made a profit? • Can the company pay its way?	• To assess whether the company is able to pay wages and salaries • To consider the stability of the company in offering employment opportunities in the future
Customers	• Is the company profitable? • What is the value of the assets? • Can the company pay its way?	• To see if the company will continue to supply its products or services • To assess the ability of the company to meet warranty liabilities, and provision of spare parts
Government and government agencies	• Has the company made a profit? • What was the revenue (sales turnover) figure?	• To calculate the tax due • To ensure that the company is registered for VAT and completes VAT returns on time • To provide a basis for government regulation and statistics • To see how grants provided have been spent
The public	• Is the company profitable? • Can the company pay its way?	• To assess employment prospects • To assess the contribution to the economy
Managers	• Is the company making a profit? • Can the company pay its way? • How efficiently is the company using its resources?	• To see if the company is expanding or declining • To see if the company will continue in the foreseeable future • To examine the efficiency of the company and to make comparisons with other, similar, companies

Internal users include company directors and managers, employees.

External users include existing and potential shareholders, lenders, suppliers and customers, government agencies, the public, etc.

Whilst each user is interested in a number of different aspects, as the diagram on the previous page shows, most users will assess the stewardship of the management of the company. By stewardship, we mean that the management of a company is accountable for the safe-keeping of the company's resources, and for their proper, efficient and profitable use.

contents of the financial statements

As financial statements are the principal means of communicating accounting information to users they must provide details of:

financial position

* they provide information about the economic resources used by the company
* they provide information about the liquidity, use of resources, and financial position of the company

financial performance

* they assess the stewardship of management
* they make possible an assessment of the effectiveness of the use of the company's resources in achieving its objectives, eg in profitability
* they allow comparison to be made with the financial performance from previous accounting periods

changes in financial position

* they provide information about the investing, financing and operating activities of the company
* they enable an assessment of the ability of the company to generate cash and how such cash flows will be used

ELEMENTS OF FINANCIAL STATEMENTS

Elements of financial statements are the 'building blocks' from which financial statements are constructed – that is, they are the classes of items which comprise financial statements.

The five main elements of financial statements are as follows:
* assets

- liabilities
- equity
- income
- expenses

Note that the elements are broad classes and, in practice, financial statements will include a number of sub-classifications – eg assets will be classified between non-current and current, each of which will be further detailed (see Chapters 2 and 3). The intention is that the company will give sufficient information to users to enable them to make economic decisions.

The way in which the elements link together in the financial statements of income statement and balance sheet, together with definitions, is shown in the diagrams on the next page.

importance of elements of financial statements

The importance of the elements of financial statements is that they define the items which can be included in financial statements. The elements are appropriate for the financial statements of limited companies:

- an income statement to show income and expenses for the accounting period
- a balance sheet to show assets, liabilities and equity at a particular date
- a cash flow statement reflects income statement elements and changes in balance sheet elements

Study the diagrams on the next page in conjunction with the note below.

---

tutorial note

Pay particular attention to the definitions of the five elements, together with profits or losses, which are given in the diagram on the next page. These are often asked in the examination for *Drafting Financial Statements* and it is important in an answer to give a full definition. For example, if asked to define an asset, you will need to say more than 'something owned'; instead, pick out and explain the three key parts of the definition:

- a resource controlled by the entity
- as a result of past events
- from which future economic benefits are expected

Applying these key parts to two example assets:

current asset: inventories (stocks)
- the entity can sell them to customers, or use them in the manufacture of products
- the inventories were bought in the past
- cash will be received when the inventories, or the manufactured products, are sold

non-current asset: machine
- the entity can decide when and how to use the asset
- the asset was bought in the past
- the asset can be used to manufacture products which can be sold and cash received

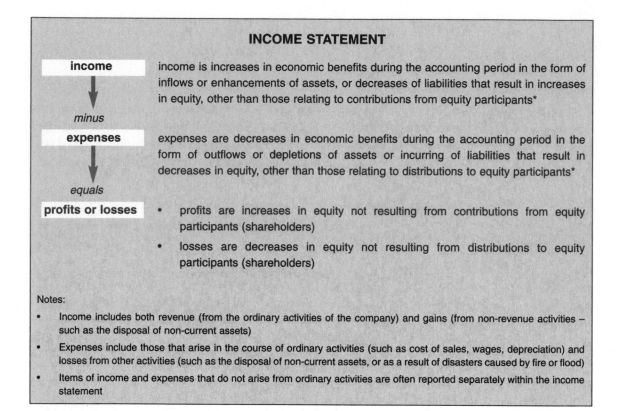

INCOME STATEMENT

income

minus

expenses

equals

profits or losses

income is increases in economic benefits during the accounting period in the form of inflows or enhancements of assets, or decreases of liabilities that result in increases in equity, other than those relating to contributions from equity participants*

expenses are decreases in economic benefits during the accounting period in the form of outflows or depletions of assets or incurring of liabilities that result in decreases in equity, other than those relating to distributions to equity participants*

• profits are increases in equity not resulting from contributions from equity participants (shareholders)

• losses are decreases in equity not resulting from distributions to equity participants (shareholders)

Notes:

• Income includes both revenue (from the ordinary activities of the company) and gains (from non-revenue activities – such as the disposal of non-current assets)

• Expenses include those that arise in the course of ordinary activities (such as cost of sales, wages, depreciation) and losses from other activities (such as the disposal of non-current assets, or as a result of disasters caused by fire or flood)

• Items of income and expenses that do not arise from ordinary activities are often reported separately within the income statement

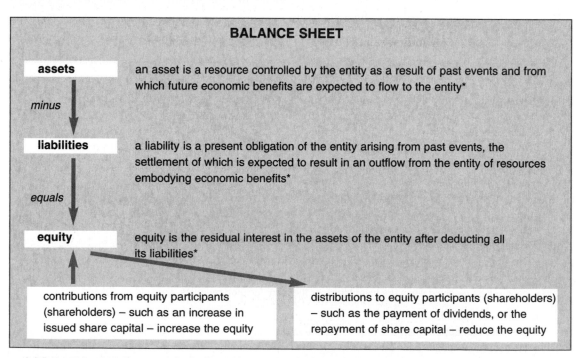

BALANCE SHEET

assets

minus

liabilities

equals

equity

an asset is a resource controlled by the entity as a result of past events and from which future economic benefits are expected to flow to the entity*

a liability is a present obligation of the entity arising from past events, the settlement of which is expected to result in an outflow from the entity of resources embodying economic benefits*

equity is the residual interest in the assets of the entity after deducting all its liabilities*

contributions from equity participants (shareholders) – such as an increase in issued share capital – increase the equity

distributions to equity participants (shareholders) – such as the payment of dividends, or the repayment of share capital – reduce the equity

* definitions taken from *Framework for the Preparation and Presentation of Financial Statements* – see page 21.

THE ACCOUNTING EQUATION

The accounting equation underlies the balance sheet of a limited company and relates to the following elements:

assets *minus* liabilities *equals* equity

Equity increases with

- profits from the activities of the company
- gains from non-revenue activities, eg revaluation of assets
- contributions from the shareholders

Equity decreases with

- losses from the activities of the company
- losses from other activities, such as a disaster caused by fire or flood, and the devaluation of assets
- distributions to shareholders, eg the payment of dividends

In the balance sheet of a limited company, the equity is represented by the share capital and reserves of the company. The income statement links to the balance sheet where profits are added to, or losses are deducted from, equity – thus the income statement explains how the change in equity came about, together with any contributions or distributions made by the shareholders – capital introduced or repaid. Some non-revenue gains or losses are reported separately from the income statement as part of the statement of changes in equity (see page 62).

To summarise, equity is represented by:

- capital from shareholders
- retained earnings from the income statement
- other gains or losses

✳ THE REGULATORY FRAMEWORK OF ACCOUNTING

The regulatory framework forms the 'rules' of accounting. When drafting company financial statements, accountants seek to follow the same set of rules – thus enabling broad comparisons to be made between the financial results of different companies.

The regulatory framework comprises

- accounting standards
- company law
- Framework for the Preparation and Presentation of Financial Statements

An important development in 2002 was the issue by the European Union (EU) of a mandatory regulation requiring all companies listed on a regulated market (eg stock market) to prepare their consolidated accounts in accordance with international accounting standards from 1 January 2005, at the latest. Furthermore, member states of the EU have the option of extending this regulation to apply to all company accounts – listed and unlisted companies, unitary and consolidated accounts.

For *Drafting Financial Statements* we will be studying international accounting standards in detail. The diagram below explains the development of the regulatory framework in the UK over the last thirty or forty years.

accounting standards

Over the last thirty to forty years, a number of accounting standards have been produced to provide a framework for accounting and to reduce the variety of accounting treatments which companies may use in their financial statements.

historical development of the regulatory framework in the UK

1970	1980	1990	2000	2010

Statements of Standard Accounting Practice (SSAPs) and Financial Reporting Standards (FRSs) issued by the Accounting Standards Board (formerly Committee)

Companies Act

1985   1989

International Accounting Standards (IASs) and International Financial Reporting Standards (IFRSs) issued by the International Accounting Standards Board (formerly Committee)

1989
Framework for the Preparation and Presentation of Financial Statements issued

2005
International accounting standards adopted by UK listed companies

Statements of Standard Accounting Practice (SSAPs) were issued by the Accounting Standards Committee between 1971 and 1990. **Financial Reporting Standards (FRSs)** have been issued by the Accounting Standards Board since 1991. Currently there are some thirty-five SSAPs and FRSs in issue which apply to company accounts which are not required to use international accounting standards. Note that the older standards are SSAPs – there are being replaced by FRSs.

International accounting standards – in the form of **International Accounting Standards (IASs)** and **International Financial Reporting Standards (IFRSs)** – have been developed by the International Accounting Standards Board (formerly the International Accounting Standards Committee) since 1973 with the aim of harmonising international financial reporting. Since 1 January 2005, all EU listed companies have been required to prepare their consolidated accounts in accordance with international accounting standards. For *Drafting Financial Statements* we will study solely the international standards; indeed it seems that it will be only a matter of time before these standards become mandatory for all UK companies.

A current list of international accounting standards, at the time of writing, is given on pages 95-96. Note that IASs are the older standards, which are being replaced with IFRSs – the collective term for both is 'international accounting standards'. You can keep up-to-date with developments on www.iasb.org.uk

Company Law

Limited companies are regulated by the Companies Act 1985 as amended by the Companies Act 1989. In particular, the 1989 Act introduced a requirement that company accounts must state that they have been prepared in accordance with applicable accounting standards and, if there have been any material departures, must give details and the reasons for such departures.

Framework for the Preparation and Presentation of Financial Statements

Although not an accounting standard, the *Framework* has been developed by the International Accounting Standards Committee (now Board) to set out the principles that should underlie the preparation and presentation of financial statements. It is designed to:

• assist in the development and review of international accounting standards

• assist in promoting harmonisation of standards by reducing the number of permissible alternative accounting treatments

- help preparers of accounts to deal with issues not yet covered by the standards

- help users of accounts to interpret the information in financial statements which have been prepared in accordance with the standards

We will be looking in more detail at the *Framework* on page 21.

THE INTERNATIONAL ACCOUNTING STANDARDS BOARD

In later chapters we will focus on the use of international accounting standards – both International Accounting Standards (IASs) and International Financial Reporting Standards (IFRSs). Here we will look in more detail at the regulatory structure for the setting of international standards. The structure is shown in the diagram below.

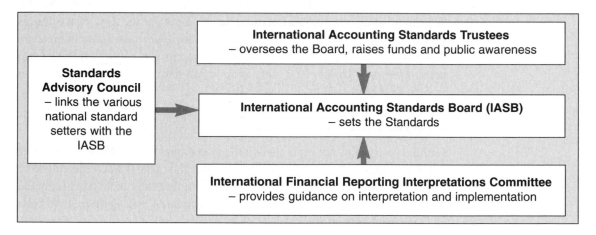

The International Accounting Standards Committee (IASC) was created in 1973. This sought to build a consensus and get agreement between the national standard-setters in many different countries. It was reorganised from 1 April 2001 and renamed the International Accounting Standards Board (IASB). It is based in London and is responsible for publishing Exposure Drafts (EDs) and International Financial Reporting Standards (IFRSs). It is advised by the Standards Advisory Council, which forms a link between the national standard-setters and the IASB.

The Trustees appoint the chairman and the other members of the IASB. The Standards Advisory Council and the International Financial Reporting Interpretations Committee both act in an advisory role in the production of IFRSs.

accounting standards – the development process

The IASs which were current at the time of the formation of the ASB in 2001 have been adopted by the Board. (The IASs had been developed by the IASB's predecessor, the International Accounting Standards Committee.) Since 2001 a number of IASs have been replaced by IFRSs.

The procedure for developing new standards is that appropriate topics are identified by the Board from either its own research or submissions made by interested parties. A discussion paper and consultation process then follows which may lead to the publication of an Exposure Draft (ED). A wider consultation process now takes place, with views being taken into account, before the ED is issued as an IFRS by the board.

authority of accounting standards

International accounting standards are not laws in themselves. However, in the UK, the Companies Act 1985 requires that, where directors of a company prepare IAS accounts, they must state in the notes to the accounts that the financial statements have been prepared in accordance with international accounting standards.

FRAMEWORK FOR THE PREPARATION AND PRESENTATION OF FINANCIAL STATEMENTS

As we have seen earlier, the *Framework* is not itself an accounting standard. It sets out the concepts which underlie the preparation and presentation of financial statements. It helps the development of future international accounting standards and the review of existing standards.

It deals with the objectives of financial statements, the qualitative characteristics of useful financial information and the definition, recognition and measurement of the elements of financial statements.

users of financial statements

The *Framework* identifies the main users of financial statements as:
- investors
- employees
- lenders
- suppliers
- customers
- government
- the public

the objective of financial statements

As we saw earlier (page 12), the objective of financial statements is *'to provide information about the financial position, performance and changes in financial position of an entity that is useful to a wide range of users in making economic decisions'*.

- Information on the *financial position* is provided by a balance sheet.

- The *performance* of an entity is usually presented in an income statement.

- *Changes in financial position* are shown by a cash flow statement.

Financial statements do not provide all the information users may need since they only show the financial effects of what has happened in the past and exclude a lot of non-financial information. Users work with financial statements to assess the stewardship of management and make economic decisions.

underlying assumptions

When preparing financial statements, it is assumed they are prepared on an accrual basis and that the entity is a going concern.

Using the *accrual* basis means that the effects of transactions are recognised when they occur (and not when cash is received or paid) and they are recorded in the accounting records and reported in the financial statements of the periods to which they relate.

Going concern means that financial statements are prepared on the assumption that the entity will continue in business for the foreseeable future. Thus there is no intention to liquidate or reduce the size of the business – if this was the case, the financial statements would have to be prepared on a different basis.

qualitative characteristics

These are the attributes that make the information provided in financial statements useful to users. The four principal qualitative characteristics identified by the *Framework* are:

- understandability
- relevance
- reliability
- comparability

The diagram on the next page shows these characteristics.

understandability

This means that the information provided in financial statements should be readily *understandable* by users.

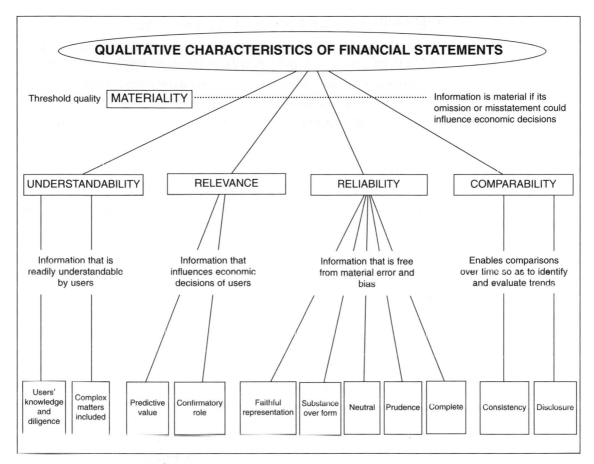

relevance

The diagram shows that, for information to be *relevant* it must have:

- the ability to influence the economic decisions of users
- predictive value, which helps users to evaluate or assess past, present or future events
- a confirmatory role, which helps users to confirm their past evaluations

reliability

For information to be *reliable* it must be:

- a faithful representation, ie it corresponds to the effect of transactions or events
- presented in accordance with the substance and economic reality of the transaction rather than its legal form, ie substance over form
- neutral, ie it is free from bias
- prudent, ie a degree of caution has been applied when making judgements and estimates
- complete, within the bounds of materiality

comparability

Comparability enables financial statements for the company from other time periods to be compared so as to identify and evaluate trends. It incorporates:

- consistency, ie the same accounting techniques have been used both within the same accounting period and also from one period to the next
- disclosure of accounting policies used in the preparation of financial statements

materiality

Under the heading for relevance, the *Framework* also incorporates the threshold or cut-off point of *materiality*. Although materiality is rarely defined in law or accounting standards, the preparer of financial statements must make judgements as to whether or not an item is material. As the *Framework* says: 'Information is material if its omission or misstatement could influence the economic decisions of users taken on the basis of the financial statements'. It goes on to say: 'Materiality depends on the size of the item or error judged in the particular circumstances or misstatement'. Thus materiality depends very much on the size of the business: a large company may consider that items of less than £1,000 are not material; a small company will use a much lower figure. What is material, and what is not, becomes a matter of judgement, based on the overall usefulness of the financial information.

true and fair view

The overall objective of financial statements is to show a true and fair view of financial position, performance and changes in financial position. The *Framework* states that application of the four qualitative characteristics – understandability, relevance, reliability, comparability – and the appropriate accounting standards, will normally result in financial statements that give a true and fair view of the entity.

the elements of financial statements

Elements of financial statements are the classes of items that financial statements comprise. They have been discussed in detail earlier in this chapter (page 14).

financial position – balance sheet

The principal elements are assets, liabilities and equity.

An **asset** is a resource controlled by the entity as a result of past events and from which future economic benefits are expected to flow.

A **liability** is a present obligation of the entity arising from past events, the settlement of which is expected to result in an outflow of resources.

Equity is the residual interest in the assets of the entity after deducting all its liabilities. It includes funds contributed by shareholders, retained earnings, and other gains and losses.

financial performance – the income statement

Profit is an increase in equity not resulting from contributions from shareholders. It is the result of comparing income and expenses.

Income is an increase in economic benefits in the form of inflows or enhancements in assets that increase equity.

Expenses are decreases in economic benefits in the form of outflows or depletions of assets or the incurring of liabilities that decrease equity.

recognition in financial statements

Recognition is the process of including something in the balance sheet or income statement. An item should be recognised:

- if it is probable that future economic benefits will flow to or from the entity; and
- it has a cost or value that can be reliably measured.

measurement bases

Measurement is the process of determining the money amounts at which the elements of the financial statements are to be recognised and carried in the balance sheet and income statement.

Traditionally assets and liabilities have been measured at their *historical cost*: assets are recorded at the amount paid at the time of acquisition; liabilities are recorded at the amount expected to be paid. As well as historical cost, other measurement bases include:

- *current cost* – what it would cost to replace assets and liabilities at today's prices
- *realisable value* – what the assets could be sold for, and the amount required to settle the liabilities, today
- *present value* – assets and liabilities are valued at the present discounted values of their future cash inflows and outflows

ACCOUNTING CONCEPTS

There are a number of accounting concepts which form the 'bedrock' of the preparation of financial statements. Some are included in the *Framework* (see previous section), while others are discussed further in IAS 1, entitled *Presentation of Financial Statements* – see Chapter 3.

Accounting concepts are illustrated in the diagram on the next page and include:

business entity

This refers to the fact that financial statements record and report on the activities of one particular entity. They do not include the personal assets and liabilities of those who play a part in owning or running the entity.

materiality

Some items are of such low value that it is not worth recording them separately in the accounting records, ie they are not 'material'. Examples include

- small expense items grouped together as sundry expenses
- small end-of-year items of office stationery not valued for the purpose of financial statements
- low-cost non-current assets being charged as an expense in the income statement

Materiality is part of the characteristic of relevance – see the *Framework* on page 21.

going concern

This presumes that the entity to which the financial statements relate will continue in the foreseeable future, ie there is no intention to reduce significantly the size of the entity or to liquidate it. Values based on break-up (realisable) amounts tend not to be relevant to users seeking to assess the entity's ability to generate cash or to adapt to changing circumstances.

Going concern is one of the underlying assumptions in the preparation of financial statements – see the *Framework* on page 21.

accruals

This means that income and expenses are matched so that they concern the same goods or services and the same time period. The income statement shows the amount of income that should have been received and the amount of expense that should have been incurred.

Accruals is one of the underlying assumptions in the preparation of financial statements – see the *Framework* on page 21.

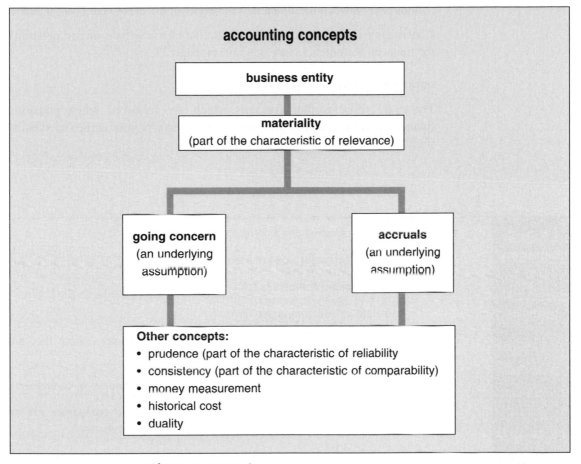

other concepts

prudence

This requires that financial statements should always, when there is any doubt, report a conservative figure for profit or the valuation of assets. To this end, profits are not to be anticipated and should only be recognised when they can be measured reliably.

Prudence is one aspect of the qualitative characteristic of reliability for financial statements – see diagram on page 23.

consistency

This requires that, when an entity adopts particular accounting methods, it should normally continue to use such methods consistently. For example, the use of straight-line depreciation for a particular class of fixed asset would normally continue to be used in the future; however, changes can be made provided there are good reasons for so doing, and a note of explanation is included in the financial statements. By application of consistency, direct comparison between the financial statements of different years can be made.

Consistency is one aspect of the qualitative characteristic of comparability for financial statements – see diagram on page 23.

money measurement, historical cost, duality

These are three further concepts which are followed when preparing financial statements. They will have been covered in your earlier accounting studies.

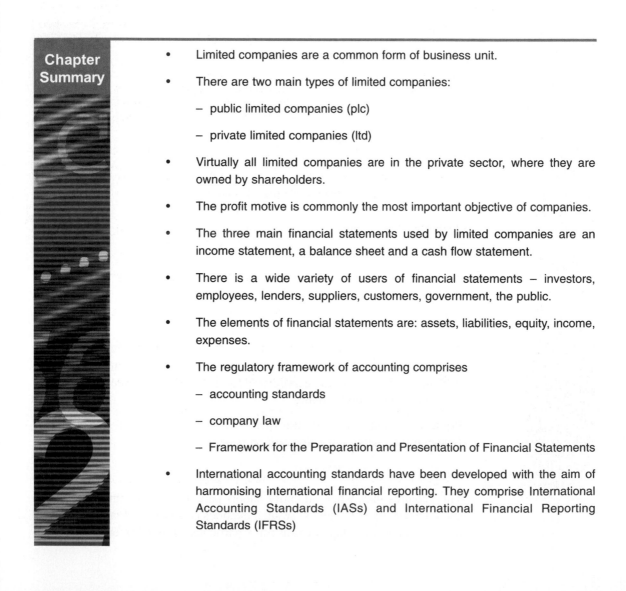

Chapter Summary

- Limited companies are a common form of business unit.

- There are two main types of limited companies:

  - public limited companies (plc)

  - private limited companies (ltd)

- Virtually all limited companies are in the private sector, where they are owned by shareholders.

- The profit motive is commonly the most important objective of companies.

- The three main financial statements used by limited companies are an income statement, a balance sheet and a cash flow statement.

- There is a wide variety of users of financial statements – investors, employees, lenders, suppliers, customers, government, the public.

- The elements of financial statements are: assets, liabilities, equity, income, expenses.

- The regulatory framework of accounting comprises

  - accounting standards

  - company law

  - Framework for the Preparation and Presentation of Financial Statements

- International accounting standards have been developed with the aim of harmonising international financial reporting. They comprise International Accounting Standards (IASs) and International Financial Reporting Standards (IFRSs)

- Framework for the Preparation and Presentation of Financial Statements sets out the concepts that underlie the preparation and presentation of financial statements.

- Accounting concepts form the 'bedrock' of the preparation of financial statements; they include: business entity, materiality, going concern and accruals.

Key Terms		
	limited company	business entity in the private sector, generally owned by shareholders who are looking for profits
	stewardship	management of a company is accountable for the safe-keeping of the company's resources, and for their proper, efficient and profitable use
	economic decisions	making use of information from financial statements to help in making decisions about investment or potential investment in the company
	elements of financial statements	the building blocks from which financial statements are constructed
	income statement	income *minus* expenses *equals* profits or losses
	balance sheet	assets *minus* liabilities *equals* equity
	IAS	International Accounting Standard
	IFRS	International Financial Reporting Standard
	financial position	information is provided by a balance sheet
	financial performance	information is provided by an income statement
	changes in financial position	information is provided by a cash flow statement

Student Activities

Osborne Books is grateful to the AAT for their kind permission to use past assessment material. This has been amended to incorporate the requirements of international accounting standards.

1.1 Which one of the following statements is correct?

(a) assets – liabilities = equity

(b) assets + liabilities = equity

(c) current assets – current liabilities = equity

(d) current assets + current liabilities = equity

1.2 Which one of the following statements is correct?

(a) assets – expenses = profits or losses

(b) income + assets = profits or losses

(c) income – expenses = profits or losses

(d) expenses + liabilities = profits or losses

1.3 Name three user groups of limited company financial statements indicating the type of financial information each group might be interested in.

1.4 Explain the following terms used in financial accounting.

(a) going concern

(b) prudence

(c) business entity

(d) accruals

1.5 In preparing the accounts of HH Limited for the year to 31 March 20-2, the managing director, Harold Hughes, has raised a number of issues. These were as follows:

(a) The company bank account paid Harold's daughters' school fees for the year.

(b) At 31 March 20-2 there was a box of pencils left in the stationery cupboard, and Harold is not sure if this should be included as closing inventories (stock).

(c) The short-term viability of HH Limited seems extremely uncertain.

(d)   During the year HH Limited paid £6,000 rent but Harold is puzzled because only £5,000 appears in the income statement and £1,000 appears in the balance sheet as a prepayment.

(e)   It is rumoured that one of HH Limited's customers has gone into liquidation, owing the company £500.

(f)   In previous years HH Limited has valued closing inventories (stock) on a FIFO (first in, first out) basis, but this year Harold believes that the company will pay less tax if it is valued on a LIFO (last in, first out) basis.

REQUIRED

State which accounting concept(s) relates to each of the above problems (a) - (f) and show how each concept should be applied in the case of HH Limited.

1.6   You have been asked to advise Jonathan Brown, managing director of JB Limited, on the accounting treatment of certain transactions which he considers might affect the company's financial statements for the year ended 31 December 20-5. The matters on which he would like your advice are set out below.

(a)   The company paid for an advertising campaign during the year at a cost of £2,800. It is estimated by Jonathan Brown that this will lead to an overall increase in income of 15%. Half of this increase was achieved in 20-5 and the other half is expected to be achieved in 20-6.

(b)   Jonathan Brown took goods costing £500 from the company at the end of the year for his own use. He removed the goods on 31 December 20-5 after the year end inventories (stock) count had taken place. No adjustment was made to the inventories balance to take account of this action.

(c)   Jonathan Brown has put his own house up as security for a loan made by the bank to the company. The loan was made specifically for the company and not for the personal use of Jonathan Brown.

REQUIRED

Advise Jonathan Brown on the accounting treatment of these transactions in the financial statements of JB Limited for the year ended 31 December 20-5. Explain your treatment, where relevant, by reference to accounting concepts.

1.7   **Task 1**

(a)   What is the objective of financial statements?

(b)   Illustrate how this objective is fulfilled by considering the financial statements of a limited company.

Task 2

(a)   Identify the elements of financial statements.

(b)   Explain how the elements are related in the balance sheet and in the income statement of a limited company and the relationship between the two financial statements.

1.8 The accounting equation is often expressed as:

ASSETS – LIABILITIES = EQUITY

(a) Explain what each of the terms 'assets', 'liabilities' and 'equity' means.

(b) Identify, in general terms only, the balances that would appear in the 'equity' section of the balance sheet of a limited company.

1.9 The directors of Machier Limited have asked you a number of questions about financial statements. Prepare notes for the directors answering the following questions:

(a) What are the elements in a balance sheet of a company? State which of the balances in the balance sheet of Machier Limited (shown below) fall under each element.

(b) How are the elements related in the accounting equation? Show numerically that the accounting equation is maintained in the balance sheet of Machier Limited.

Machier Limited

Balance Sheet as at 31 March 20-9

	£000
Non-current (Fixed) assets	4,282
Current assets	
Inventories (Stocks)	448
Trade receivables (Debtors)	527
Cash	–
	975
Current liabilities	
Trade payables (Creditors)	(381)
Tax	(165)
Bank overdraft	(203)
	(749)
Net current assets	226
Non-current (Long-term) loan	(2,800)
	1,708
Share capital	200
Share premium	100
Retained earnings	1,408
	1,708

1.10   Which one of the following statements is correct?

	Assets	Liabilities	Equity
	£	£	£
(a)	80,250	35,000	45,000
(b)	75,400	15,100	90,500
(c)	68,350	26,800	41,550
(d)	96,850	37,500	49,350

1.11   Which accounting concepts are described by each of the following sentences?

(a)   Some items are of such low value that it is not worth recording them separately in the accounting records.

(b)   The financial statements record and report on the activities of one particular entity.

(c)   Income and expenses are matched so that they concern the same goods or services and the same time period.

(d)   The presumption is that the entity to which the financial statements relate will continue in the foreseeable future.

1.12   The International Accounting Standards Board's *Framework for the Preparation and Presentation of Financial Statements* states that:

'The objective of financial statements is to provide information about the financial position, performance and changes in financial position of an entity that is useful to a wide range of users in making economic decisions.'

You are to:

(a)   State the financial statement that reports on each of the following:

- financial position

- financial performance

- changes in financial position

(b)   What is meant by the term 'entity'?

(c)   Give four examples of users of financial statements. Suggest an economic decision that might be made by each and which is helped by information contained in the financial statements.

Introduction to limited company accounts

In this chapter we focus on the financial statements of limited companies and look at:

- the terms used in limited company accounts

- the advantages of forming a limited company

- the differences between a private limited company, a public limited company, and a company limited by guarantee

- the information contained in a company's Memorandum of Association and Articles of Association

- the differences between ordinary shares and preference shares

- the concept of reserves, and the difference between capital reserves and revenue reserves

- the layout of limited company financial statements

PERFORMANCE CRITERIA COVERED

unit 11: DRAFTING FINANCIAL STATEMENTS

element 11.1

draft limited company financial statements

A   draft limited company financial statements from the appropriate information

B   correctly identify and implement subsequent adjustments and ensure that discrepancies, unusual features or queries are identified and either resolved or referred to the appropriate person

E   ensure that confidentiality procedures are followed at all times

TERMS USED IN LIMITED COMPANY ACCOUNTS

The implementation of international accounting standards (IAS) to limited company accounts has an effect on some of the terminology used in accounts. When you prepared the final accounts of sole traders and partnerships in Unit 5, *Maintaining Financial Records and Preparing Accounts*, you used terms such as profit and loss account, stocks, debtors and creditors. For limited company accounts, prepared in accordance with international accounting standards, these terms become 'income statement', 'inventories', 'trade receivables' and 'trade payables'. The table which follows shows the main changes to terminology (including some terms used in company accounts prior to the introduction of international accounting standards) and will help in the transition from sole trader and partnership financial statements to those of limited companies.

Changes to accounting terminology

Pre IAS terms	IAS terms
Profit and loss account	*Income statement*
Turnover (sales)	Revenue
Operating profit	Profit from operations
Balance sheet	*Balance sheet*
Fixed assets	Non-current assets
Tangible assets	Property, plant and equipment
Stocks	Inventories
Debtors	Trade receivables
Cash at bank and in hand	Cash and cash equivalents (explained in more detail in Chapter 6, page 170)
Creditors: amounts falling due within one year	Current liabilities
Trade creditors	Trade payables
Creditors: amounts falling due after more than one year/Provisions for liabilities and charges	Non-current liabilities
Capital and reserves	Equity
Profit and loss balance	Retained earnings

It is expected that these new terms will become more widely used over the next two or three years. During this transition period it is likely that unincorporated businesses – sole traders and partnerships – will use the 'old' terms, while companies – especially the larger ones – will use the 'new' terms. Over time there will be a gradual change towards the IAS terms.

In this chapter we will study the 'internal use' accounts, rather than being concerned with the detailed requirements of international accounting standards. However, we will use the IAS terminology so that you become familiar with it before we study the published accounts of limited companies in Chapter 3.

ADVANTAGES OF FORMING A LIMITED COMPANY

A limited company is a separate legal entity, owned by shareholders and managed by directors.

The limited company is often chosen as the legal status of a business for a number of reasons:

limited liability

The shareholders (members) of a company can only lose the amount of their investment, being the money paid already, together with any money unpaid on their shares (unpaid instalments on new share issues, for example). Thus, if the company became insolvent (went 'bust'), shareholders would have to pay any unpaid instalments to help pay the liabilities. As this happens very rarely, shareholders are usually in a safe position: their personal assets, unless pledged as security to a lender (as in the case of a director/shareholder), are not available to pay the company's liabilities.

separate legal entity

A limited company is a separate legal entity from its owners. Anyone taking legal action proceeds against the company and not the individual shareholders.

ability to raise finance

A limited company can raise substantial funds from outside sources by the issue of shares:

- for the larger public company – from the public and investing institutions on the Stock Exchange or similar markets

- for the smaller company – privately from venture capital companies, relatives and friends

Companies can also raise finance by means of debentures (see page 41).

membership

A member of a limited company is a person who owns at least one share in that company. A member of a company is the same as a shareholder.

other factors

A limited company is usually a much larger business unit than a sole trader or partnership. This gives the company a higher standing and status in the business community, allowing it to benefit from economies of scale, and making it of sufficient size to employ specialists for functions such as production, marketing, finance and human resources.

THE COMPANIES ACT

TUTORIAL NOTE

Company law in the UK is currently under review in order to update it and to bring it into line with international accounting standards. Keep a look out for developments by visiting www.companieshouse.gov.uk

Limited companies are regulated by the Companies Act 1985, as amended by the Companies Act 1989.

Under the terms of the 1985 Act there are two main types of limited company: the larger public limited company (abbreviated to 'Plc'), which is defined in the Act, and the smaller company, traditionally known as a private limited company (abbreviated to 'Ltd'), which is any other limited company. A further type of company is limited by guarantee.

public limited company (Plc)

A company may become a public limited company if it has:

- issued share capital of over £50,000

- at least two members (shareholders) and at least two directors

A public limited company may raise capital from the public on the Stock Exchange or similar markets – the new issues and privatisations of recent years are examples of this. A public limited company does not have to issue shares on the stock markets, and not all do so.

private limited company (Ltd)

The private limited company is the most common form of limited company. The term *private* is not set out in the Companies Act 1985, but it is a traditional description, and well describes the smaller company, often in family ownership. A private limited company has:

- no minimum requirement for issued share capital
- at least one member (shareholder) and at least one director who may be the sole shareholder

The shares are not traded publicly, but are transferable between individuals, although valuation will be more difficult for shares not quoted on the stock markets.

company limited by guarantee

A company limited by guarantee is not formed with share capital, but relies on the guarantee of its members to pay a stated amount in the event of the company's insolvency. Examples of such companies include charities, and artistic and educational organisations.

GOVERNING DOCUMENTS OF COMPANIES

There are a number of documents required by the Companies Act in the setting-up of a company. Two essential governing documents are the **Memorandum of Association** and the **Articles of Association**.

The **Memorandum of Association,** the constitution of the company, regulates the affairs of the company to the outside world and contains five main clauses:

1 the name of the company (together with the words 'public limited company' or 'limited', as appropriate)
2 capital of the company (the amount that can be issued in shares: the authorised share capital)
3 'objects' of the company, ie what activities the company can engage in; under the Companies Act the objects can be stated as being those of 'a general commercial company', ie the company can engage in any commercial activity
4 registered office of the company (not the address, but whether it is registered in England and Wales, or in Scotland)
5 a statement that the liability of the members is limited

The **Articles of Association** regulate the internal administration of the company, including the powers of directors and the holding of company meetings.

TYPES OF SHARES ISSUED BY LIMITED COMPANIES

The **authorised share capital** – also known as the nominal or registered capital – is stated in the Memorandum of Association and is the maximum share capital that the company is allowed to issue. The authorised share capital may not be the same as the **issued share capital** – also known as the called up capital. Under company law the issued capital cannot exceed the amount authorised. If a company which has issued the full extent of its authorised share capital wishes to make an increase, it must first pass the appropriate resolution at a general meeting of the shareholders.

The authorised share capital is shown on the balance sheet (or as a note to the accounts) 'for information', but is not added into the balance sheet total, as it may not be the same amount as the issued share capital. By contrast, the issued share capital – showing the classes and number of shares that have been issued – is included in the balance sheet figures.

The authorised and issued share capital may be divided into a number of classes or types of share; the main types are **ordinary shares** and, less commonly, **preference shares**.

ordinary (equity) shares

These are the most commonly issued class of share which carry the main 'risks and rewards' of the business: the risks are of losing part or all of the value of the shares if the business loses money or becomes insolvent; the rewards are that they take a share of the profits – in the form of **dividends** – after allowance has been made for all expenses of the business, including finance costs (eg loan and debenture interest), tax, and after preference dividends (if any). When a company makes large profits, it will have the ability to pay higher dividends to the ordinary shareholders; when losses are made, the ordinary shareholders may receive no dividend.

Companies rarely pay out all of their profits in the form of dividends; most retain some profits as reserves. These can always be used to enable a dividend to be paid in a year when the company makes little or no profit, always assuming that the company has sufficient cash in the bank to make the payment. Ordinary shareholders, in the event of the company becoming insolvent, will be the last to receive any repayment of their investment: other liabilities will be paid off first.

Ordinary shares usually carry voting rights – thus shareholders have a say at the annual general meeting and at any other shareholders' meetings.

preference shares

Whereas ordinary share dividends will vary from year-to-year, preference shares usually carry a fixed percentage rate of dividend – for example, ten per cent of nominal value. Their dividends are paid in preference to those of ordinary shareholders; but they are only paid if the company makes profits. In the event of the company ceasing to trade, the preference shareholders will also receive repayment of capital before the ordinary shareholders.

Preference shares do not normally carry voting rights.

nominal and market values of shares

Each share has a **nominal value** – or face value – which is entered in the accounts. Shares may be issued with nominal values of 5p, 10p, 25p, 50p or £1, or indeed for any amount. Thus a company with an authorised share capital of £100,000 might state in its Memorandum of Association that this is divided up into:

100,000 ordinary shares of 50p each	£50,000
50,000 ten per cent preference shares of £1 each	£50,000
	£100,000

The nominal value usually bears little relationship to the **market value**. The market value is the price at which issued – or 'secondhand' – shares are traded. Share prices of a quoted public limited company may be listed in the *Financial Times* and other business newspapers.

issue price

This is the price at which shares are issued to shareholders by the company – either when the company is being set up, or at a later date when it needs to raise more funds. The issue price is either **at par** (ie the nominal value), or above nominal value. In the latter case, the amount of the difference between issue price and nominal value is known as a **share premium** (see page 44): for example – nominal value £1.00; issue price £1.50; therefore share premium is 50p per share.

LOANS AND DEBENTURES

In addition to money provided by shareholders, who are the owners of the company, further funds can be obtained by borrowing in the form of loans or debentures:

- **Loans** are monies borrowed by companies from lenders – such as banks – on a medium or long-term basis. Generally repayments are made throughout the period of the loan, but can often be tailored to suit the needs of the borrower. Invariably lenders require security for loans so that, if the loan is not repaid, the lender has an asset – such as property – that can be sold.

  Smaller companies are sometimes also financed by directors' loans.

- **Debentures** are formal certificates issued by companies raising long-term finance from lenders and investors. Debenture certificates issued by large public limited companies are often traded on the Stock Exchange. Debentures are commonly secured against assets such as property that, in the event of the company ceasing to trade, could be sold and used to repay the debenture holders.

Loans and debentures usually carry fixed rates of interest that must be paid, just like other overheads, whether a company makes profits or not. Loan and debenture interest is shown in the income statement as 'finance costs'. In the event of the company ceasing to trade, loan and debenture-holders would be repaid before any shareholders. On the balance sheet, loans and debentures are usually shown as non-current (long-term) liabilities.

INCOME STATEMENT

The income statement of a limited company is the equivalent of the profit and loss account of a sole trader or partnership. However there are two overhead items commonly found in the income statement of a limited company that are not found in the profit statements of other business types:

- **directors' remuneration** – as directors are employed by the company, the amount paid to them appears amongst the overheads of the company
- **debenture interest** – as already noted, when debentures are issued by companies, the interest is shown under the heading of 'finance costs'

The income statement concludes with the profit for the year. Limited company accounts require a further statement – a statement of changes in equity – to show how the profit for the year has been distributed and to provide a link to the balance sheet. The statement of changes in equity will be covered in more detail in Chapter 3. For the time being, we will use the following layout to demonstrate some of the changes in equity:

Statement of changes in equity (extract)

	£
*Retained earnings**	
Balance at start of year	x
Profit for the year	x
Transfers from other reserves	x
	x
Dividends paid	(x)
Transfers to other reserves	(x)
Balance at end of year	x

* retained earnings is a revenue reserve – see page 44

Notes:

- dividends paid – all dividends *paid* during the accounting period; these include *interim dividends* (usually paid just over half-way through the financial year) and the previous year's *final dividends* (proposed at the end of the previous year, but paid early in the current financial year)
- transfers to and from other reserves – see below
- the balance at the end of the year is shown on the balance sheet as 'retained earnings' in the equity section

The diagram on pages 46 and 47 shows the income statement (for internal use) of Orion Limited as an example.

BALANCE SHEET

Balance sheets of limited companies follow the same layout as those for sole traders and partnerships, but the equity section is more complex with the issued shares and various reserves. The diagram on pages 48 and 49 shows the balance sheet (for internal use) of Orion Limited as an example (published accounts are covered in the next chapter).

Note that, for *Drafting Financial Statements*, the pro-forma layout of the balance sheet used in the examination includes lines for amounts to be shown for *total assets* and *total liabilities*. The total assets comprise the non-current assets and current assets, while the total liabilities comprise current liabilities and non-current liabilities – both totals are arrowed and shaded in the example balance sheet on page 49. It is important to note that the amounts shown for total assets and total liabilities are *for information only* – they are not themselves added or deducted in the balance sheet. They confirm the accounting equation of assets minus liabilities equals equity.

RESERVES

A limited company rarely distributes all its profits to its shareholders. Instead, it will often keep part of the profits earned each year in the form of reserves. As the balance sheet of Orion Limited shows (page 49), there are two types of reserves:

- capital reserves, which are created as a result of a non-trading profit
- revenue reserves, which include retained earnings from the income statement

capital reserves

Examples of capital reserves (which cannot be used to fund dividend payments, ie they are non-distributable) include:

- **Revaluation reserve.** This occurs when a non-current asset, most probably property, is revalued (in an upwards direction) in the balance sheet. The amount of the revaluation is placed in a revaluation reserve where it increases the value of the shareholders' investment in the company. Note, however, that this is purely a 'book' adjustment – no cash has changed hands.

  In the example below a company revalues its property upwards by £250,000 from £500,000 to £750,000.

BALANCE SHEET (EXTRACTS)

	£
Before revaluation	
Non-current asset: property at cost	500,000
Share capital: ordinary shares of £1 each	500,000
After revaluation	
Non-current asset: property at revaluation	750,000
Share capital: ordinary shares of £1 each	500,000
Capital reserve: revaluation reserve	250,000
	750,000

- **Share premium account.** An established company may issue additional shares to the public at a higher amount than the nominal value. For example, Orion Ltd (page 49) seeks finance for further expansion by issuing additional ordinary shares. Although the shares have a nominal value of £1 each, because Orion is a well-established company, the shares are issued at £1.50 each. Of this amount, £1 is recorded in the issued share capital section, and the extra 50p is the share premium.

revenue reserves

Revenue reserves are profits generated from trading activities; they have been retained in the company to help build the company for the future. Revenue reserves include the balance of retained earnings from the statement of changes in equity (see page 42). Also, there may be named revenue reserve accounts, such as *general reserve*, or a revenue reserve for a specific purpose, such as *reserve for the replacement of machinery*. Transfers to or from these named revenue reserve accounts are made in the statement of changes in equity. Revenue reserves are distributable, ie they can be used to fund dividend payments.

reserves: profits not cash

It should be noted that reserves – both capital and revenue – are not cash funds to be used whenever the company needs money, but are in fact represented by assets shown on the balance sheet. The reserves record the fact that the assets belong to the shareholders via their ownership of the company.

EXAMPLE ACCOUNTS

On pages 46 to 49 are set out the income statement and balance sheet for Orion Limited, a private limited company. Note that these are the 'internal use' accounts – the detailed layouts required by international accounting standards are covered in Chapter 3.

Explanations of the financial statements are set out in each case on the left-hand page.

ACCESSIBILITY AND CONFIDENTIALITY OF ACCOUNTS

accessibility

Limited company accounts are far more readily accessible to interested parties than the accounts of sole traders and partnerships:

- all limited companies must submit accounts to Companies House where they are available for public inspection

- a copy of the accounts is available to all shareholders, together with a report on the company's activities during the year

- the income statements and balance sheets of larger public limited companies are commented on and discussed in the media

- the accounts of larger public limited companies are freely available to potential investors, lenders and other interested parties

confidentiality

Although company accounts are readily accessible, great care must be taken when they are being prepared. Confidentiality procedures must be observed at all times:

- during the preparation of year-end financial statements

- during the period after the accounts have been prepared but before they are sent to the shareholders and disclosed to the public

- for information that has been used in the preparation of the accounts but which is not required to be disclosed under international accounting standards (see also Chapter 3, which follows)

Confidentiality means only discussing aspects of the financial statements with those people who are entitled to know about the accounts, eg work colleagues and managers. Such matters cannot be discussed with others, such as family and friends.

With all aspects of financial statements any discrepancies, unusual features or queries that you identify should be either resolved or referred to the appropriate person, such as your line manager.

The **overheads** of a limited company are usually split between distribution costs and administrative expenses.

The company has recorded a **profit from operations** of £49,000, before deduction of finance costs (such as debenture interest, bank and loan interest).

Tax, the corporation tax that a company has to pay, based on its profits, is shown. We shall not be studying the calculations for corporation tax in this book. It is, however, important to see how the tax is recorded in the financial statements.

Profit for the year, ie after deducting finance costs and tax is taken to the statement of changes in equity.

The **statement of changes in equity**, of which an extract is shown here, demonstrates how profit for the year is added to the brought forward balance of retained earnings (a revenue reserve), while dividends paid during the year are deducted. The resultant balance of retained earnings at the end of the year is shown in the balance sheet in the equity section. There is more on the statement of changes in equity in Chapter 3.

ORION LIMITED

Income Statement for the year ended 31 December 2006

	£	£
Revenue		725,000
Opening inventories	45,000	
Purchases	381,000	
	426,000	
Closing inventories	(50,000)	
Cost of sales		(376,000)
Gross profit		349,000
Overheads:		
Distribution costs	(75,000)	
Administrative expenses	(225,000)	
		(300,000)
Profit from operations		49,000
Finance costs (debenture interest)		(6,000)
Profit before tax		43,000
Tax		(15,000)
Profit for the year		28,000

Statement of changes in equity (extract)

Retained earnings

Balance at 1 January 2006	41,000
Profit for the year	28,000
	69,000
Dividends paid	(20,000)
Balance at 31 December 2006	49,000

The **non-current assets** section of a limited company balance sheet usually distinguishes between:

intangible non-current assets, which do not have material substance but belong to the company and have value, eg goodwill (the amount paid for the reputation and connections of a business that has been taken over), patents and trademarks; the intangible non-current assets are amortised (depreciated) and/or are subject to impairment reviews.

property, plant and equipment, which are tangible (ie have material substance) non-current assets and are depreciated over their useful lives and may be subject to impairment reviews.

As well as the usual **current liabilities**, for limited companies, this section also contains the amount of tax to be paid within the next twelve months.

Non-current liabilities are those that are due to be repaid more than twelve months from the date of the balance sheet, eg loans and debentures.

Authorised share capital is included on the balance sheet 'for information', but is not added into the balance sheet total, as it may not be the same amount as the issued share capital. It can also be disclosed as a note to the accounts.

Issued share capital shows the shares that have been issued. In this balance sheet, the shares are described as being fully paid, meaning that the company has received the full amount of the value of each share from the shareholders. Sometimes shares will be partly paid, eg ordinary shares of £1, but 75p paid. This means that the company can make a call on the shareholders to pay the extra 25p to make the shares fully paid.

Capital reserves are created as a result of non-trading profit and are non-distributable.

Revenue reserves are retained earnings from the statement of changes in equity and are distributable.

Total equity represents the stake of the shareholders in the company. It comprises share capital, plus capital and revenue reserves.

ORION LIMITED
Balance sheet as at 31 December 2006

Non-current Assets	Cost £	Dep'n to date £	Net £
Intangible			
Goodwill	50,000	20,000	30,000
Property, plant and equipment			
Freehold land and buildings	280,000	40,000	240,000
Machinery	230,000	100,000	130,000
Fixtures and fittings	100,000	25,000	75,000
	660,000	185,000	475,000
Current Assets			
Inventories		50,000	
Trade receivables		38,000	
Cash and cash equivalents		21,000	
		109,000	
Total assets *(see note below)*			**584,000**
Current Liabilities			
Trade payables		(30,000)	
Tax liabilities		(15,000)	
		(45,000)	
Net Current Assets (or Working Capital)			64,000
			539,000
Non-current Liabilities			
10% debentures			(60,000)
Total liabilities *(see note below)*			**105,000**
Net Assets			479,000
EQUITY			
Authorised Share Capital			
600,000 ordinary shares of £1 each			600,000
Issued Share Capital			
400,000 ordinary shares of £1 each, fully paid			400,000
Capital Reserve			
Share premium account			30,000
Revenue Reserve			
Retained earnings (see page 44)			49,000
TOTAL EQUITY			479,000

Note: The amounts shown for total assets and total liabilities (arrowed and shaded above) are *for information only* – they are not themselves added or deducted in the balance sheet. They confirm the accounting equation of assets minus liabilities equals equity, here £584,000 – £105,000 = £479,000.

Chapter Summary

- A limited company has a separate legal entity from its owners.

- A company is regulated by the Companies Act 1985 (as amended by the Companies Act 1989), and is owned by shareholders and managed by directors.

- A limited company may be either a public limited company or a private limited company.

- The liability of shareholders is limited to any money unpaid on their shares.

- The main types of shares that may be issued by companies are ordinary shares and preference shares.

- Borrowings in the form of loans and debentures are a further source of finance.

- The income statement of a company concludes with profit for the year. A further statement – a statement of changes in equity – shows how the profit has been distributed and provides a link to the balance sheet.

- The balance sheet of a limited company is similar to that of sole traders and partnerships but the equity section reflects the ownership of the company by its shareholders:

  – a statement of the authorised and issued share capital

  – details of capital reserves and revenue reserves

Key Terms

limited company	a separate legal entity owned by shareholders and managed by directors
limited liability	shareholders of a company are liable for company debts only to the extent of any money unpaid on their shares
shareholder	person who owns at least one share in a limited company; a shareholder is also a member of a company
public limited company	a company, registered as a plc, with an issued share capital of over £50,000 and at least two members and at least two directors; it may raise funds on the stock markets
private limited company	any limited company with share capital other than a public limited company
Memorandum of Association	the document setting out the constitution of the company, which regulates the affairs of the company to the outside world
Articles of Association	the document regulating the internal administration of the company

ordinary shares	commonly issued type of shares which take a share in the profits of the company, in the form of dividends, but which also carry the main risks
preference shares	shares which carry a fixed rate of dividend paid, subject to sufficient profits, in preference to ordinary shareholders; in event of repayment of capital, rank before the ordinary shareholders
debentures	issued by companies raising long-term finance; debenture interest is a finance cost in the income statement
nominal value	the face value of the shares entered in the accounts
issue price	the price at which shares are issued to shareholders by the company
market value	the price at which shares are traded
directors' remuneration	amounts paid to directors as employees of the company; an overhead in the income statement
corporation tax	tax paid by a company on its profit
statement of changes in equity	statement which shows how the profit for the year has been distributed and provides a link to the retained earnings figure shown in the balance sheet
dividends	amounts paid to shareholders from the profit of the company; an interim dividend is paid just over half-way through a financial year; a final dividend is paid early in the following year
authorised share capital	amount of share capital authorised by the company's Memorandum of Association
issued share capital	the classes and number of shares that have been issued by the company; cannot exceed the authorised share capital
reserves	profits retained by the company; two main types: – capital reserves, created as a result of a non-trading profit, are non-distributable – revenue reserves, eg retained profits from the income statement, are distributable
revaluation reserve	capital reserve created by the upwards revaluation of a non-current asset, most usually property; cannot be used to fund dividend payments
share premium account	capital reserve created by the issue of shares at a price higher than nominal value, the excess being credited to share premium; cannot be used to fund dividend payment

Student Activities

Blank photocopiable pro-formas of the income statement and balance sheet are included in the Appendix – it is advisable to enlarge them to full A4 size.

2.1   In limited company financial statements, directors' salaries are:

(a)   debited to the statement of changes in equity

(b)   debited to the income statement

(c)   credited to the statement of changes in equity

(d)   credited to the income statement.

2.2   The authorised share capital of a limited company is:

(a)   the amount of shares issued to shareholders

(b)   the amount paid for shares by the shareholders

(c)   the maximum amount of shares that can be issued

(d)   the minimum amount of shares that can be issued

2.3   Which one of these items would not appear in the income statement of a limited company?

(a)   finance costs

(b)   ordinary dividends

(c)   directors' salaries

(d)   tax

2.4   What are the main differences between preference shares and ordinary shares?

2.5   List three differences between the income statement of a limited company and that of a sole trader business.

2.6   The following trial balance has been extracted from the books of account of Gretton plc as at 31 March 20-2

	Dr	Cr
	£000	£000
Administrative expenses	210	
Issued share capital (ordinary shares of £1 fully paid)		600
Trade receivables	670	
Cash and cash equivalents	15	
Share premium		240
Distribution costs	420	
Rent, rates and insurance	487	
Dividends paid	60	
Non-current assets		
At cost	950	
Accumulated depreciation (at 1 April 20-1)		220
Retained earnings (at 1 April 20-1)		242
Purchases	960	
Inventories (at 1 April 20-1)	140	
Trade payables		260
Revenue		2,350
	3,912	3,912

Additional information

Closing Stock
- Inventories at 31 March 20-2 are valued at £180,000.

- The tax liabilities based on the profits for the year are £32,000.

- It is company policy to depreciate the non-current assets based on an annual rate of 10% on cost.
95

REQUIRED

Prepare the financial statements of Gretton plc for the year ended 31 March 20-2.

2.7   Hickson plc prepares its accounts to 30 September each year. At 30 September 20-2 its trial balance was as follows:

	Dr £	Cr £
Equipment at cost	140,000	
Depreciation to 1 October 20-1		20,000
Fixtures and fittings at Cost	40,000	
Depreciation to 1 October 20-1		10,000
Vehicles at cost	80,000	
Depreciation to 1 October 20-1		30,000
Inventories at 1 October 20-1	25,000	
Purchases	125,000	
Revenue		280,000
Wages and salaries	40,000	
Directors fees	29,000	
Printing, telephone and stationery	7,000	
General expenses	6,000	
Rent, rates and insurance	11,000	
Dividends paid	6,400	
Trade receivables	26,000	
Trade payables		14,000
Cash and cash equivalents	6,000	
Ordinary shares of 25p each		80,000
Share premium account		36,000
Retained earnings at 1 October 20-1		21,400
8% Debenture loan		50,000
	541,400	541,400

Additional information

- Closing inventories are valued at £49,000

- The interest on the debenture loan needs to be accrued for, for the whole year.

- Depreciation of the non-current assets is to be provided for as follows:
  - Equipment   10% on cost
  - Fixtures & fittings   15% on cost
  - Vehicles   25% reducing balance method

- Provision of £8,000 for tax is to be made.

REQUIRED

Prepare the financial statements of Hickson plc for the year ended 30 September 20-2.

2.8   The following list of balances has been extracted from the books of Grayson plc as at 31 December 20-2:

	Dr £	Cr £
Revenue		2,640,300
Administrative expenses	120,180	
Distribution costs	116,320	
Wages and salaries	112,800	
Directors' salaries and fees	87,200	
Interest paid on loan stock	10,000	
Postage and telephone	7,900	
Bank loan		50,000
Purchases	2,089,600	
Inventories at 1 January 20-2	318,500	
Cash and cash equivalents	20,640	
Trade receivables	415,800	
Provision for doubtful receivables at 1 January 20-2		10,074
Bad debts	8,900	
Trade payables		128,250
10% Loan stock		200,000
Motor expenses	12,280	
Bank interest	7,720	
Dividends paid	60,000	
Office equipment at net book value	110,060	
Vehicles at net book value	235,000	
Ordinary shares of 50p each		260,000
Retained earnings at 1 January 20-2		144,276
	3,732,900	3,732,900

Additional information

- Provide for £10,000 loan stock interest which is payable on 1 January 20-3.

- Provide for administrative expenses paid in advance at 31 December 20-2 £12,200 and distribution costs of £21,300 owing at 31 December 20-2.

- Provision for doubtful receivables is to be maintained at 3% of trade receivables.

- Inventories at 31 December 20-2 are valued at £340,600.

- Provide for tax of £45,000 payable on 1 October 20-3.

- Depreciation on the non-current assets has already been calculated for the year and charged to administrative expenses and distribution costs accordingly.

REQUIRED

Prepare the financial statements of Grayson plc for the year ended 31 December 20-2.

3 Published accounts of limited companies

- *the purpose and components of financial statements*
- *the format of published accounts*
- *dealing with dividends in the financial statements*
- *interpretation of the auditors' report*
- *the accounting policies followed by a particular company*
- *bonus issues and rights issues of shares*

Towards the end of the chapter (page 78) we see how a trial balance for a company is converted into the layout of published accounts.

PERFORMANCE CRITERIA COVERED

unit 11: DRAFTING FINANCIAL STATEMENTS

element 11.1

draft limited company financial statements

A   *draft limited company financial statements from the appropriate information*

B   *correctly identify and implement subsequent adjustments and ensure that discrepancies, unusual features or queries are identified and either resolved or referred to the appropriate person*

C   *ensure that limited company financial statements comply with relevant accounting standards and domestic legislation and with the organisation's policies, regulations and procedures*

E   *ensure that confidentiality procedures are followed at all times*

INTRODUCTION

All limited companies have shareholders. Each shareholder owns a part of the company and, although they do not take part in the day-to-day running of the company (unless they are also directors), they are entitled to know the financial results of the company.

Every limited company, whether public or private, is required by law to produce financial statements, which are also available for anyone to inspect if they so wish. We need to distinguish between the *statutory accounts* and the *annual report and accounts*. The **statutory accounts** are those which are required to be produced under company law, and a copy of these is filed with the Registrar of Companies.

The **annual report and accounts** – often referred to as the **corporate report** – is available to every shareholder and contains:

* income statement

* balance sheet

* cash flow statement

* statement of changes in equity

* notes to the financial statements, including a statement of the company's accounting policies

* directors' report

* auditors' report

The annual report and accounts of large well-known companies are often presented in the form of a glossy booklet, well illustrated with photographs and diagrammatic presentations. Some companies, by agreement with individual shareholders, issue a simpler form of annual review, including a **summary financial statement**, the full report and accounts being available on request.

Companies often include the report and accounts on their web sites, where they are readily accessible.

RESPONSIBILITIES OF DIRECTORS

The directors of a limited company are responsible for ensuring that the provisions of the Companies Act 1985 which relate to accounting records and statements are followed. The main provisions of the Act are that:

- a company's accounting records must:
  - show and explain the company's transactions
  - disclose with reasonable accuracy at any time the financial position of the company
  - enable the directors to ensure that the company's income statement and balance sheet give a true and fair view of the company's financial position
- a company's accounting records must contain:
  - day-to-day entries of money received and paid, together with details of the transactions
  - a record of the company's assets and liabilities
  - details of inventories held at the end of the year
- a company's financial statements must be prepared in accordance with the Companies Act and with either UK accounting standards or international accounting standards (note that, for *Drafting Financial Statements*, we shall study only accounts which comply with IASs).

Every company director has a responsibility to ensure that the statutory accounts are produced and filed with the Registrar of Companies, where they are available for public inspection. The annual accounts must be approved by the company's board of directors and the copy of the balance sheet filed with the Registrar of Companies must be signed by one of the directors on behalf of the board. The directors must prepare a directors' report (see page 70) – this must be approved by the board and the copy to be filed with the Registrar of Companies signed on behalf of the board by a director (or the company secretary). The statutory accounts must be laid before the company at the annual general meeting, and they must be circulated beforehand to shareholders, debenture holders and any other persons entitled to attend the meeting.

The statutory accounts are normally included in the corporate report (see page 57), together with a range of other financial and general information about the company.

IAS 1 – PRESENTATION OF FINANCIAL STATEMENTS

The objective of this standard is to set out how financial statements should be presented to ensure comparability with previous accounting periods and with other entities. The standard includes material covered in the *Framework* (see Chapter 1), including that the purpose of financial statements is to *'provide information about the financial position, financial performance and cash flows of an entity that is useful to a wide range of users in making economic decisions'.*

components of financial statements

IAS 1 states that a complete set of financial statements comprises:

- balance sheet
- income statement
- statement of changes in equity
- cash flow statement
- accounting policies and explanatory notes

overall considerations

The financial statements must present fairly the financial position, financial performance, and cash flows of an entity. The application of international accounting standards – supported by appropriate additional disclosures – is presumed to result in financial statements that achieve a fair presentation. IAS 1 requires that an entity whose financial statements comply with the standards should make an explicit and unreserved statement of such compliance in the notes. In extremely rare circumstances, it may be necessary to depart from compliance with a particular standard in order to achieve a fair presentation – this is allowed subject to disclosure of the name of the standard, the reasons for the non-compliance, and the financial impact of the departure.

IAS 1 requires compliance with a number of accounting concepts (see also pages 26-28) and other considerations:

- *going concern* – when an entity's financial statements are prepared in accordance with international accounting standards, the presumption is that the entity is a going concern, ie it will not cease to trade in the immediate future

- *accrual basis of accounting* – financial statements, except for cash flow information, are prepared under the accruals concept, ie income and expenses are matched to the same accounting period

- *consistency of presentation* – generally the presentation and classification of items in financial statements is to be consistent from one period to the next, eg consistency in depreciation and inventories valuation

- *materiality and aggregation* – each material class of similar items is to be presented separately in the financial statements, eg the classification of assets as non-current and current

- *offsetting* – generally it is not permitted to set off assets and liabilities, and income and expenses against each other in order to show a net figure, eg cash at bank is not netted off against a bank overdraft

- *comparative information* – a requirement to show the figures from previous periods for all amounts shown in the financial statements in order to help users of the statements

structure and content – general principles

IAS 1 sets out the detailed disclosures to be shown on the face of the income statement, balance sheet, and statement of changes in equity. We shall be covering these later in this chapter.

There are some general principles that the standard requires. These include the identification of:

- the financial statements, which are to be distinguished from other information in the corporate report
- the name of the reporting entity
- whether the financial statements are for an individual entity or for a group (see Chapter 8)
- the period covered by the financial statements, eg for the year ended 31 December 2006
- the currency of the financial statements, £s, €s, etc
- the level of rounding used for money amounts, thousands, millions, etc

Generally, financial statements are to be prepared at least annually. However, if the reporting period changes, the financial statements will be prepared for longer or shorter than a year. In these circumstances the entity must disclose the reason for the change and give a warning that figures may not be comparable with those of previous periods.

INCOME STATEMENT

The published income statement does not have to detail every single overhead or expense incurred by the company – to do so would be to disclose important management information to competitors. Instead, the main items are summarised; however, IAS 1 requires that certain items must be detailed on the face of the income statement, including:

- revenue
- finance costs
- share of the profit or loss of associates (see Chapter 8) and joint ventures accounted for using the equity method
- tax expense
- the after-tax profit or loss for the period from discontinued operations

Note that further detail may be needed to give information relevant to an understanding of financial performance.

The income statement concludes by showing the profit or loss for the period attributable to equity holders.

Note that the income statement must include all items of income and expense recognised in the period (unless an alternative treatment is permitted by other Standards).

Expenses must be analysed either by nature (raw materials, employee costs, depreciation, etc) or by function (cost of sales, distribution costs, administrative expenses, etc) – depending on which provides the more reliable and relevant information. The analysis by nature is often appropriate for manufacturing companies, while the analysis by function is commonly used by trading companies. The example income statement on the next page (with specimen figures) shows an analysis by function (only this form of analysis is assessable for *Drafting Financial Statements*); it is adapted to take note of the requirements of IFRS 5, *Non-current Assets Held for Sale and Discontinued Operations* – see below and page 66.

Much of the detail shown in the income statement is summarised. For example:

- revenue incorporates the figures for sales and sales returns
- cost of sales includes opening inventories, purchases, purchases returns, carriage inwards and closing inventories
- distribution costs include warehouse costs, post and packing, delivery drivers' wages, running costs of vehicles, depreciation of vehicles, etc
- administrative expenses include office costs, rent and rates, heating and lighting, depreciation of office equipment, etc.

A recent income statement for InBev, a Belgian limited company, is shown on page 63. This gives the consolidated (or group) income statement, together with the figures for the previous year. Group accounts are covered in Chapter 8.

discontinued operations

While most of the figures given in the income statement relate to the day-to-day continuing operations of the company, it is a requirement of IFRS 5, *Non-current Assets Held for Sale and Discontinued Operations*, to show the financial effects of discontinued operations, eg the sale of part of the business. To this end the income statement must disclose:

- the post-tax profit or loss from discontinued operations
- the post-tax gain or loss on the disposal of assets relating to the discontinued operation

These amounts are required to be further analysed either on the face of the income statement or as a note to the accounts. The cash flow statement (see Chapter 6) also has to give information about the cash flows from discontinued operations.

The objective of these requirements is to give more information to users of financial statements.

XYZ PLC

Income Statement for the year ended 31 December 2006

	£000
Continuing Operations	
Revenue	30,000
Cost of sales	(16,500)
Gross profit	13,500
Distribution costs	(4,250)
Administrative expenses	(4,000)
Profit/(loss) from operations	5,250
Finance costs	(200)
Profit/(loss) before tax	5,050
Tax	(1,225)
Profit/(loss) for the year from continuing operations	3,825
Discontinued Operations	
Profit/(loss) for the year from discontinued operations	(500)
Profit/(loss) for the year attributable to equity holders	3,325

Notes:
- IAS 1 does not permit items of income and expense to be described as 'extraordinary items'.
- All material items of income and expense are to be disclosed separately, either on the face of the income statement or in the notes – examples include disposals of property, plant and equipment, disposals of investments, litigation settlements.

STATEMENT OF CHANGES IN EQUITY

IAS 1 requires that a statement of changes in equity is one of the components of financial statements. As its name implies, it shows the changes that have taken place to the shareholders' stake in the company – not only the *realised* profit or loss from the income statement, but also *unrealised* profits (such as the gain on the upward revaluation of property) which are taken directly to reserves.

Consolidated financial statements and notes

CONSOLIDATED INCOME STATEMENT

For the year ended 31 December
Million euro

	Notes	2004	2003
Net turnover		**8,568**	**7,044**
Cost of sales		(3,996)	(3,385)
Gross Profit		**4,572**	**3,659**
Distribution expenses		(953)	(778)
Sales and marketing expenses		(1,544)	(1,377)
Administrative expenses		(728)	(615)
Other operating income/expenses	4	(96)	(50)
Profit from operations, before non-recurring items		**1,251**	**839**
Non-recurring items	5	59	-
Profit from operations		**1,310**	**839**
Net financing costs	8	(172)	(131)
Income from associates		23	35
Profit before tax		**1,161**	**743**
Income tax expense	9	(263)	(185)
Profit after tax		**898**	**558**
Minority interests		(179)	(53)
Net profit		**719**	**505**
Weighted average number of ordinary shares (million shares)		480	432
Fully diluted weighted average number of ordinary shares (million shares)		483	434
Year-end number of ordinary shares (million shares)		576	432
Basic earnings per share		1.50	1.17
Diluted earnings per share		1.49	1.16
Earnings per share before goodwill and non-recurring items		1.69	1.45
Diluted earnings per share before goodwill and non-recurring items		1.68	1.44
Earnings per share before goodwill		1.95	1.45

Income statement of InBev, a Belgian limited company
Note that, for comparison, figures for both the current year and last year are shown.

The information to be given is:

- profit or loss for the period
- items of income and expense for the period that are recognised directly in equity (eg gains or losses on the revaluation of property)
- the total of income and expense for the period (the sum of the first two items)
- the effects on equity of any changes in accounting policies and correction of errors

IAS 1 allows alternative set-outs for the statement of changes in equity. The required information can be given in the form of a 'statement of recognised income and expense' which is as follows (with sample figures):

XYZ PLC

Statement of Recognised Income and Expense
for the year ended 31 December 2006

	£000
Gains/(losses) on revaluation of properties	500
Tax on items taken directly to equity	(150)
Net income recognised directly in equity	350
Transfers	
eg the transfer to gain or loss on the sale	
of some types of assets	
Profit/(loss) for the year	3,325
Total recognised income and expense for the year	3,675

For *Drafting Financial Statements*, a pro-forma of this statement will always be given in the examination when it is required.

Note that IAS 1 requires information to be given, either on the face of the statement of changes in equity, or in the notes to the financial statements, on:

- details of transactions with shareholders, showing separately dividends paid to shareholders

- opening and closing balances of retained earnings and changes during the period (see Chapter 2, page 42)

- opening and closing balances of each reserve and changes during the period

BALANCE SHEET

IAS 1 specifies the items to be shown on the face of the balance sheet as a minimum. The Standard does not, however, state the order in which the items are to be presented.

The items to be shown on the face of the balance sheet include:

- property, plant and equipment
- investment property
- intangible assets
- financial assets (excluding investments, cash and receivables)
- investments accounted for using the equity method
- inventories
- trade and other receivables
- cash and cash equivalents
- trade and other payables
- provisions
- financial liabilities
- tax liabilities
- issued capital and reserves

In their balance sheets, IAS 1 requires most companies to separate out current and non-current assets and liabilities. IAS 1 does, however, permit a presentation based on liquidity where it provides information that is reliable and more relevant – the order of liquidity of assets and liabilities is often used by banks and other financial institutions.

Current assets are

- cash or cash equivalent
- those to be realised, sold or used within the normal operating cycle
- assets held for trading and expected to be realised within twelve months

All other assets are non-current.

Examples of current assets are trade receivables, inventories, and cash and cash equivalents.

Current liabilities are:

- those expected to be settled within the normal operating cycle
- liabilities held for trading and expected to be settled within twelve months
- where the company does not have an unconditional right to defer payment beyond twelve months

All other liabilities are non-current.

Examples of current liabilities are trade payables, tax liabilities and bank overdraft.

Further detail can be given about balance sheet items – either on the face of the balance sheet or in the notes. Examples include:

- property, plant and equipment may be shown by different classes – such as land and buildings, machinery, motor vehicles, office equipment, etc
- receivables may be split into amounts due from trade customers, prepayments, etc
- inventories can be sub-classified into raw materials, work-in-progress, finished goods, etc
- share capital and reserves can be shown by the various classes of shares and reserves

In particular, IAS 1 requires the following disclosures about share capital (either on the face of the balance sheet or in the notes):

- the number of shares authorised
- the number of shares issued and fully paid, and issued but not fully paid
- the par (or nominal) value

---

tutorial note

IAS 1 does not set out a required format for balance sheets: assets can be presented first, then liabilities and equity; or, in a version common in the UK, non-current assets can be followed by net current assets (current assets minus current liabilities), then non-current liabilities, all balanced against equity. This latter layout is shown in the example balance sheet (with specimen figures) on the next page.

---

assets as held for sale

The example balance sheet on the next page includes a line for 'assets as held for sale'. This relates to IFRS 5, *Non-current Assets Held for Sale and Discontinued Operations*, which states that non-current assets are to be classified as held for sale when their value will be recovered principally through a sale transaction rather than their continuing use. For valuation purposes, such assets are to be shown on the balance sheet at the lower of their carrying amount (net book value) and their fair value*, less costs to sell. Both IFRS 5 and IAS 1 require that non-current assets held for sale are to be shown separately on the face of the balance sheet.

* 'fair value' is defined by IFRS 5 as 'the amount for which an asset could be exchanged, or a liability settled, between knowledgeable, willing parties in an arm's length transaction'.

XYZ PLC
Balance Sheet as at 31 December 2006

	£000	£000
Non-current Assets		
Goodwill		50
Other intangible assets		–
Property, plant and equipment		9,750
Investments in subsidiaries*		–
Investments in associates*		–
Non-current assets as held for sale		=
		9,800
Current Assets		
Inventories	1,190	
Trade and other receivables	1,600	
Cash and cash equivalents	10	
	2,800	
Total assets		**12,600**
Current Liabilities		
Trade and other payables	(900)	
Tax liabilities	(850)	
Bank overdrafts and loans	(50)	
	(1,800)	
Net Current Assets		1,000
		10,800
Non-current Liabilities		
Bank loans	(1,500)	
Long-term provisions	(100)	
		(1,600)
Total liabilities		**3,400**
Net Assets		9,200
EQUITY		
Share capital		4,000
Share premium account		400
Revaluation reserve		500
Retained earnings		4,300
TOTAL EQUITY		9,200

* accounting for subsidiaries and associates is covered in Chapter 8.

Note: The amounts shown for total assets and total liabilities are *for information only* – they are not themselves added or deducted in the balance sheet. They confirm the accounting equation of assets minus liabilities equals equity, here £12,600 – £3,400 = £9,200.

A recent balance sheet for InBev, a Belgian limited company, is shown on the next page. This gives the consolidated (or group) balance sheet, together with the figures for the previous year; group accounts are covered in Chapter 8.

DEALING WITH DIVIDENDS IN THE FINANCIAL STATEMENTS

Dividends are distributions to the shareholders, who own the company, as a return on their investment. Many companies pay dividends twice a year – an *interim dividend*, which is usually paid just over halfway through the financial year, and a *final dividend* which is paid early in the next financial year. The interim dividend is based on the profits reported by the company during the first half of the year, while the final dividend is based on the profits reported for the full year. The final dividend is proposed by the directors but has to be approved by shareholders at the Annual General Meeting of the company. Thus the financial calendar for a company with a financial year end of 31 December 2006 might take the following form:

January 2006	Directors propose final dividend for year ended 31 December 2005
March 2006	Annual General Meeting of the company approves final dividend
April 2006	Final dividend paid for year ended 31 December 2005
August 2006	Interim dividend paid for year ended 31 December 2006, based on reported profit for the first half of the year
December 2006	Financial year ends on 31 December
January 2007	Directors propose final dividend for year ended 31 December 2006

Only the dividends paid during the year can be recorded in the financial statements (see IAS 10, *Events after the Balance Sheet Date*, page 153). In the above example, the dividends paid in April 2006 (final dividend for the previous year) and August 2006 (interim dividend for the current year) are recorded in the financial statements. The proposed final dividend for the year ended 31 December 2006 is disclosed as a note to the accounts, stating that it is subject to approval by the shareholders at the company's Annual General Meeting. An example of a note to the published accounts for dividends is as follows:

continued on page 70

CONSOLIDATED BALANCE SHEET

As at 31 December
Million euro

	Notes	2004	2003
ASSETS			
Non-current assets			
Property, plant and equipment	11	5,298	3,342
Goodwill	12	7,459	3,744
Intangible assets other than goodwill	13	246	228
Interest-bearing loans granted		49	9
Investments in associates	14	6	443
Investment securities	15	274	247
Deferred tax assets	16	743	169
Employee benefits	23	39	31
Trade and other receivables	18	550	324
		14,664	**8,537**
Current assets			
Interest-bearing loans granted		11	2
Investment securities	15	2	-
Inventories	17	847	460
Income tax receivable		119	30
Trade and other receivables	18	1,977	1,509
Cash and cash equivalents	19	976	445
		3,932	**2,446**
Total assets		**18,596**	**10,983**
EQUITY AND LIABILITIES			
Capital and reserves			
Issued capital	20	444	333
Share premium	20	6,471	3,215
Reserves	20	(353)	(232)
Retained earnings	20	1,968	1,404
		8,530	**4,720**
Minority interests		**412**	**410**
Non-current liabilities			
Interest-bearing loans and borrowings	22	2,217	2,200
Employee benefits	23	371	300
Trade and other payables	25	401	40
Provisions	24	502	200
Deferred tax liabilities	16	314	251
		3,805	**2,991**
Current liabilities			
Bank overdrafts	19	100	85
Interest-bearing loans and borrowings	22	2,074	612
Income tax payables		310	122
Trade and other payables	25	3,284	1,956
Provisions	24	81	87
		5,849	**2,862**
Total liabilities		**18,596**	**10,983**

Balance sheet of InBev, a Belgian limited company

(note that consolidated accounts are covered in Chapter 8)

DIVIDENDS
(note for published accounts

	£000
Amounts recognised as distributions to equity holders during the year:	
• *Final dividend* for the year ended 31 December 2005 of 7.5p per share	375
• *Interim dividend* for the year ended 31 December 2006 of 5p per share	250
	625
Proposed final dividend for the year ended 31 December 2006 of 10p per share	500

The proposed final dividend is subject to approval by shareholders at the Annual General Meeting and has not been included as a liability in these financial statements

---

The amount of £625,000 will be shown as part of the Statement of Changes in Equity, and will also be recorded in the cash flow statement (see Chapter 6). The proposed final dividend is shown as a note only for this year, but will form part of dividends paid for the year ended 31 December 2007.

The reason for treating proposed dividends in this way is that, until they are approved at the AGM, they are not liabilities of the company and should not, therefore, be shown in the financial statements.

DIRECTORS' REPORT

The report contains details of the following:

- a statement of the principal activities of the company
- review of the activities of the company over the past year and of likely developments in the future, including research and development activity
- directors' names and their shareholdings
- proposed dividends
- significant differences between the book value and market value of land and buildings
- political and charitable contributions
- policy on employment of disabled people
- health and safety at work of employees
- action taken on employee involvement and consultation
- policy on payment of suppliers

CASH FLOW STATEMENTS

IAS 7 requires that limited companies must include, as part of their accounts, a cash flow statement, which we will look at in detail in Chapter 6. Such a statement shows an overall view of money flowing in and out during an accounting period. It links profit with changes in assets and liabilities and the effect on the cash of the company. A recent cash flow statement for InBev, a Belgian limited company, is shown on page 72.

AUDITORS' REPORT

Larger companies must have their accounts audited by external auditors, who are appointed by the shareholders to check the accounts. The auditors' report, which is printed in the published accounts, is the culmination of their work. The three main sections of the auditors' report are:

* **respective responsibilities of directors and auditors** – the directors are responsible for preparing the accounts, while the auditors are responsible for forming an opinion on the accounts

* **basis of opinion** – the framework of auditing standards within which the audit was conducted, other assessments, and the way in which the audit was planned and performed

* **opinion** – the auditors' view of the company's accounts

An *'unqualified'* auditors' opinion will read as follows:

> *'In our opinion, the financial statements give a true and fair view of the financial position of the Company at .... 20.., and of the results of its operations and its cash flows for the year then ended, in accordance with the Companies Act 1985, or in accordance with international accounting standards.'*

A *'qualified'* auditors' report will raise points that the auditors consider have not been dealt with correctly in the accounts. Where such points are not too serious, the auditors will use the phrase 'except for ... the financial statements give a true and fair view'. Much more serious is where the auditors' statement says that the accounts 'do not show a true and fair view' or 'we are unable to form an opinion ...'. These indicate a major disagreement between the company and the auditors, and a person involved with the company – such as an investor or supplier – should take serious note.

Note that smaller private companies are exempt from audit requirements.

CONSOLIDATED CASH FLOW STATEMENT

For the year ended 31 December
Million euro

	2004	2003
OPERATING ACTIVITIES		
Net profit from ordinary activities	719	505
Depreciation	621	504
Amortization and impairment of goodwill	216	120
Amortization of intangible assets	49	37
Impairment losses (other than goodwill)	135	(1)
Write-offs on non-current and current assets	3	1
Unrealized foreign exchange losses/(gains)	(25)	26
Net interest (income)/expense	196	107
Net investment (income)/expense	(39)	(5)
Loss/(gain) on sale of investment in associates	(488)	-
Loss/(gain) on sale of plant and equipment	(31)	(19)
Loss/(gain) on sale of intangible assets	3	-
Income tax expense	263	185
Income from associates	(23)	(35)
Minority interests	179	53
Profit from operations before changes in working capital and provisions	**1,778**	**1,478**
Decrease/(increase) in trade and other receivables	(194)	-
Decrease/(increase) in inventories	(63)	(25)
Increase/(decrease) in trade and other payables	329	-
Increase/(decrease) in provisions	(60)	(96)
Cash generated from operations	**1,790**	**1,357**
Interest paid	(252)	(139)
Interest received	75	33
Dividends received	8	58
Income tax (paid)/received	(237)	(158)
CASH FLOW FROM OPERATING ACTIVITIES	**1,384**	**1,151**
INVESTING ACTIVITIES		
Proceeds from sale of property, plant and equipment	135	83
Proceeds from sale of intangible assets	-	3
Proceeds from sale of investments	1,155	100
Repayments of loans granted	3	7
Sale of subsidiaries, net of cash disposed of	7	-
Acquisition of subsidiaries, net of cash acquired	(899)	(383)
Acquisition of property, plant and equipment	(812)	(544)
Acquisition of intangible assets	(48)	(137)
Acquisition of other investments	(12)	(62)
Payments of loans granted	(32)	(6)
CASH FLOW FROM INVESTING ACTIVITIES	**(503)**	**(939)**
FINANCING ACTIVITIES		
Proceeds from the issue of share capital	29	7
Purchase of own shares of an affiliate	(74)	-
Reimbursement of capital	(6)	-
Proceeds from borrowings	4,941	6,228
Repayment of borrowings	(5,015)	(5,985)
Payment of finance lease liabilities	(7)	(9)
Dividends paid	(229)	(168)
CASH FLOW FROM FINANCING ACTIVITIES	**(361)**	**73**
Net increase/(decrease) in cash and cash equivalents	**520**	**285**
Cash and cash equivalents less bank overdrafts at beginning of year	360	93
Effect of exchange rate fluctuations	(4)	(18)
Cash and cash equivalents less bank overdrafts at end of year	**876**	**360**

Cash flow statement of InBev, a Belgian limited company

(note that cash flow statements are covered in Chapter 6)

ACCOUNTING POLICIES

IAS 1 requires companies to include details of the specific accounting policies used. IAS 8, *Accounting Policies, Changes in Accounting Estimates and Errors*, provides further details and defines accounting policies as *'the specific principles, bases, conventions, rules and practices applied by an entity in preparing and presenting financial statements.'* Included in the definition are accounting principles and accounting bases:

* accounting principles are the broad concepts that apply to almost all financial statements, eg going concern, accruals, prudence, consistency and materiality
* accounting bases are the methods developed for applying the accounting principles to financial statements, and which are intended to reduce subjectivity by identifying the acceptable methods, eg the value of assets based on cost or revaluation

Accounting policies are the specific accounting bases selected by the directors and followed by a company, such as the method of depreciation. In selecting and applying accounting policies, IAS 8 requires that:

* where an accounting policy is given in a standard (IAS and IFRS) or an interpretation (of the International Financial Reporting Interpretations Committee) for a particular transaction, then that policy must apply
* where there is no standard or interpretation to give guidance, the management of the company must use its judgement to give information that is relevant and reliable; management may refer firstly to other standards, interpretations, then to the *Framework* document, and lastly to guidance from other standard-setting bodies (provided that the guidance does not result in conflicts with the international standards and interpretations)

Once adopted by a company, accounting policies are to be applied consistently for similar transactions – unless a standard or interpretation allows differing policies to be applied to categories of items. Changes of accounting policies can only occur:

* if the change is required by a standard or interpretation; or
* if the change results in the financial statements providing reliable and more relevant information

When there are changes in accounting policies, they are to be applied retrospectively. Any changes require the figure for equity and other figures from the income statement and balance sheet to be altered for previous financial statements – subject to the practicalities of calculating the relevant amounts.

An extract from the accounting policies of InBev is shown on the next page.

IAS 8 also deals with the effect of errors on the financial statements. It defines errors as '*omissions from, and misstatements in, the entity's financial statements for one or more prior periods arising from a failure to use, or misuse of, reliable information that:*

- *was available when financial statements for those periods were authorised for issue; and*
- *could reasonably be expected to have been obtained and taken into account in the preparation and presentation of those financial statements.*'

Note that such errors can result from mathematical mistakes, mistakes in applying accounting policies, oversights or misinterpretations of facts, and fraud.

The general principle of dealing with errors is that the entity must correct material errors from prior accounting periods retrospectively in the next set of financial statements by restating the comparative amounts for the prior period(s) presented in which the error occurred. If, however, the error occurred before the earliest prior period presented, then it will be necessary to restate the opening balances for assets, liabilities and equity for the earliest prior period presented. Note that correction of errors from prior periods is subject to the practicalities of calculating the relevant amounts.

NOTES TO THE FINANCIAL STATEMENTS

IAS 1 requires a number of notes to the financial statements. These include:

- information about the basis of preparation of the financial statements and the specific accounting policies used
- disclosure of information required by international accounting standards that is not already included in the income statement, statement of changes in equity, balance sheet, or cash flow statement
- the provision of additional information that is relevant to an understanding of the financial statements

Notes are to be presented systematically, with cross-referencing from the financial statements to the relevant note.

continued on page 76

1. SIGNIFICANT ACCOUNTING POLICIES (EXTRACTS)

InBev SA is a company domiciled in Belgium. The consolidated financial statements of the company for the year ended 31 December 2004 comprise the company and its subsidiaries (together referred to as "InBev" or the "company") and the company's interest in associates and jointly controlled entities. The financial statements were authorized for issue by the board of directors on 1 March 2005.

(A) STATEMENT OF COMPLIANCE
The consolidated financial statements have been prepared in accordance with International Financial Reporting Standards (formerly named IAS) issued by the International Accounting Standards Board (IASB), and interpretations issued by the International Financial Reporting Interpretations Committee (IFRIC), as adopted by the European Union up to 31 December 2004. InBev has not applied any standards and interpretations issued up to 31 December 2004 but with an effective date after 31 December 2004.

(B) BASIS OF PREPARATION
The financial statements are presented in euro, rounded to the nearest million. They are prepared on the historical cost basis except for derivative financial instruments, investments held for trading and investments available-for-sale which are stated at fair value. Investments in equity instruments or derivatives linked to and to be settled by delivery of an equity instrument are stated at cost when such equity instrument does not have a quoted market price in an active market and for which other methods of reasonably estimating fair value are clearly inappropriate or unworkable. Recognized assets and liabilities that are hedged are stated at fair value in respect of the risk that is hedged.

The accounting policies have been applied consistently, except for accounting for jointly controlled entities (refer to note 10).

The consolidated financial statements are prepared as of and for the period ending 31 December 2004.

They are presented before the effect of the profit appropriation of the parent company proposed to the general assembly of shareholders.

(G) PROPERTY, PLANT AND EQUIPMENT
(1) Owned assets
All property, plant and equipment is recorded at historical cost less accumulated depreciation and impairment losses (refer accounting policy M). Cost includes the purchase price and other direct acquisition costs (e.g. non refundable tax, transport). The cost of self-constructed assets includes the cost of materials, direct labor and an appropriate proportion of production overheads.

(2) Subsequent expenditure
Subsequent expenditure is capitalized only when it increases the future economic benefits embodied in the item of property, plant and equipment. Repairs and maintenance, which do not increase the future economic benefits of the asset to which they relate, are expensed as incurred.

(3) Depreciation
Depreciation is calculated from the date the asset is available for use, using the straight-line method over the estimated useful lives of the assets.

(J) INVENTORIES
Inventories are valued at the lower of cost and net realizable value. Cost is determined by the weighted average method.

The cost of finished products and work in progress comprises raw materials, other production materials, direct labor, other direct cost and an allocation of fixed and variable overhead based on normal operating capacity. Net realizable value is the estimated selling price in the ordinary course of business, less the estimated costs of completion and selling costs.

(K) TRADE RECEIVABLES
Trade receivables are carried at cost less impairment losses. An estimate is made for doubtful receivables based on a review of all outstanding amounts at the year-end. Bad debts are written off during the year in which they are identified.

(L) CASH AND CASH EQUIVALENTS
Cash and cash equivalents comprise cash balances and call deposits. For the purpose of the statement of cash flows, cash and cash equivalents are presented net of bank overdrafts.

Extract from the accounting policies of InBev, a Belgian limited company

Included in the notes is to be a summary of significant accounting policies followed, including:

- the measurement basis (or bases) – eg historical cost basis – used in preparing the financial statements, and
- the other accounting policies used that are relevant to an understanding of the financial statements.

With regard to dividends, there must be disclosed in the notes the amount of dividends proposed or declared before the financial statements were authorised for issue but not recognised as a distribution to shareholders during the period, and the related amount per share (see page 70 for an example of this note).

BONUS ISSUES AND RIGHTS ISSUES

Limited companies – and particularly plcs – quite often increase their capital by means of either **bonus issues** or **rights issues** of shares. Whilst both of these have the effect of increasing the number of shares in issue, they have quite different effects on the structure of the company balance sheet.

bonus issues

A bonus issue is made when a company issues free shares to existing shareholders; it does this by using reserves that have built up and capitalising them (ie they are turned into permanent share capital). The bonus issue is distributed on the basis of existing shareholdings – for example, one bonus share for every two shares already held.

With a bonus issue no cash flows in or out of the company. The shareholders are no better off: with more shares in issue the stock market price per share will fall in proportion to the bonus issue, ie the company's net assets are now spread among a greater number of shares.

Bonus issues are made in order to acknowledge the fact that reserves belong to shareholders. Often a build-up of reserves occurs because a company hasn't the cash to pay dividends, so a bonus issue is a way of passing the reserves to shareholders.

Note that capital or revenue reserves can be used for bonus issues. If there is a choice, then capital reserves are used first – this is because it is one of the few uses of a capital reserve, which cannot be used to fund the payment of dividends.

rights issues

A rights issue is used by a company seeking to raise further finance through the issue of shares. Instead of going to the considerable expense of offering additional shares to the public, it is cheaper to offer shares to existing shareholders at a favourable price (usually a little below the current market price). As with a bonus issue the extra shares are offered in proportion to the shareholders' existing holding. The shareholder may take up the rights by subscribing for the shares offered; alternatively the rights can often be sold on the stock market.

Case Study

SEVERN PLC AND WYE PLC: BONUS ISSUES AND RIGHTS ISSUES

situation

The following are the summary balance sheets of Severn plc and Wye plc:

	Severn	Wye
	£	£
Non-current assets	300,000	300,000
Current assets (including bank)	100,000	100,000
	400,000	400,000
Ordinary shares of £1 each	200,000	200,000
Reserves (capital and revenue)	200,000	200,000
	400,000	400,000

Severn is planning a one-for-two bonus issue.

Wye is seeking finance for a capital expenditure programme through a one-for-two rights issue at a price of £1.80 per share (the current market price is £2.10).

solution

After the issues, the balance sheets appear as:

	Severn	Wye
	£	£
Non-current assets	300,000	300,000
Current assets (including bank)	100,000	280,000
	400,000	580,000
Ordinary shares of £1 each	300,000	300,000
Share premium account (capital reserve)	–	80,000
Reserves	100,000	200,000
	400,000	580,000

The changes are:

Severn   Reserves are reduced by £100,000, whilst share capital is increased by the same amount; the ordinary share capital is now more in balance with fixed assets; no cash has been received.

Wye   The bank balance has increased by £180,000, being 100,000 shares (assuming that all shareholders took up their rights) at £1.80; share capital has increased by £100,000, whilst 80p per share is the share premium, ie £80,000 in total. The company now has the money to finance its capital expenditure programme. There are also significant reserves which could be used for a bonus issue in the future.

PREPARING FOR THE EXAMINATION

In the AAT Examination for *Drafting Financial Statements* you will often be presented with a limited company's trial balance (or sometimes an extended trial balance). Points of further information will also be given to you.

You will then be required to produce an income statement and/or a balance sheet using the figures from the trial balance and incorporating the further information. A specimen layout of the financial statement(s) is normally provided in the answer booklet.

In the Case Study which follows we will see how the income statement and balance sheet are prepared in published accounts format from the figures given in a trial balance.

Case Study

AMARILLO LIMITED: PREPARING THE ACCOUNTS FROM A TRIAL BALANCE

situation

You have been asked to help prepare the financial statements of Amarillo Limited for the year ended 30 June 2006. The trial balance of the company as at 30 June 2006 is set out below.

Amarillo Limited
Trial balance as at 30 June 2006

	Debit £000	Credit £000
Interest	200	
Distribution costs	5,468	
Administrative expenses	2,933	

continued on next page

Trade receivables	4,235	
Trade payables		1,872
Dividends paid	625	
Ordinary share capital		5,000
Revenue		25,840
Long-term loan		4,000
Land – cost	6,000	
Buildings – cost	2,298	
Fixtures and fittings – cost	1,865	
Vehicles – cost	2,145	
Office equipment – cost	1,783	
Purchases	12,965	
Cash and cash equivalents	609	
Retained earnings as at 1 July 2005		3,875
Inventories as at 1 July 2005	4,285	
Share premium		1,500
Buildings – accumulated depreciation		424
Fixtures and fittings – accumulated depreciation		597
Vehicles – accumulated depreciation		1,410
Office equipment – accumulated depreciation		893
	45,411	45,411

Further information available to you:

- The authorised share capital of the company, all of which has been issued, consists of ordinary shares with a nominal value of £1.

- During the year the company paid a final dividend of 7.5p per share for the year to 30 June 2005, and an interim dividend of 5p per share for the current year. The proposed final dividend for the year to 30 June 2006 is 10p per share.

- The inventories at the close of business on 30 June 2006 were valued at cost at £5,162,000.

- The tax charge for the year has been calculated as £1,475,000.

- An advertising campaign was undertaken during the year at a cost of £22,000. No invoices have yet been received for this campaign.

- Interest on the long-term loan has been paid for six months of the year. No adjustment has been made for the interest due for the final six months of the year. Interest is charged on the loan at a rate of 10% per annum.

- The land has been revalued by professional valuers at £7,000,000. The revaluation is to be included in the financial statements for the year ended 30 June 2006.

- All of the operations are continuing operations.

From the further information given above you are to make the journal entries required (dates and narratives are not required), together with the note for the published accounts in respect of dividends.

Notes:

* show any workings relevant to these adjustments

* ignore any effect of these adjustments on the tax charge for the year given above

Draft an income statement (including a statement of the change in retained earnings) for the year ended 30 June 2006, and a balance sheet for Amarillo Limited as at that date, making any adjustments required as a result of the further information given above (the only note to the accounts that is required is that in respect of dividends).

solution

JOURNAL ENTRIES

			£000	£000
1.	DR	Inventories – Balance sheet	5,162	
	CR	Inventories – Income statement		5,162
2.	DR	Tax – Income statement	1,475	
	CR	Tax payable – Balance sheet		1,475
3.	DR	Distribution expenses – Income statement	22	
	CR	Accruals – Balance sheet		22
4.	DR	Finance costs – Income statement	200	
	CR	Accruals – Balance sheet		200
5.	DR	Land – Balance sheet	1,000	
	CR	Revaluation reserve – Balance sheet		1,000

tutorial notes:
(all figures £000)
Interest: £4,000 x 10% x 6 months = £200
Revaluation: £7,000 – £6,000 = £1,000 to revaluation reserve

AMARILLO LIMITED
Income statement for the year ended 30 June 2006

	£000
Continuing operations	
Revenue	25,840
Cost of sales (note 1)	(12,088)
Gross profit	13,752
Distribution costs (note 2)	(5,490)
Administrative expenses	(2,933)
Profit from operations	5,329
Finance costs (note 3)	(400)
Profit before tax	4,929
Tax	(1,475)
Profit for the year attributable to equity holders	3,454

Statement of changes in equity (extract)

Retained earnings	£000
Balance at 1 July 2005	3,875
Profit for the year	3,454
	7,329
Dividends paid (see note on next page)	(625)
Balance at 30 June 2006	6,704

Revaluation reserve

	£000
Revaluation of land	1,000

Balance Sheet as at 30 June 2006

	£000	£000
Non-current Assets (note 4)		
Property, plant and equipment		11,767
Current Assets		
Inventories	5,162	
Trade receivables	4,235	
Cash and cash equivalents	600	
	10,006	
Total assets		21,773
Current liabilities		
Trade and other payables (note 5)	(2,094)	
Tax liabilities	(1,475)	
	(3,569)	
Net Current Assets		6,437
		18,204
Non-current Liabilities		
Long-term loan		(4,000)
Total liabilities		7,569
		14,204
EQUITY		
Share capital		5,000
Share premium account		1,500
Revaluation reserve		1,000
Retained earnings		6,704
TOTAL EQUITY		14,204

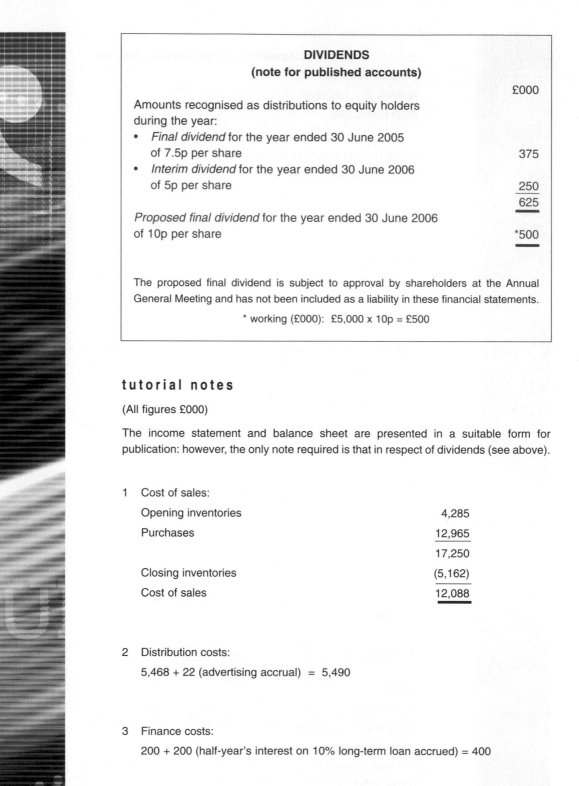

DIVIDENDS
(note for published accounts)

	£000
Amounts recognised as distributions to equity holders during the year:	
• *Final dividend* for the year ended 30 June 2005 of 7.5p per share	375
• *Interim dividend* for the year ended 30 June 2006 of 5p per share	250
	625
Proposed final dividend for the year ended 30 June 2006 of 10p per share	*500

The proposed final dividend is subject to approval by shareholders at the Annual General Meeting and has not been included as a liability in these financial statements.

* working (£000): £5,000 x 10p = £500

tutorial notes

(All figures £000)

The income statement and balance sheet are presented in a suitable form for publication: however, the only note required is that in respect of dividends (see above).

1   Cost of sales:

Opening inventories	4,285
Purchases	12,965
	17,250
Closing inventories	(5,162)
Cost of sales	12,088

2   Distribution costs:

5,468 + 22 (advertising accrual) = 5,490

3   Finance costs:

200 + 200 (half-year's interest on 10% long-term loan accrued) = 400

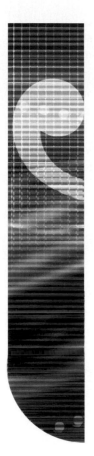

4   Non-current assets:

Property, plant and equipment	Cost	Accumulated depreciation	Net book value
Land	7,000	–	*7,000
Buildings	2,298	424	1,874
Fixtures and fittings	1,865	597	1,268
Vehicles	2,145	1,410	735
Office equipment	1,783	893	890
	15,091	3,324	11,767

* Land: 6,000 + 1,000 = 7,000

5   Trade and other payables:

Trade payables	1,872
Advertising accrual	22
Interest accrual	200
	2,094

This Case Study asked you to prepare the income statement and balance sheet from a trial balance. However, if an examination question asks you to prepare a balance sheet only, you need to think about how you are going to get the figure for retained earnings which goes in the balance sheet. In such circumstances you will need to do a working note which summarises the income statement transactions, ie revenue, less cost of sales, costs and expenses, and taxation, together with a note of dividends paid and their effect on the figure for retained earnings.

CONFIDENTIALITY PROCEDURES

The published accounts of limited companies are readily available to shareholders and interested parties either from the company itself or from Companies House (www.companieshouse.gov.uk). Nevertheless, as noted in this chapter, only certain information has to be disclosed in the published accounts.

For those involved in the preparation of the accounts, confidentiality procedures must be observed at all times:

– during the preparation of published accounts

– during the period after the accounts have been prepared but before they are sent to the shareholders, filed at Companies House, and disclosed to the public

– for detailed information that is needed in the preparation of the accounts but is not required to be disclosed under accounting standards and the Companies Acts

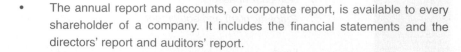

Chapter Summary

- The annual report and accounts, or corporate report, is available to every shareholder of a company. It includes the financial statements and the directors' report and auditors' report.

- The directors are responsible for ensuring that the company keeps accounting records and that financial statements are prepared.

- IAS 1, *Presentation of Financial Statements*, sets out how financial statements should be prepared to ensure comparability. IAS 1 requires compliance with a number of accounting concepts and other considerations:

  - going concern
  - accruals basis of accounting
  - consistency of presentation
  - materiality and aggregation
  - offsetting
  - comparative information

- For larger companies, external auditors report to the shareholders on the state of affairs of the company.

- The directors establish the accounting policies which the company follows.

- Bonus issues and rights issues increase the number of shares in issue – only the latter brings in cash to the company.

Key Terms

statutory accounts	financial statements required by law, a copy of which is filed at Companies House, where it can be inspected
report and accounts	the corporate report of the company which is available to every shareholder
set of financial statements	IAS 1 states that a complete set of financial statements comprises: – balance sheet – income statement – statement of changes in equity – cash flow statement – accounting policies and explanatory notes
auditors' report	gives the auditors' opinion on the company's financial statements as to whether they give a true and fair view of the financial position of the company

accounting policies the specific principles, bases, conventions, rules and practices applied by an entity in preparing and presenting financial statements

errors omissions from, and misstatements in, the entity's financial statements for one or more prior periods arising from a failure to use, or misuse of, reliable information

bonus issue the capitalisation of reserves – either capital or revenue – in the form of free shares issued to existing shareholders in proportion to their holdings; no cash flows into the company

rights issue the raising of cash by offering shares to existing shareholders, in proportion to their holdings, at a favourable price

Student Activities

Osborne Books is grateful to the AAT for their kind permission to use past assessment material, which has been amended to incorporate the requirements of international accounting standards.

Blank photocopiable pro-formas of the income statement and balance sheet are included in the Appendix – it is advisable to enlarge them to full A4 size.

3.1 Which one of the following statements is not part of the corporate report?

(a) income statement

(b) auditors' report

(c) directors' report

(d) chairman's statement

3.2 According to IAS 1, *Presentation of Financial Statements*, what comprises a complete set of financial statements?

3.3 How does IFRS 5, *Non-current Assets Held for Sale and Discontinued Operations*, describe assets which are to be classified as held for sale?

    (a)   when their net realisable value is lower than their cost

    (b)   when their value will be recovered principally through a sale transaction rather than their continuing use

    (c)   when their carrying value (net book value) falls to zero

    (d)   when their fair value, less costs to sell, is lower than their carrying value (net book value)

3.4 Which one of the following transactions does not involve the movement of cash?

    (a)   bonus issue of shares

    (b)   rights issue of shares

    (c)   repayment of shares

    (d)   issue of debentures

3.5 Briefly outline the benefits to a company's shareholders of the statement of changes in equity.

3.6 List four items that need to be included in a directors' report.

3.7 The following trial balance has been extracted from the books of account of Proudlock PLC as at 31 March 20-2.

	£000	£000
Administrative expenses	240	
Share capital (£1 ordinary shares)		700
Trade receivables	600	
Cash and cash equivalents	75	
Accruals		15
Share premium		200
Distribution costs	500	
Non-current asset investments	600	
Plant and machinery at cost	1,000	
Accumulated depreciation at 31 March 20-2		500
Retained earnings at 1 April 20-1		350
Purchases	1,200	
Inventories at 1 April 20-1	160	
Trade payables		300
Other payables		80
Revenue		2,295
Dividends received		75
Dividends paid	140	
	4,515	4,515

Additional information

- Inventories at 31 March 20-2 were valued at £180,000.

- The tax charge based on the profits for the year is £65,000.

Note that depreciation has already been provided for in the list of balances above and allocated to administrative expenses and distribution costs accordingly.

REQUIRED

Task 1

Prepare journal entries for the adjustments listed above under 'additional information'.

Task 2

In so far as the information permits, prepare the company's published income statement (including a statement of the change in retained earnings) for the year to 31 March 20-2 and a balance sheet as at that date.

Note: Where relevant, working notes should be attached to your answer.

3.8 The following information has been extracted from the books of Broadfoot plc for the year to 31 March 20-2.

	Dr £000	Cr £000
Administrative expenses	185	
Share capital (£1 ordinary shares)		200
Cash and cash equivalents	15	
Accruals		90
Distribution costs	240	
Land and buildings: at cost	210	
accumulated depreciation (at 1 April 20-1)		48
Plant and machinery: at cost	125	
accumulated depreciation (at 1 April 20-1)		75
Retained earnings (at 1 April 20-1)		350
Purchases	470	
Revenue		1,300
Inventories (at 1 April 20-1)	150	
Trade payables		60
Trade receivables	628	
Dividends paid	100	
	2,123	2,123

Additional information

- Inventories at 31 March 20-2 were valued at £250,000.

- Buildings and plant and machinery are depreciated on a straight-line basis (assuming no residual value) at the following rates:

On cost:	%
Buildings	5
Plant and machinery	20

  Land at cost was £110,000. Land is not depreciated.

  There were no purchases or sales of non-current assets during the year to 31 March 20-2.

  The depreciation charges for the year to 31 March 20-2 are to be apportioned as follows:

	%
Cost of sales	60
Distribution costs	20
Administrative expenses	20

- Tax for the year to 31 March 20-2 is £135,000.

REQUIRED

Task 1

Prepare journal entries for the adjustments listed above under 'additional information'.

Task 2

As far as the information permits, prepared Broadfoot plc's published income statement (including a statement of the change in retained earnings), for the year to 31 March 20-2 and a balance sheet as at that date. (Where relevant, working notes should be attached to your answer.)

3.9   The following list of balances was extracted from the books of Grandware plc on 31 December 20-2

	£
Revenue	2,640,300
Administrative expenses	220,180
Distribution costs	216,320
Interest paid on loan stock	10,000
Dividends received	2,100
Dividends paid	20,000
Share premium	40,000
Purchases	2,089,600
Inventories at 1 January 20-2	318,500
Cash and cash equivalents	20,640

Trade receivables	415,800
Provision for doubtful receivables at 1 January 20-2	10,074
Bad debts	8,900
Trade payables	428,250
10% Loan stock	200,000
Non-current investments in listed companies	20,000
Office equipment	110,060
Vehicles	235,000
Share capital (£1 ordinary shares)	200,000
Retained earnings at 1 January 20-2	164,276

Notes:

• Accrue for the six months £10,000 loan stock interest due, which is payable 1 January 20-3.

• Provide for administrative expenses of £12,200 paid in advance at 31 December 20-2 and distribution costs of £21,000 owing at 31 December 20-2.

• Provision for doubtful receivables is to be maintained at 3% of receivables.

• Inventories at 31 December 20-2 were valued at £340,600.

• Provide for tax of £45,000 which is payable on 1 October 20-3.

• Depreciation on tangible non-current assets has already been allocated for the year and apportioned to the respective expense accounts in the list of balances provided.

REQUIRED

Task 1

Prepare journal entries for the adjustments listed above under 'notes'.

Task 2

Prepare for presentation to the shareholders a published income statement (including a statement of the change in retained earnings), for the year ended 31 December 20-2 and a balance sheet as at that date.

Working notes should be attached to your answer.

3.10 You have been asked to help prepare the financial statements of Hightink Limited for the year ended 31 March 20-2. The trial balance of the company as at 31 March 20-2 is set out below.

	Dr £000	Cr £000
Interest	240	
Distribution costs	6,852	
Administrative expenses	3,378	
Trade receivables	5,455	
Trade payables		2,363
Dividends paid	400	
Ordinary share capital		4,000
Revenue		31,710
Long-term loan		6,000
Land – cost	5,000	
Buildings – cost	3,832	
Fixtures and fittings – cost	2,057	
Motor vehicles – cost	3,524	
Office equipment – cost	2,228	
Purchases	15,525	
Cash and cash equivalents	304	
Retained earnings		6,217
Inventories as at 1 April 20-1	6,531	
Share premium		2,000
Buildings – accumulated depreciation		564
Fixtures and fittings – accumulated depreciation		726
Motor vehicles – accumulated depreciation		1,283
Office equipment – accumulated depreciation		463
	55,326	55,326

Further information:

- The authorised share capital of the company, all of which has been issued, consists of ordinary shares with a nominal value of £1.

- During the year the company paid a final dividend of 7.5p per share for the year to 31 March 20-1, and an interim dividend of 2.5p per share for the current year. The proposed final dividend for the year to 31 March 20-2 is 10p per share.

- The inventories at the close of business on 31 March 20-2 were valued at cost at £7,878,000.

- The corporation tax charge for the year has been calculated as £1,920,000.

- Credit sales relating to April 20-2 amounting to £204,000 had been entered incorrectly into the accounts in March 20-2.

- Interest on the long-term loan has been paid for six months of the year. No adjustment has been made for the interest due for the final six months of the year. Interest is charged on the loan at a rate of 8% per annum.

•   The land has been revalued by professional valuers at £5,500,000. The revaluation is to be included in the financial statements for the year ended 31 March 20-2.

•   All of the operations are continuing operations.

REQUIRED

Task 1

Make the journal entries required as a result of the further information given above. Dates and narratives are not required.

•   You must show any workings relevant to these adjustments.

•   Ignore any effect of these adjustments on the tax charge for the year given above.

Task 2

Making any adjustments required as a result of the further information given above, draft an income statement (including a statement of the change in retained earnings) for the year ended 31 March 20-2, and a balance sheet for Hightink as at that date.

Task 3

Show the note that is required to be included in the published accounts of Hightink for the year in respect of dividends.

3.11   You have been asked to assist in the preparation of the financial statements of Wyvern Office Products Limited for the year ended 31 December 20-4. The company sells office equipment and supplies to businesses and individuals through its shops and warehouses.

You have been provided with the extended trial balance of Wyvern Office Products Limited as at 31 December 20-4 as shown on the next page.

The following information is available to you:

•   the authorised share capital of the businesses, all of which has been issued, consists of ordinary shares with a nominal value of £1

•   depreciation has been calculated on the non-current assets of the business and has already been transferred into the balances for distribution costs and administrative expenses shown on the extended trial balance

•   the corporation tax charge for the year has been calculated as £215,000

•   interest on the 10% debentures has been paid for the first six months of the year only

REQUIRED

From the extended trial balance, and the information provided above, you are to draft an income statement (including a statement of the change in retained earnings) for the year ended 31 December 20-4 and a balance sheet as at that date.

Notes:

•   journal entries are not required for any necessary adjustments to the figures in the extended trial balance

•   ignore the effect of any of the adjustments to the tax charge for the year

•   show workings relevant to the figures appearing in the financial statements

EXTENDED TRIAL BALANCE — WYVERN OFFICE PRODUCTS LIMITED — 31 DECEMBER 20-4

Description	Trial balance Dr £000	Trial balance Cr £000	Adjustments Dr £000	Adjustments Cr £000	Income statement Dr £000	Income statement Cr £000	Balance sheet Dr £000	Balance sheet Cr £000
Revenue		10,641				10,641		
Purchases	7,028				7,028			
Returns inwards	65				65			
Returns outwards		48				48		
Inventories	2,220		2,533	2,533	2,220	2,533	2,533	
Distribution costs	1,524		176		1,700			
Administrative expenses	1,103		308		1,411			
Accruals				67				67
Prepayments			24				24	
Interest	80				80			
Land – cost	510						510	
Buildings – cost	1,490						1,490	
Fixtures and fittings – cost	275						275	
Vehicles – cost	316						316	
Office equipment – cost	294						294	
Investments (non-current)	1,850						1,850	
Buildings – accumulated depn		407		298				705
Fixtures and fittings – accumulated depn		142		55				197
Vehicles – accumulated depn		124		48				172
Office equipment – accumulated depn		107		30				137
Trade receivables	1,592						1,592	
Provision for doubtful receivables		70		10				80
Cash and cash equivalents	44						44	
Trade payables		2,051						2,051
10% Debentures		1,600						1,600
Dividends paid*	120				120			
Share capital		2,000						2,000
Share premium		750						750
Retained earnings		571						571
Profit					598			598
	18,511	18,511	3,041	3,041	13,222	13,222	8,928	8,928

* to be deducted from retained earnings

3.12 Teme plc is a company which sells furniture. The following information has been extracted from the books of account for the year to 31 March 20-6.

	£000
Auditors' remuneration	25
Tax: based on the accounting profit for the year to 31 March 20-6	1,400
Delivery expenses	2,160
Dividends paid	2,000
Non-current assets at cost:	
Delivery vans	300
Office cars	80
Showroom premises and equipment	6,000
Office expenses	900
Office rent, rates, heat and light	400
Purchases	30,000
Revenue	40,000
Inventories at cost:	
at 1 April 20-5	6,000
at 31 March 20-6	7,000
Showroom costs	1,600
Wages and salaries:	
Delivery staff	800
Directors	400
Office staff	200
Showroom staff	500
Interest paid on bank loan	150
Retained earnings at 1 April 20-5	2,550

Additional information

1   *Depreciation policy*

Depreciation is provided at the following annual rates on a straight-line basis: delivery vans 20%; office cars 25%; showroom premises and equipment 10%.

2   The Directors' salaries can be split as follows:

	£000
Managing Director	150
Chairman	50
Sales Director	90
Finance Director	110

REQUIRED

Prepare for presentation to the shareholders a published income statement (including a statement of the change in retained earnings), for the year ended 31 March 20-6. Note that a published balance sheet is not required.

Working notes should be attached to your answer to show cost of sales, distribution costs and administrative expenses.

this chapter covers . . .

In this chapter we focus on the international accounting standards that impact on the way in which assets are accounted for in both the income statement and the balance sheet. We focus on assets, to cover:

- property, plant and equipment (IAS 16)
- intangible assets (IAS 38)
- impairment of assets (IAS 36)
- investment property (IAS 40)
- leases
- inventories (IAS 2)

PERFORMANCE CRITERIA COVERED

unit 11: DRAFTING FINANCIAL STATEMENTS
element 11.1
draft limited company financial statements

A   draft limited company financial statements from the appropriate information

B   correctly identify and implement subsequent adjustments and ensure that discrepancies, unusual features or queries are identified and either resolved or referred to the appropriate person

C   ensure that limited company financial statements comply with relevant accounting standards and domestic legislation and with the organisation's policies, regulations and procedures

E   ensure that confidentiality procedures are followed at all times

HOW TO STUDY THE ACCOUNTING STANDARDS

As we have seen in earlier chapters, international accounting standards – in the form of International Accounting Standards (IASs) and International Financial Reporting Standards (IFRSs) – play a major role in the presentation and detail of financial statements. *Drafting Financial Statements* requires knowledge of a large number of standards – in this book we have attempted, as far as possible, to group standards together where they relate to particular topics. Accordingly, this chapter focuses on those standards that relate to assets. The next chapter looks at the standards covering liabilities and the income statement; Chapter 8 deals with consolidated accounts, so the standards which cover group accounts (and also associated companies) are covered there. The cash flow statement is detailed in an accounting standard (IAS 7) and this is detailed in Chapter 6. A few standards do not fit readily to such groupings and so these have been included at what seems to be the most logical place. We believe that this 'grouping' approach is preferable to explaining the standards in their numerical order, which results in a long 'list' where often unrelated topics follow one another.

the international accounting standards

The table that follows shows the current international accounting standards, together with their titles and the page in this book where each is covered. The index of standards (page 341) also shows relevant page numbers. Note that not all standards are assessed in *Drafting Financial Statements*.

International Financial Reporting Standards (IFRSs)

IFRS 1	First-time Adoption of International Financial Reporting Standards	not assessable
IFRS 2	Share-based Payment	not assessable
IFRS 3	Business Combinations	page 240
IFRS 4	Insurance Contracts	not assessable
IFRS 5	Non-current Assets Held for Sale and Discontinued Operations	pages 61 and 66
IFRS 6	Exploration for and Evaluation of Mineral Resources	not assessable

International Accounting Standards (IASs)

IAS 1	Presentation of Financial Statements	page 58
IAS 2	Inventories	page 127

continued on the next page

IAS 7	Cash Flow Statements	page 169
IAS 8	Accounting Policies, Changes in Accounting Estimates and Errors	page 73
IAS 10	Events after the Balance Sheet Date	page 153
IAS 11	Construction Contracts	not assessable
IAS 12	Income Taxes	page 141
IAS 14	Segment Reporting	page 159
IAS 16	Property, Plant and Equipment	page 98
IAS 17	Leases	page 120
IAS 18	Revenue	page 155
IAS 19	Employee Benefits	not assessable
IAS 20	Accounting for Government Grants and Disclosure of Government Assistance	not assessable
IAS 21	The Effects of Changes in Foreign Exchange Rates	not assessable
IAS 23	Borrowing Costs	page 156
IAS 24	Related Party Disclosures	not assessable
IAS 26	Accounting and Reporting by Retirement Benefit Plans	not assessable
IAS 27	Consolidated and Separate Financial Statements	page 240
IAS 28	Investments in Associates	page 266
IAS 29	Financial Reporting in Hyperinflationary Economies	not assessable
IAS 30	Disclosures in the Financial Statements of Banks and Similar Financial Institutions	not assessable
IAS 31	Interests in Joint Ventures	not assessable
IAS 32	Financial Instruments: Disclosure and Presentation	not assessable
IAS 33	Earnings per Share	page 157
IAS 34	Interim Financial Reporting	not assessable
IAS 36	Impairment of Assets	page 112
IAS 37	Provisions, Contingent Liabilities and Contingent Assets	page 147
IAS 38	Intangible Assets	page 108
IAS 39	Financial Instruments: Recognition and Measurement	not assessable
IAS 40	Investment Property	page 118
IAS 41	Agriculture	not assessable

Note: gaps in the numbers represent standards that have been withdrawn

organising your study of accounting standards

In this textbook we cover the aspects of each international accounting standard that are assessable under *Drafting Financial Statements*. Note, however, that some standards are not assessable, while others cover more detailed issues that are not assessable. The texts of all current standards are available from the International Accounting Standards Board (www.iasb.org.uk).

For learning the key points of accounting standards, it is strongly recommended that you use a system of index cards: put the number and name of each standard on the top of an index card and then outline the key points of the standards on the cards, using bullet point format, together with a cross-reference to the relevant pages of this textbook. The set of index cards (don't use very small cards!) then forms a useful learning and revision aid which can be carried around and easily referred to at almost any time.

It is also important to keep up-to-date with any changes to accounting standards – on a monthly basis use accountancy magazines and web sites (see the Web Directory on page 6).

ACCOUNTING FOR ASSETS

This chapter explains the accounting treatment of assets – non current and current – as specified by the relevant international accounting standards. The diagram which follows shows the questions to be asked when dealing with assets:

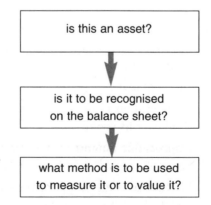

It is well worth going back to the *Framework* document for the definition of an asset (page 16): *'a resource controlled by the entity as a result of past events and from which future economic benefits are expected to flow to the entity.'*

The definition refers to a resource being *controlled* (and not necessarily owned). Thus a company which leases an asset – such as a machine – from a leasing company may well recognise the asset on its balance sheet, even though it is not the legal owner. Note that there is also the requirement for the asset to generate future economic benefits for the entity.

In order to be recognised (ie shown) on the balance sheet, assets must be capable of being reliably measured at either their cost or their value.

Once an asset is recognised on the balance sheet, there is then the question of how it is to be subsequently measured – for example, at cost less depreciation/amortisation, or revaluation. The international accounting standards which follow in the chapter set out the recognition and measurement criteria of different classes of assets: *Property, Plant and Equipment* (IAS 16), *Intangible Assets* (IAS 38), *Investment Property* (IAS 40) and *Inventories* (IAS 2), together with *Impairment of Assets* (IAS 36) and *Leases* (IAS 17).

IAS 16 – PROPERTY, PLANT AND EQUIPMENT

This standard sets out the accounting treatment for property, plant and equipment (PPE). These are non-current tangible assets such as land and buildings, machinery, office equipment, shop fittings and vehicles.

The principal issues covered by the standard are the recognition of the assets, the determination of their carrying amounts (see below), and the depreciation charges and impairment losses (see IAS 36, *Impairment of Assets*, page 112) to be recognised in relation to them.

definitions

Property, plant and equipment are tangible assets held for use in the production or supply of goods and services, which are expected to be used for more than one period.

Depreciation is the systematic allocation of the depreciable amount of an asset over its useful life.

Depreciable amount is the cost or valuation of the asset, less any residual value.

Useful life is the length of time, or the number of units of production, for which an asset is expected to be used.

Residual value is the net amount the entity expects to obtain for an asset at the end of its useful life after deducting the expected costs of disposal.

Fair value is the amount for which an asset could be exchanged between knowledgeable, willing parties in an arm's length transaction.

Carrying amount is the amount at which an asset is recognised in the balance sheet, after deducting any accumulated depreciation or impairment losses.

recognition

An item of property, plant and equipment is to be recognised as an asset when

– it is probable that *future economic benefits* will flow to the entity; and

– the cost of the asset can be *measured reliably*

IAS 16 acknowledges that, after the initial purchase cost, there will often be further costs spent on PPE – the standard sets out the following guidelines for such subsequent expenditure:

• the costs of day-to-day servicing of the asset, including the cost of small parts, are to be recognised in the income statement

• where parts of the asset require replacement at regular intervals – eg the seats of a bus or a train – the costs incurred can be recognised in the carrying amount of the PPE (subject to the recognition criteria – see above – of future economic benefits and reliable measurement)

• where regular inspections have to be carried out to continue operating an asset – for example, an aircraft – the costs of the inspection can be recognised in the carrying amount (subject to the recognition criteria – see above)

Note that *derecognition* (which occurs when assets are disposed of) is explained on page 102.

measurement of property, plant and equipment

Initially PPE are measured at cost in the balance sheet.

Cost includes the purchase price, including any import duties and other taxes, plus any costs directly attributable (see below) to bring the asset to the location and condition for its intended use, plus the estimated costs of dismantling and removing the asset at the end of its useful life.

Attributable costs which *can be included* in the cost of the asset include:

– costs of site preparation

– initial delivery and handling costs

– installation and assembly costs

– costs of testing the asset

– professional fees, eg engineers, architects

Costs which *cannot be included* in the cost of the asset include administration and other general overhead costs, start-up costs of a new business or section of the business, start-up costs for introducing a new product or service – such as advertising and promotional costs.

After acquisition of PPE an entity must choose either the cost model or the revaluation model as its accounting policy – which is then applied to an entire class of PPE. The two models are defined as follows:

- **Cost model** – the asset is carried at cost less accumulated depreciation and impairment losses

- **Revaluation model** – the asset is carried in the balance sheet at a revalued amount, being its fair value* less any subsequent depreciation and impairment losses (see IAS 36, *Impairment of Assets*, page 112); revaluations are to be made regularly to ensure that the carrying amount does not differ materially from its fair value at the balance sheet date

  * fair value is defined on the previous page; its use is subject to the fair value being able to be measured reliably

IAS 16 gives guidance on the use of fair values in the revaluation model:

- for land and buildings, the fair value is usually determined from market-based evidence and is undertaken by professional valuers

- for plant and equipment, the fair value is usually their market value

- where items of PPE are specialist and there is no market-based evidence, other methods may be needed to determine fair value – for example, by applying depreciation to the replacement cost

- the regularity of revaluations depends upon changes in the fair values – when changes are frequent, annual revaluations are required; where changes are insignificant, revaluations can be made every three to five years

When an item of PPE is revalued, the entire class of assets to which it belongs must be revalued. Note that classes are groups of similar assets, for example land, buildings, machinery, vehicles, fixtures and fittings, office equipment, etc. Revaluations are dealt with as follows:

- any increase in value is credited directly within equity to a *revaluation surplus* (although an increase which reverses part or all of a previous decrease for the same asset is recognised as income in the income statement)

- any reduction in value is recognised as an expense in the income statement (although a decrease which reverses part or all of a previous increase for the same asset is debited to the revaluation surplus) – see also Step 3 of the impairment review on page 115

depreciation

The depreciable amount (cost less residual value) of an asset is to be allocated on a systematic basis over its useful life.

Note the following points:

- the residual value and the useful life of an asset are to be reviewed at least annually and, if they differ from previous estimates, any change is to be accounted for as a change in an estimate under IAS 8, *Accounting Policies, Changes in Accounting Estimates and Errors*
- depreciation continues to be recognised even if the fair value of an asset exceeds its carrying amount (but there is no need for depreciation when the residual value is greater than the carrying amount)
- spending money on repair and maintenance of an asset does not remove the need for depreciation
- when calculating depreciable amount, the residual values of assets are often low or immaterial – for example, the scrap value of a machine is often negligible
- depreciation can be applied to separate parts of an asset where each part is a significant cost – for example, the engines of an aircraft are often depreciated separately from the body of the aircraft
- depreciation for the period is recognised in the income statement (unless it is included in the carrying value of another asset)
- when determining the useful life of an asset, the following factors need to be considered (even if the asset is not being used):
  - expected usage of the asset, ie the expected capacity or output
  - expected physical wear and tear, which depends on operational factors and the repair and maintenance programme
  - technical or commercial obsolescence, eg the introduction of new technology, changes in demand for the product or service
  - legal or similar limits on the use of the asset, eg the period for which an asset is leased

Freehold land is shown at cost and is not depreciated because it has an unlimited useful life (unless it is a mine or a quarry); note that leasehold land will be depreciated.

Land and buildings are separated out and accounted for separately – the land is not depreciated, but buildings have a limited useful life and are depreciated. An increase in the value of the land on which a building stands does not affect the depreciable amount of the building.

Depreciation methods include the straight-line method, the diminishing (reducing) balance method, and the units of production (output) method –

you will be familiar with some of these from your studies at Intermediate Level. Key features of each of these are:

- straight-line depreciation results in a constant depreciation charge over the asset's useful life
- diminishing (reducing) balance depreciation results in a decreasing depreciation charge over the useful life (ie the depreciation in the early years is greater than in later years) – see also sum of the digits depreciation in the Case Study which follows
- units of production (or service) depreciation results in a depreciation charge based on the expected use or output

An entity chooses the depreciation method which best reflects the pattern in which the asset's economic benefits are consumed. The depreciation method is to be reviewed at least annually and, if there has been a change in the pattern of consumption of benefits, the method should be changed (this would be a change in an accounting estimate – see IAS 8, page 73).

Derecognition occurs when an item of PPE is disposed of, or when no future economic benefits are expected from its use or disposal. Any gain or loss on disposal (ie the difference between the net disposal proceeds and the carrying value) is recognised as income or expense in the income statement.

For example, an item of PPE has a carrying value (cost/revaluation less accumulated depreciation) of £1,500 and is now sold for £800: the loss on disposal of £700 is recognised as an expense in the income statement.

disclosure in the financial statements

For each class of property, plant and equipment the financial statements are to show:

- the basis for determining the carrying amount
- the depreciation method(s) used
- the useful lives or depreciation rates
- the gross carrying amount (eg cost of the asset) and the accumulated depreciation and impairment losses at the beginning and end of the period
- a reconciliation of the carrying amount at the beginning and end of the period showing:
  - additions
  - disposals
  - acquisitions through business combinations (see Chapter 8)
  - revaluation increases
  - impairment losses
  - reversal of impairment losses

- depreciation
- other changes

As depreciation methods and the estimation of useful lives are matters of judgement, it is important to provide users of financial statements with information that enables them to review the policies selected by management and to enable comparison to be made with other companies. To this end it is necessary to disclose in the financial statements:

• the depreciation for the period

• the accumulated depreciation at the end of the period

Case Study

BROCKEN LIMITED: CALCULATING DEPRECIATION

situation

You are an accounts assistant at Brocken Limited, an engineering company. The company has recently bought a new computer-controlled cutting machine for use in the factory. You have been asked by the finance director to prepare depreciation calculations, based on the following information:

CUTTING MACHINE	
Cost price on 1 January 2006	£20,000 (net of VAT)
Estimated life	4 years
Estimated production:	
2006	60,000 units
2007	50,000 units
2008	25,000 units
2009	25,000 units
total	160,000 units
Estimated residual value at end of four years	£4,000

The finance director wants to know which methods of depreciation are available to the company, and for you to prepare a table for each method showing the amount of depreciation expense per year recognised in the income statement, and the net book value of the asset for the balance sheet.

solution

You decide to calculate figures for four depreciation methods:

• straight-line depreciation

• diminishing (reducing) balance depreciation

• units of production depreciation

• sum of the digits depreciation

straight-line depreciation

With this method, a fixed percentage is written off the original cost of the asset each year. For this machine, twenty-five per cent of the depreciable amount will be written off each year by the straight-line method.

The method of calculating straight-line depreciation, taking into account the asset's estimated residual value at the end of its useful life, is:

$$\frac{\text{cost of asset} - \text{estimated residual (scrap or salvage) value}}{\text{number of years' expected use of asset}}$$

The machine is expected to have a residual value of £4,000, so the depreciation amount will be:

$$\frac{£20,000 - £4,000}{4 \text{ years}} = £4,000 \text{ per year}$$

diminishing (reducing) balance depreciation

With this method, a fixed percentage is written off the diminished balance each year. The diminished (reduced) balance is cost of the asset less depreciation to date. The machine is to be depreciated by 33.3% (one-third) each year, using the diminishing balance method (see calculations below). The depreciation amounts for the four years of ownership are:

	£
Original cost of machine	20,000
2006 depreciation: 33.3% of £20,000	6,667
Value at end of 2006	13,333
2007 depreciation: 33.3% of £13,333	4,444
Value at end of 2007	8,889
2008 depreciation: 33.3% of £8,889	2,963
Value at end of 2008	5,926
2009 depreciation: 33.3% of £5,926	1,926
Residual value at end of 2009	4,000

Note that the figures have been rounded to the nearest £, and depreciation for 2009 has been adjusted by approximately £50 to leave a residual value of £4,000.

The formula to calculate the percentage of reducing balance depreciation is:

$$r = 1 - \sqrt[n]{\frac{s}{c}}$$

In this formula:

r	=	percentage rate of depreciation
n	=	number of years
s	=	residual value
c	=	cost of asset

For the machine above, the 33.3% is calculated as:

$$r = 1 - \sqrt[4]{\frac{4,000}{20,000}}$$

$$r = 1 - \sqrt[4]{0.2}$$ (to find the fourth root press the square root key on the calculator twice)

$$r = 1 - 0.669$$

$$r = 0.331 \text{ or } 33.1\% \text{ (which is close to the 33.3\% used above)}$$

units of production depreciation

This method uses the estimated number of units to be produced by the machine over its useful life. (In other circumstances it can be based on the number of hours' operation of a machine, or the number of miles/kilometres of a vehicle.)

Depreciation for a given year is calculated by reference to the number of units for that year.

The machine is to be depreciated by £16,000 (ie £20,000 – £4,000 residual value). As the total number of units to be produced by the machine is expected to be 160,000, then each year's depreciation will be calculated at £1,000 for every 10,000 units produced (£16,000 ÷ 160,000 units).

Depreciation amounts will be:

2006	£6,000	depreciation for year
2007	£5,000	depreciation for year
2008	£2,500	depreciation for year
2009	£2,500	depreciation for year
	£16,000	total depreciation

This method has the benefit of linking usage (ie units) to the depreciation amount. In years of high usage, depreciation is higher than in years of low usage. As the asset gets older, so the usage may be lower, but repair costs may be increasing: in this way the total expense (depreciation + repair costs) will probably be a similar amount from year-to-year.

sum of the digits depreciation

This method is often used as an approximation of diminishing (reducing) balance. Here the depreciation amount each year is calculated on the sum of the number of years of useful life. As the machine is expected to last for four years: the sum of the digits is 1 + 2 + 3 + 4 = 10. Depreciation is applied to the depreciable amount, £16,000 (ie £20,000 – £4,000 residual value) as follows:

2006	4/10 x £16,000	=	£6,400	depreciation for year
2007	3/10 x £16,000	=	£4,800	depreciation for year
2008	2/10 x £16,000	=	£3,200	depreciation for year
2009	1/10 x £16,000	=	£1,600	depreciation for year
			£16,000	total depreciation

In using this method, the digits count down from the number of years of useful life, ie the depreciation for year 1 is higher than that for year 2, etc. In this way, sum of the digits depreciation is similar to the diminishing (reducing) balance method.

depreciation methods compared

The following tables use the depreciation amounts calculated above.

	1	2	3	4
straight-line depreciation				
Year	Original cost	Depreciation for year	Depreciation to date	Net book value (ie column 1-3)
	£	£	£	£
2006	20,000	4,000	4,000	16,000
2007	20,000	4,000	8,000	12,000
2008	20,000	4,000	12,000	8,000
2009	20,000	4,000	16,000	4,000

Note: Net book value (carrying amount) is cost, less depreciation to date, ie column 1, less column 3.

These calculations will be used in the financial statements as follows: taking 2007 as an example, the income statement will recognise £4,000 (column 2) as an expense, while the balance sheet will carry £12,000 (column 4) as the net book value (carrying amount).

	1	2	3	4
diminishing balance depreciation				
Year	Original cost	Depreciation for year	Depreciation to date	Net book value (ie column 1-3)
	£	£	£	£
2006	20,000	6,667	6,667	13,333
2007	20,000	4,444	11,111	8,889
2008	20,000	2,963	14,074	5,926
2009	20,000	1,926	16,000	4,000

	1	2	3	4
units of production depreciation				
Year	Original cost	Depreciation for year	Depreciation to date	Net book value (ie column 1-3)
	£	£	£	£
2006	20,000	6,000	6,000	14,000
2007	20,000	5,000	11,000	9,000
2008	20,000	2,500	13,500	6,500
2009	20,000	2,500	16,000	4,000

sum of the digits depreciation				
	1	2	3	4
Year	Original cost	Depreciation for year	Depreciation to date	Net book value (ie column 1-3)
	£	£	£	£
2006	20,000	6,400	6,400	13,600
2007	20,000	4,800	11,200	8,800
2008	20,000	3,200	14,400	5,600
2009	20,000	1,600	16,000	4,000

COMPARISON OF DEPRECIATION METHODS

METHOD	depreciation amount	depreciation rate	suitability
straight-line	same money amount each year	lower depreciation percentage required to achieve same residual value	best used for non-current assets likely to be kept for the whole of their useful lives, eg machines, office equipment
diminishing balance	different money amounts each year: more than straight-line in early years, less in later years	higher depreciation percentage required to achieve same residual value – but can never reach nil value	best used for non-current assets which depreciate more in early years and which are not kept for whole of useful lives, eg vehicles
units of production	invariably different money amounts each year	depreciation is linked to production	allocates depreciation on a systematic basis over asset's useful life – suitable for non-current assets where units can be ascertained reliably, eg machinery, vehicles
sum of the digits	similar to diminishing balance	depreciation is linked to number of years of useful life, eg, for a four-year life, 1 year + 2 + 3 + 4 = 10 digits	often used as an approximation of diminishing balance depreciation

Note: Whichever depreciation method is selected, the total profits of the company over the life of the asset will be the same. The various methods will cause the profit for individual years to be different but, overall, the same total depreciation is recognised as an expense in the income statement. IAS 16 requires that the depreciable amount (cost less residual value) of an asset is to be allocated on a systematic basis over its useful life. As depreciation is 'non-cash' there is no effect on the bank balance.

IAS 38 – INTANGIBLE ASSETS

This standard sets out the accounting treatment of expenditure on acquiring, developing, maintaining or enhancing intangible assets such as scientific or technical knowledge, design and implementation of new processes, licences, intellectual property, market knowledge, and trademarks (including brand names). Note that goodwill is not covered – see IFRS 3, *Business Combinations* (page 240).

definition

An intangible asset is defined as '*an identifiable non-monetary asset without physical substance*'. An asset is a resource:

– controlled by an entity as a result of past events (eg a purchase transaction), and

– from which future economic benefits (eg cash inflows) are expected to flow to the entity

Thus examples of intangible assets include computer software, patents, copyrights, customer lists, licences and marketing rights.

The definitions, above, give the three key elements of an intangible asset as being:

• *identifiability* – the asset is either separable from the entity and is capable of being sold or transferred, or it arises from contractual or other legal rights

• *control* – the entity has the power to obtain future economic benefits from the asset

• *future economic benefits* – include revenue from the sale of products or services, cost savings, or other benefits

recognition

Intangible assets come about from two main sources: either they are purchased, or they are internally generated (ie created within the business). In both cases the intangible asset is recognised initially in the financial statements at cost price when:

– it is probable that the expected future economic benefits that are attributable to the asset will flow to the entity; and

– the cost of the asset can be measured reliably

Note that neither internally generated goodwill nor internally generated brands can be recognised as assets. (For goodwill which may feature in consolidated accounts, see IFRS 3, *Business Combinations*.)

research and development

Many companies are involved in the research and development of new products or processes. Such activities often lead to the creation of internally generated intangible assets. In financial statements, we must be careful to distinguish between the research phase and the development phase by noting the definitions given in IAS 38:

- **research** is original and planned investigation undertaken with the prospect of gaining new scientific or technical knowledge and understanding

- **development** is the application of research findings or other knowledge to a plan or design for the production of new or substantially improved materials, devices, products, processes, systems or services before the start of commercial production or use

Thus research is experimental or theoretical work undertaken to gain new knowledge for its own sake, while development takes new knowledge in order to create new or improved products, services and systems up to the point of commercial use.

IAS 38 requires that revenue expenditure on research is to be recognised as an expense in the income statement of the year in which it is incurred. However, capital expenditure on non-current assets – such as a new research laboratory   is to be recorded as non-current assets and depreciated over the useful lives of the assets.

Development costs are either recognised as an expense in the income statement when they are incurred, or they are to be capitalised (ie recognised on the balance sheet) as an intangible asset if the entity can demonstrate all of the following:

- the technical feasibility of completing the intangible asset so that it will be available for use or sale

- its intention to complete the intangible asset and to use or sell it

- its ability to use or sell the intangible asset

- the way in which the intangible asset will generate probable future economic benefits

- the availability of resources to complete the development and to use or sell the intangible asset

- its ability to measure the development expenditure reliably

Included in the development cost of internally generated intangible assets are the direct costs (eg materials, labour, fees to register legal rights); excluded are costs for general overheads (eg administrative expenses).

measurement of intangible assets

Initially, intangible assets are measured at cost in the balance sheet. However, after acquisition, an entity can choose either the cost model or the revaluation model as its accounting policy. The two models are defined – using similar terms to those seen already in IAS 16, *Property, Plant and Equipment* – as follows:

- **Cost model** – the intangible asset is carried at cost less any accumulated amortisation (depreciation) and impairment losses.

- **Revaluation model** – the intangible asset is carried at a revalued amount, being its fair value* less any subsequent amortisation and impairment losses (see IAS 36, *Impairment of Assets*, page 112); revaluations are to be made regularly to ensure that the carrying value does not differ materially from its fair value at the balance sheet date.

  * fair value of an asset is defined by IAS 38 as 'the amount for which an asset could be exchanged between knowledgeable, willing parties in an arm's length transaction.'

With the revaluation model and its requirement for regular revaluations:

- any increase in value is credited directly within equity to a *revaluation surplus* (although an increase which reverses part or all of a previous decrease for the same asset is recognised as income in the income statement)

- any reduction in value is recognised as an expense in the income statement (although a decrease which reverses part or all of a previous increase for the same asset is debited to the revaluation surplus) – see also Step 3 of the impairment review on page 115

An entity must classify the useful lives of intangible assets as either

- finite, ie having a limited useful life; or
- indefinite, ie having no foreseeable limit to the period over which the asset is expected to generate net cash inflows

An intangible asset with a *finite life* is to be amortised over its useful life:

- the method of amortisation should reflect the pattern of benefits expected by the entity (if the pattern cannot be determined reliably, then the straight-line method should be used)

- the amount of amortisation is to be recognised as an expense in the income statement

- the residual value should be assumed to be zero (unless there is an agreement for a third party to buy it at the end of its useful life, or where a residual value can be determined by reference to a market in such assets)

- the amortisation period (and method) should be reviewed at least annually, with appropriate changes being made where necessary

An asset with an *indefinite life* is not amortised. Instead, it is to be tested for impairment annually, and whenever there is an indication that the asset may be impaired. The useful life is to be reviewed each accounting period to determine whether or not it is still indefinite. If necessary, a change from indefinite to finite should be made and accounted for as a change in an accounting estimate (see IAS 8, *Accounting Policies, Changes in Accounting Estimates and Errors*, page 73).

Case Study	POMONA AGROCHEMICAL COMPANY: RESEARCH AND DEVELOPMENT COSTS

POMONA AGROCHEMICAL COMPANY: RESEARCH AND DEVELOPMENT COSTS

situation

Pomona Agrochemical Company has the following account in its book-keeping system:

Dr		Research and Development Expenditure Account		Cr
2006		£	2006	£
24 Mar	Bank (research)	24,000		
18 Nov	Bank (development)	40,000		

The development costs have been incurred in respect of a new agricultural chemical, WACL X123. This product has been on sale since 1 January 2007; revenue in the first few weeks look very promising and the company is forecasting good profits from it.

It is now February 2007 and you are preparing the company's financial statements for the year ended 31 December 2006. How will you deal with the research and development expenditure?

solution

research

The research costs of £24,000 will be recognised as an expense in the income statement for the year ended 31 December 2006.

development

The development costs of £40,000 should be recognised as an expense in the income statement unless they meet the criteria set out in IAS 38. Here, the development costs of the new chemical do appear to fit the definition of intangible asset, ie 'an identifiable non-monetary asset without physical substance.' The asset is a resource

– controlled by an entity as a result of past events

– from which future economic benefits are expected to flow to the entity

Provided that the company can demonstrate all of the points which follow, then the development costs are to be recognised on the balance sheet:

• the technical feasibility of completing the intangible asset so that it will be available for use or sale

• its intention to complete the intangible asset and use or sell it

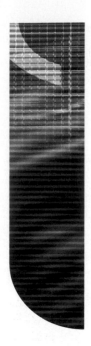

- its ability to use or sell the intangible asset
- the way in which the intangible asset will generate probable future economic benefits
- the availability of resources to complete the development and to use or sell the intangible asset
- its ability to measure the development expenditure reliably

As the new chemical is already on sale and the company is forecasting good profits, it seems most likely that the development costs can be capitalised and recognised on Pomona's balance sheet as an intangible non-current asset with a value of £40,000 at 31 December 2006.

As the new chemical is now in production, the asset must now be amortised over its useful life, so the question for the following year's accounts (2007) will be to decide how long revenue from the product will last – this will determine the amount of amortisation to be recognised in the income statement for the year ended 31 December 2007, and the reduced value of the intangible asset for the year end balance sheet.

If the company believes that the asset has an indefinite life, it will not be amortised. Instead, it will be tested for impairment annually, and also whenever there is an indication that the asset may be impaired.

IAS 36 – IMPAIRMENT OF ASSETS

This standard sets out the accounting procedures to ensure that assets are carried in the balance sheet at no more than their value, or recoverable amount. If the recoverable amount of an asset is less than its carrying amount, then the carrying value is to be reduced. This is an impairment loss, which is recognised as an expense in the income statement.

definitions

Carrying amount is the amount at which an asset is recognised after deducting any accumulated depreciation (amortisation and accumulated impairment losses

Depreciation (Amortisation) is the systematic allocation of the depreciable amount of an asset over its useful life

Note: the term 'amortisation' is customarily used in relation to intangible assets instead of 'depreciation' – however, the two terms have the same meaning

Depreciable amount is the cost of an asset less its residual value

Impairment loss is the amount by which the carrying amount of an asset exceeds its recoverable amount

Fair value, less costs to sell is the amount obtainable from the sale of an asset (or cash generating unit – see below) in an arm's length transaction between knowledgeable, willing parties, less the costs of disposal

Recoverable amount of an asset is the higher of its fair value, less costs to sell, and its value in use (these terms are explained on page 115)

Useful life is either

- the period of time over which an asset is expected to be used by the entity; or
- the number of production units expected to be obtained from the asset by the entity

Cash-generating unit is the smallest identifiable group of assets that generates cash inflows that are largely independent of the cash inflows from other assets or groups of assets

scope of the standard

IAS 36 applies to most non-current assets, such as land and buildings, plant and machinery, vehicles, goodwill, other intangible assets, investments in subsidiary and associated companies (see Chapter 8). It does not apply to certain assets, including:

- inventories (see IAS 2, *Inventories*, page 127)
- assets held for sale (see IFRS 5, *Non-current Assets Held for Sale and Discontinued Operations*, page 66)
- investment property carried at fair value (see IAS 40, *Investment Property*, page 118)
- deferred tax assets (see IAS 12, *Income Taxes*, page 141)

Impairment occurs when the recoverable amount is less than the asset's carrying amount. The principle of IAS 36 is that assets need to be reviewed at each balance sheet date to see if there is any indication of impairment. The standard provides a number of indicators of impairment (see below). Certain assets have to be tested for impairment annually by comparing carrying value with recoverable amount – these assets include

- an intangible asset with an indefinite useful life
- an intangible asset not yet available for use
- goodwill acquired in a business combination (see Chapter 8)

indicators of impairment

IAS 36 gives a number of external and internal indicators of impairment, including:

External sources

- a significant fall in the asset's market value

- adverse effects on the entity caused by technology, markets, the economy, laws
- increases in interest rates
- the stock market value of the entity is less than the carrying amount of net assets

Internal sources

- obsolescence or physical damage to the asset
- adverse effects on the asset of a significant reorganisation within the entity
- the economic performance of the asset is worse than expected

There may well be other indicators – in particular, evidence from internal financial statements can indicate that an asset may be impaired. Examples include:

- a fall in the profit (or an increase in the loss) from operations
- a fall in the cash flows from operations, or a negative cash flow
- a fall in budgeted cash flows, or budgeted profit from operations

The normal expectation is that there will be no indication of impairment but, where there is, the entity must carry out an impairment review.

the impairment review

An impairment review involves comparing the asset's carrying amount with the recoverable amount. The three steps are as follows (see also the Case Study, on page 116):

STEP 1   What is the asset's carrying amount (net book value, ie cost/revaluation less depreciation/amortisation to date)?

STEP 2   What is the asset's recoverable amount? See diagram below.

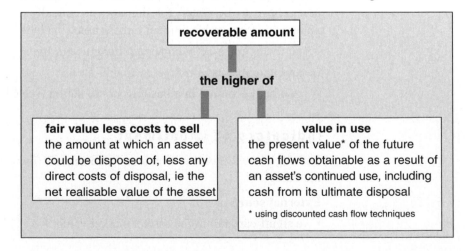

STEP 3   If carrying value is greater than recoverable amount, then the asset is impaired and should be written down to its recoverable amount in the balance sheet. The amount of the impairment loss is recognised as an expense in the income statement unless it relates to a previously revalued asset, when it is debited to the revaluation surplus within equity (to the extent of the revaluation surplus for that particular asset).

Some of the points from the three-step impairment review need a note or two of explanation.

Fair value, less costs to sell

IAS 36 gives guidance as follows:

- the best evidence of fair value is a binding sale agreement, less disposal costs
- if there is an active market (evidenced by buyers and sellers, and prices readily available), then the market price can be used, less disposal costs
- where there is no active market, the entity uses an estimate based on the best information available of the selling price, less disposal costs
- costs of disposal are direct costs only, eg legal costs, removal costs

Value in use

The calculation of an asset's value in use should consider the following:

- estimated future cash flows from the asset
- expectations of possible variations – either in amount or timing – of the future cash flows
- current interest rates
- the effect of the uncertainty inherent in the asset

The value in use is the discounted present value of the future net cash flows from the asset, including cash from its ultimate disposal. The discount rate used in the discounted cash flow calculations is to be a pre-tax rate that reflects the current market view of the time value of money, and includes any risks specific to the asset which have not been adjusted in the cash flow estimates.

recognition of impairment losses

An impairment loss is to be recognised when the recoverable amount is less than the carrying amount. The asset is reduced to its recoverable amount and the impairment loss is recognised immediately as an expense in the income statement (unless it relates to a previously revalued asset when it is debited to the revaluation surplus within equity).

After recognition of an impairment loss, depreciation/amortisation will need to be adjusted for future financial periods.

cash-generating units

For many assets it is difficult to determine the individual recoverable amount which specifically relates to them. This is because the asset belongs to a group of assets – a cash-generating unit (CGU) – which generates revenue and cash flows. A cash-generating unit (defined on page 113) is the smallest group of assets of the entity that can generate revenue and cash flows independently. IAS 36 requires that the recoverable amount should be estimated for an individual asset whenever possible; however, if this is not possible, then it will be necessary to determine the recoverable amount of the CGU to which the asset belongs. The recoverable amount of the CGU can then be compared with its carrying value to see if there has been an impairment loss.

Notes:

- Where a CGU includes goodwill amongst the assets, then IAS 36 requires that an impairment test should be carried out annually. The impairment test can be undertaken at any time during the year (not necessarily at the year end) but must be carried out at the same time as the previous year. In the year of acquisition, the impairment test must be carried out before the end of the accounting period for that year.

- Where there are impairment losses, ie the recoverable amount is less than the carrying amount of the CGU, they are to be used as follows:

  - firstly, to reduce the carrying amount of the goodwill within the CGU

  - then to reduce the carrying amount of the other assets of the CGU on a pro-rata basis

disclosure in the financial statements

The financial statements must disclose the amount of impairment losses recognised in the income statement and the line item(s) of the income statement which include the impairment losses.

Case Study

INITIAL TRAINING PLC: THE IMPAIRMENT REVIEW

situation

Initial Training plc is a large training organisation providing government-sponsored 'return-to-work' courses.

You are helping to prepare the company's year end financial statements and have been asked by your boss, the company accountant, to carry out an impairment review of non-current assets held at the training centre at Rowcester. Today you have obtained details of the two photocopiers in the print room at Rowcester:

- **Machine 1** is six years old and is a relatively slow photocopier based on old technology. The cost of this machine was £8,000 and depreciation to date (the year end) is £4,800, giving it a net book value of £3,200. Since the arrival of the other photocopier, this machine has been relegated to 'standby' use.

- **Machine 2** is only a few months old. It is a digital copier incorporating the latest technology. It is very fast and versatile, and has the capacity to meet the needs of the entire training centre. It cost £15,000 and depreciation to the end of the financial year will be £1,500, giving it a net book value of £13,500. This machine is much preferred by the staff who use it as a first choice.

solution

The impairment review you carry out is as follows:

Machine 1

- Carrying value (ie net book value): £3,200
- The company accountant has given you the following information to enable you to calculate the recoverable amount:

  the higher of

  - fair value: £1,000 resale value of machine on the secondhand market (there would be no selling costs on disposal)

  - value in use: £2,000 being the present value of the future benefits from continued use as a standby machine

  Therefore the recoverable amount is £2,000.

- As carrying value (£3,200) is greater than the machine's recoverable amount (£2,000), the asset is impaired. Accordingly, the amount of the impairment loss (£1,200) is to be recognised as an expense in the income statement, and the value of the machine will be recognised on the company's balance sheet at the recoverable amount of £2,000.

Machine 2

- Carrying value (ie net book value): £13,500
- You are given the following information to enable you to calculate the recoverable amount:

  the higher of

  - fair value: £10,000 resale value of machine on the secondhand market (there would be no selling costs on disposal)

  - value in use: £55,000 being the present value of the future benefits from continued use as the main machine

  Therefore recoverable amount is £55,000.

- As carrying value (£13,500) is less than the machine's recoverable amount (£55,000), the asset is not impaired. Accordingly, the machine will be recognised on the company's balance sheet at cost price less depreciation to date.

IAS 40 – INVESTMENT PROPERTY

Earlier in this chapter we have seen how IAS 16, *Property, Plant and Equipment*, requires that such non-current assets are to be subject to a systematic depreciation charge. For investment property – land and buildings held for rental income or capital appreciation – the IAS 16 requirement is not considered to be an appropriate accounting treatment. Accordingly, IAS 40 sets out the accounting treatment, and disclosure requirements, for investment property.

definitions

Investment property is property held to earn rent or for capital appreciation, but not being used in the ordinary course of business

Owner-occupied property is property being used in the ordinary course of business

Investment property can be land and/or a building (or a part of a building). Examples include:

- land being held for long-term capital appreciation

- land being held for undecided future use

- a building leased out under an operating lease (see IAS 17, *Leases*, page 120)

- a vacant building which is being held to be leased out under an operating lease

recognition

Investment property is to be recognised as an asset when

- it is probable that the *future economic benefits* that are associated with the property will flow to the entity, and

- the cost of the investment property can be *measured reliably*

IAS 40 requires that investment property is to be measured initially at cost, including transaction costs (eg legal fees).

After acquisition of investment property an entity must choose either the fair value model or the cost model. Whichever model is used must be applied to all of the entity's investment property. The two models are explained further as follows:

- **Fair value model**. Following initial recognition, the investment property is measured at fair value (the amount for which an asset could be exchanged between knowledgeable, willing parties in an arm's length transaction). Any gain or loss arising from a change in fair value is recognised in the income statement for the period to which it relates (note that this is different from the accounting treatment for property, plant and equipment where increases in values are credited to a revaluation surplus).

• **Cost model**. Following initial recognition, the investment property is measured at cost less accumulated depreciation and impairment losses (note that this is the same as the accounting treatment for property, plant and equipment set out in IAS 16).

disposals

Derecognition occurs when the investment property is disposed of, or when it is permanently withdrawn from use and no future economic benefits are expected from its disposal. Gains or losses on disposal are the difference between the net disposal proceeds and the carrying amount of the assets. They are to be recognised as either income or an expense in the income statement.

disclosure in the financial statements

The financial statements must disclose whether the fair value model or the cost model is being used.

Case Study

WYVERN CARS LIMITED:
ACCOUNTING FOR INVESTMENT PROPERTIES

situation

Wyvern Cars Limited is a 'niche' manufacturer of hand-built sports cars. On 1 January 2005 it buys an office block near to the works for £2m. The office block will not be used by Wyvern Cars, but is to be held as an investment property.

During the next two years the fair value of the office block at 31 December (the financial year end of Wyvern Cars) is as follows:

31 December 2005	£2.4m
31 December 2006	£2.2m

The company has decided to adopt the fair value model for its investment property.

Show how the investment property will be shown in the balance sheets of Wyvern Cars.

solution

Year ended 31 December 2005

Non-current Assets	£m
Investment property at cost	2.0
Gain for year	0.4
Fair value at 31 December 2005	2.4

- The gain in value is credited to the income statement (ie not to a revaluation surplus).
- The £0.4m gain in value is recognised on the balance sheet.

Year ended 31 December 2006

Non-current Assets	£m
Investment property	2.4
Loss for year	(0.2)
Fair value at 31 December 2006	2.2

- The loss in value is debited to the income statement (ie not to revaluation surplus).
- The £0.2m loss in value is recognised on the balance sheet.

IAS 17 – LEASES

Leasing is the means by which companies obtain the right to use assets, such as machinery or vehicles. The lessee makes agreed payments for a period of time to a lessor (often a finance company). There may be provision in a lease contract for legal title of the leased asset to pass to the lessee.

IAS 17 sets out the accounting treatment where assets are obtained for use by a business under:

- a **finance lease** (usually a longer term lease, under which substantially all the risks and rewards of ownership are transferred to the lessee)

- an **operating lease** (usually a shorter term lease, where there is no transfer of the risks and rewards of ownership to the lessee)

A simple example illustrates the difference between these: hiring a van for the weekend to move some furniture is an operating lease; a business that leases a van under a four or five year contract does so under a finance lease.

Deciding whether a lease is a finance lease or an operating lease depends on the substance of the transaction rather than the form of the contract. However, a finance lease is usually characterised by *one or more* of the following:

- the lease transfers ownership of the asset to the lessee by the end of the lease term

- the lessee has the option to purchase the asset at a price that is expected to be sufficiently lower than the fair value* at the date the option becomes exercisable for it to be reasonably certain, at the inception of the lease, that the option will be exercised

- the lease term is for the major part of the economic life of the asset, even if the title is not transferred

- at the inception of the lease, the present value of the minimum lease payments amounts to at least substantially all of the fair value* of the leased asset

- the leased assets are of such a specialised nature that only the lessee can use them without major modifications

* fair value: the amount for which an asset could be exchanged, or a liability settled, between knowledgeable, willing parties in an arm's length transaction

These characteristics can be summarised in the diagram which follows but do note that the judgement as to how a lease is classified is a matter of overall balance.

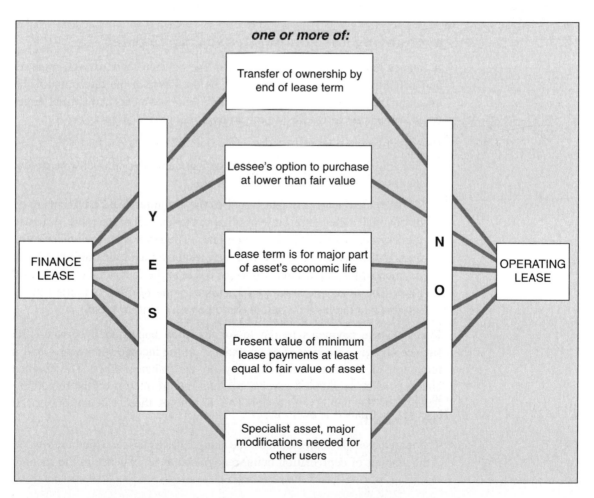

Other indications of a finance lease include one or more of the following:

- if the lessee can cancel the lease, the lessor's losses associated with the cancellation are borne by the lessee

- gains or losses from fluctuations in the fair value of the residual value accrue to the lessee (eg by means of a rebate of lease payments)

- the lessee has the ability to continue the lease for a secondary period at substantially lower lease payments

Note that for leases of land and buildings the following apply:

- the two elements – land and buildings – are normally considered separately

- land is normally classified as an operating lease (because land normally has an indefinite economic life, and a lease can only ever be for a short part of that life), unless title passes to the lessee by the end of the lease term

- buildings can be either a finance lease or an operating lease, depending on the characteristics (see above) set out in IAS 17

accounting for finance leases by lessees

A finance lease is initially recognised in the balance sheet as both an asset and a liability. The amount shown will be the lower of the fair value of the asset and the present value of the minimum lease payments. Any initial direct costs of the lessee are added to the amount recognised as an asset.

Note the following points:

- The minimum lease payments are the payments over the lease term that the lessee is, or can be, required to make.

- To calculate the present value requires the minimum lease payments to be discounted at the interest rate implicit in the lease, if practicable, or to use the lessee's incremental borrowing rate. (The *interest rate implicit in the lease* is the discount rate at which the present value of the minimum lease payments plus the residual value are equal to the fair value of the leased asset. The *lessee's incremental borrowing rate of interest* is the rate of interest that the lessee would have to pay on a similar lease.)

Finance lease payments to the lessor are then apportioned between the finance charge – recognised as an expense in the income statement – and a reduction of the outstanding liability on the balance sheet. The finance charge is to be such that it gives a constant rate of interest on the remaining balance of the liability (although IAS 17 allows these calculations to be approximated).

The leased asset is depreciated on the same basis as assets which are owned – the amount of depreciation being recognised as an expense in the income statement. If there is the possibility that the lessee will not obtain ownership at the end of the lease period, then the asset is to be depreciated over the shorter of the lease term or the useful life of the asset.

accounting for operating leases by lessees

With an operating lease, lease payments are recognised as an expense in the income statement on a straight-line basis over the lease term (unless another basis is more representative of the time pattern of the user's benefit).

Case Study

WYVERN ENGINEERING LIMITED: ACCOUNTING FOR LEASING

Tutorial note

In the examination for *Drafting Financial Statements* there will be no computational questions on accounting for leases. This Case Study is used to illustrate the practical application of IAS 17, *Leases*, to a lessee's financial statements.

situation

Wyvern Engineering Limited is leasing two machines for use in its business:

1   A **portable compressor** is leased from The Hire Shop as and when it is needed at a cost of £100 per week; usage was as follows:

2005	5 weeks
2006	3 weeks
2007	6 weeks
2008	10 weeks

When the machine is not being used, Wyvern Engineering returns it to The Hire Shop where it is available for hire by other customers. The estimated useful life of the machine is six years.

2   A **pressing machine** is leased from Mercia Finance plc from 1 January 2005. The details are:

cost price of machine	£10,000
leasing period	4 years
estimated useful life	4 years
leasing payments	£3,500 per year (payable monthly on 1st of each month in advance)
Wyvern Engineering's borrowing rate	10%

Explain how these two leases will be recorded in the financial statements of the lessee. Show relevant extracts from the income statement and balance sheet for the years ending 31 December 2005, 2006, 2007 and 2008.

solution

1   The **portable compressor** is being leased under an operating lease because

- the lessee is leasing the machine for a period which is substantially less than its total useful life

- the lessor retains the risks and rewards of ownership of the asset and is responsible for the costs of repairs and maintenance

The only accounting entries will be an expense in the income statement of the lease payments in each financial year. These are recognised at their actual cost each year (rather than on a straight-line basis) as this is more representative of the time pattern of the benefit to Wyvern Engineering.

2   The **pressing machine** is being leased under a finance lease because

- the present value of the leasing payments amounts to substantially all of the asset's fair value, ie *£14,000 (£3,500 x 4 years), compared with £10,000

- substantially all the risks and rewards of ownership are transferred to the lessee

The accounting entries are shown below.

* For simplicity, the £14,000 has not been discounted; at a 10% discount rate the present value would be approximately £12,000 – above the asset's fair value.

accounting entries: operating lease for the portable compressor
Debit income statement with actual lease payments, ie

	£
2005	500
2006	300
2007	600
2008	1,000

accounting entries: finance lease for the pressing machine
The first step is to apportion the leasing payments between finance charges and capital payments. With total leasing payments of £14,000 and the cost price of the machine at £10,000, the finance charges and capital payments are as follows:

	leasing payment	finance charge	capital payment
	£	£	£
2005	3,500	1,600	1,900
2006	3,500	1,200	2,300
2007	3,500	800	2,700
2008	3,500	400	3,100
	14,000	4,000	10,000

The finance charge has been calculated here using the sum-of-the-digits method (see page 105). This is acceptable under IAS 17, being a form of approximation. The calculations are as follows:

2005	4/(1 + 2 + 3 + 4) x £4,000	=	£1,600
2006	3/(1 + 2 + 3 + 4) x £4,000	=	£1,200
2007	2/(1 + 2 + 3 + 4) x £4,000	=	£800
2008	1/(1 + 2 + 3 + 4) x £4,000	=	£400

Depreciation on the machine (using the straight-line method) is:

$$\frac{£10,000}{4 \text{ years}} = £2,500 \text{ per year}$$

income statement extracts

£

2005

Operating lease	500
Finance charge under finance lease	1,600
Depreciation of machinery	2,500
	4,600

2006

Operating lease	300
Finance charge under finance lease	1,200
Depreciation of machinery	2,500
	4,000

2007

Operating lease	600
Finance charge under finance lease	800
Depreciation of machinery	2,500
	3,900

2008

Operating lease	1,000
Finance charge under finance lease	400
Depreciation of machinery	2,500
	3,900

balance sheet extracts

Notes:

- only the finance lease is recognised on the balance sheet
- the balance sheet extracts do not balance until the last year (2008) because of the expense of the finance charge in the income statement

2005	£
Non-current Assets	
Machinery under finance lease at cost	10,000
Less depreciation to date	2,500
	7,500
Liabilities	
Current – obligation under finance lease	*2,300
Non-current – obligation under finance lease	5,800
	8,100

* next year's payments are a current liability

2006	£
Non-current Assets	
Machinery under finance lease at cost	10,000
Less depreciation to date	5,000
	5,000
Liabilities	
Current – obligation under finance lease	2,700
Non-current – obligation under finance lease	3,100
	5,800

2007	£
Non-current Assets	
Machinery under finance lease at cost	10,000
Less depreciation to date	7,500
	2,500
Liabilities	
Current – obligation under finance lease	3,100

2008 This balance sheet will show neither asset nor liability, as the leasing contract will terminate on 31 December 2008. The leasing payment of £3,500 made in this year will be split £400 to the finance charge and £3,100, so eliminating the liability for the lease.

accounting for finance leases by lessors

Lessors – often finance companies – recognise assets held under a finance house in their balance sheets as a receivable. The amount shown is equal to the net investment in the finance lease.

Subsequent payments made by the lessee are recognised as income – based on a constant rate of interest on the net investment in the finance lease.

accounting for operating leases by lessors

With operating leases, the assets of the lease are presented in the lessor's balance sheet according to the nature of the asset.

Lease income is recognised in the income statement on a straight-line basis over the lease term (unless another basis is more representative of the time pattern in which use benefit from the leased asset is diminished).

The leased asset is depreciated by the lessor on the same basis as assets which are owned – the amount of depreciation being recognised as an expense in the income statement.

IAS 2 – INVENTORIES

Companies often have inventories in various forms:

* raw materials, for use in a manufacturing process
* work-in-progress (partly manufactured goods)
* finished goods, made by the business and ready for resale to customers
* finished goods, which have been bought in by the business for resale

Note that IAS 2 applies to all types of inventories, except for the valuation of construction contracts, and certain other specialist assets.

The principle of inventory valuation, as set out in IAS 2, is that inventories should be valued at *'the lower of cost and net realisable value'*. This valuation applies the prudence concept and is illustrated by the following diagram:

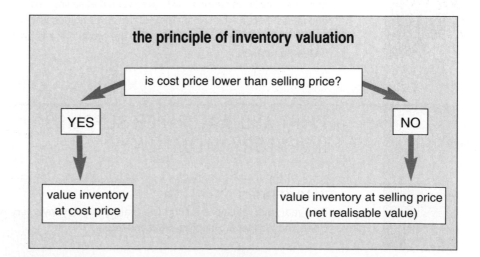

Thus two different inventory values are compared:

- cost, including additional costs to bring the product or service to its present location and condition

- net realisable value (the estimated selling price less the estimated costs of completion and the estimated costs necessary to make the sale)

The lower of these two values is taken, and different items or groups of inventory are compared separately. These principles are illustrated in the two Case Studies which follow.

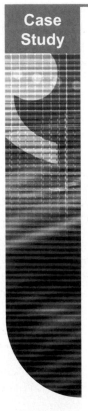

Case Study

THE CLOTHING STORE: INVENTORY VALUATION

situation

The Clothing Store bought in a range of 'designer' beachwear in the Spring, with each item costing £15 and retailing for £30. Most of the goods sell well but, by Autumn, ten items remain unsold. These are put on the 'bargain rail' at £18 each. On 31 December, at the end of the store's financial year, five items remain unsold. At what price will they be included in the year end inventories valuation?

Twelve months later, three items still remain unsold and have been reduced further to £10 each. At what price will they now be valued in the year end inventories valuation?

solution

- At 31 December, the five items will be valued at a cost of £15 each,

  ie 5 x £15 = £75.

- Twelve months later, the three items remaining unsold will be valued at a net realisable value of £10 each, ie 3 x £10 = £30.

Important note: Inventories are never valued at selling prices when selling prices are above cost prices. The reason for this is that selling prices includes profit, and to value inventories in this way would recognise the profit in the financial statements before it has been realised.

Case Study

PAINT AND WALLPAPER SUPPLIES: INVENTORY VALUATION

situation

The year end valuations for the two main groups of inventory held by the business Paint and Wallpaper Supplies are found to be:

	Cost	Net Realisable Value
	£	£
Paints	2,500	2,300
Wallpapers	5,000	7,500
	7,500	9,800

Which of the following inventories valuations do you think is correct?

(a)   £7,500

(b)   £9,800

(c)   £7,300

(d)   £10,000

solution

Inventory valuation (o) is correct, because it has taken the 'lower of cost and net realisable value' for each group of stock, ie

Paints (at net realisable value)	£2,300
Wallpapers (at cost)	£5,000
	£7,300

You will also note that this valuation is the lowest of the four possible choices, indicating that inventory valuation follows the *prudence concept*.

inventory valuation methods

IAS 2 allows two different methods to be used to calculate the cost price of inventories.

- **FIFO** (first in, first out) – this method assumes that the first items acquired are the first to be used, so that the valuation of inventory on hand at any time consists of the most recently acquired items.

- **AVCO** (average cost), or **weighted average cost method** – here the average cost of items held at the beginning of the period is calculated; as new inventory is acquired a new average cost is calculated (usually based on a weighted average, using the number of units bought as the weighting).

Notes:

- LIFO (last in, first out) cannot be used under IAS 2

- the same inventory valuation is to be used for all inventories having a similar nature and use to the entity; where there are inventories with a different nature or use, different valuations may be justified

The use of a valuation method does not necessarily correspond with the method of physical distribution adopted in a firm's stores. For example, in a car factory, one car battery of type X is the same as another, and no-one will be concerned if the storekeeper issues one from the latest batch received, even if the FIFO method has been adopted. However, perishable goods are always physically handled on the basis of first in, first out, even if the inventory records use the AVCO method.

Having chosen a suitable inventory valuation method, a business would continue to use that method unless there were good reasons for making the change. This is in line with the consistency concept of accounting.

closing inventory valuation for a manufacturer

The principles of IAS 2 are applied to a manufacturer, who may hold three types of inventories at the year-end:

- raw materials
- work-in-progress
- finished goods

For **raw materials,** the comparison is made between cost (which can be found using either FIFO or AVCO) and net realisable value.

For **work-in-progress** and **finished goods**, IAS 2 requires that the cost valuation includes expenditure not only on direct materials but also on direct labour, direct expenses and production overheads. Thus for work-in-progress and finished goods, 'cost' comprises:

- direct materials
- direct labour
- direct expenses
- production overheads (to bring the product to its present location or condition)
- other overheads, if any, attributable to bringing the product or service to its present location and condition

Note that the inventory valuation cannot include abnormal waste (eg of materials and labour), storage costs, administrative overheads not related to production, and selling costs.

The 'cost' is then compared with net realisable value, and the lower figure is taken as the inventory valuation.

Case Study

XYZ MANUFACTURING: INVENTORIES VALUATION

situation

XYZ Manufacturing started in business on 1 July 2005 producing security devices for doors and windows. During the first year 2,000 units were sold and at the end of the year, on 30 June 2006, there were 200 finished units in the warehouse and 20 units which were exactly half-finished as regards direct materials, direct labour and production overheads.

Costs for the first year were:	£
Direct materials used	18,785
Direct labour	13,260
Production overheads	8,840
Non-production overheads	4,420
TOTAL COST FOR YEAR	45,305

At 30 June 2006 it was estimated that the net realisable value of each completed security device was £35. At the same date, the company holds raw materials as follows:

	cost £	not realisable value £
Material X	1,400	1,480
Material Y	400	360
Material Z	260	280

Calculate the inventories valuation at 30 June 2006 for:

- raw materials
- work-in-progress
- finished goods

solution

RAW MATERIALS

Using the IAS 2 rule of 'the lower of cost and net realisable value' the total value is:

	£	
Material X	1,400	(cost)
Material Y	360	(net realisable value)
Material Z	260	(cost)
	2,020	

WORK-IN-PROGRESS

To calculate the value of work-in-progress and finished goods we need to know the production cost, ie direct materials, direct labour and production overheads. This is:

	£
Direct materials used	18,785
Direct labour	13,260
Production overheads	8,840
PRODUCTION COST FOR YEAR	40,885

All these costs must be included because they have been incurred in bringing the product to its present location or condition. Non-production overheads are not included because they are not directly related to production. Thus, a production cost of £40,885 has produced:

Units sold	2,000
Closing inventory of completed units	200
Closing inventory of work-in-progress –	
20 units exactly half-finished equals	
10 completed units	10
PRODUCTION FOR YEAR	2,210

The **cost per unit** is: $\dfrac{£40,885}{2,210}$ = **£18.50 per unit**

The 20 half-finished units have a cost of (20 ÷ 2) x £18.50 = **£185**. They have a net realisable value of (20 ÷ 2) x £35 = £350. The value of work-in-progress will, therefore, be recognised in the financial statements as £185, which is the lower of cost and net realisable value.

FINISHED GOODS
The completed units held at the end of the year have a production cost of 200 x £18.50 = £3,700, compared with a net realisable value of 200 x £35 = £7,000. Applying the rule of lower of cost and net realisable value, finished goods inventory will be valued at **£3,700**.

CONFIDENTIALITY PROCEDURES

It is a requirement of the Companies Act for directors of companies to disclose whether the financial statements have been prepared in accordance with accounting standards, particulars of any material departure from the standards and the reasons for the departure. Whilst this information is readily available to users, for those involved in the preparation of the financial statements, confidentiality procedures must be observed at all times:

• regarding any discussion about accounting standards with the directors

- regarding how the standards have been applied to a particular set of financial statements

- concerning any figures used but not disclosed in the financial statements; for example, the calculation of inventory valuations at cost price and net realisable value

- concerning any investigations to determine whether to treat an item in one way rather than another; for example, confidential information about the development costs of a new product, the outcome of which will determine whether costs are to be capitalised on the balance sheet or, alternatively, recognised as an expense in the income statement

Chapter Summary

- International accounting standards comprise IASs and IFRSs.

- IAS 16, *Property, Plant and Equipment*, sets out the principles of accounting for non-current assets such as land and buildings, machinery, office equipment, shop fittings and vehicles. It covers

  - recognition
  - initial measurement
  - cost and revaluation models
  - depreciation
  - derecognition

- IAS 38, *Intangible Assets*, sets out the accounting treatment of expenditure on acquiring, developing, maintaining or enhancing intangible assets. It covers

  - recognition
  - initial measurement
  - cost and revaluation models
  - amortisation of intangible assets with finite lives

- IAS 36, *Impairment of Assets*, sets out the accounting procedures to ensure that assets are carried in the balance sheet at no more than their value, or recoverable amount. The standard requires an impairment review to be carried out when there is evidence that impairment has taken place. The standard gives a number of indicators of impairment.

- IAS 40, *Investment Property*, gives the accounting treatment for land and buildings held for rental income or capital appreciation. The standard offers two models – the fair value model or the cost model. Under the fair value model, investment properties are measured at fair value, with any gains or losses being recognised in the income statement. Under the cost model, investment properties are measured at cost less accumulated depreciation and impairment losses.

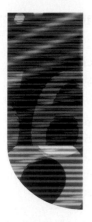

- IAS 17, *Leases*, sets out the accounting treatment for
  - operating leases
  - finance leases

  for both the lessee (the user of the leased asset) and the lessor (the owner – often a finance company – of the asset)

- IAS 2, *Inventories*, requires that inventories are valued at the lower of cost and net realisable value. Valuation methods include:
  - FIFO (first in, first out)
  - AVCO (average cost, based as a weighted average cost)

  LIFO (last in, first out) cannot be used under IAS 2.

Key Terms		
	IAS	International Accounting Standard (part of the rules of accounting)
	IFRS	International Financial Reporting Standard (part of the rules of accounting)
	asset	a resource controlled by the entity as a result of past events and from which future economic benefits are expected to flow to the entity
	property, plant and equipment	tangible assets held for use in the production or supply of goods and services, which are expected to be used for more than one period
	depreciable amount	the cost of the asset, less any residual value
	fair value	the amount for which an asset could be exchanged between knowledgeable, willing parties in an arm's length transaction
	carrying amount	the amount at which an asset is recognised in the balance sheet, after deducting any accumulated depreciation or impairment losses
	cost model	asset is carried at cost less accumulated depreciation and impairment losses
	revaluation model	asset is carried at a revalued amount, being its fair value less any subsequent depreciation and impairment losses
	intangible asset	an identifiable non-monetary asset without physical substance
	research	original and planned investigation undertaken with the prospect of gaining new scientific or technical knowledge and understanding
	development	the application of research findings or other knowledge to a plan or design for the production of new or substantially improved materials,

	devices, products, processes, systems or services before the start of commercial production or use
depreciation/amortisation	the systematic allocation of the depreciable amount of an asset over its useful life (note: the term 'amortisation' is customarily used in relation to intangible assets)
impairment loss	the amount by which the carrying amount of an asset exceeds its recoverable amount
recoverable amount	the higher of an asset's fair value, less costs to sell, and its value in use
value in use	the present value of the future cash flows obtainable as a result of an asset's continued use, including cash from its ultimate disposal
investment property	property held to earn rent or for capital appreciation, but not being used in the ordinary course of business
operating lease	a shorter-term lease, where there is no transfer of the risks and rewards of ownership to the lessee
finance lease	a longer-term lease, under which substantially all the risks and rewards of ownership are transferred to the lessee
first in, first out (FIFO)	inventory valuation method which assumes that the first items acquired are the first to be used
average cost (AVCO)	inventory valuation method which calculates an average cost (based on a weighted average) whenever new inventory is acquired

Student Activities

Osborne Books is grateful to the AAT for their kind permission to use past assessment material, which has been amended to incorporate the requirements of international accounting standards.

4.1   Which of the following statements, according to IAS 2, *Inventories*, best describes the valuation of inventories at the end of the financial year?

(a)   the lower of cost and net realisable value

(b)   the higher of cost and net realisable value

(c)   all inventories should be valued at cost

(d)   all inventories should be valued at net realisable value

4.2 Joe Yates runs a garage buying and selling second-hand cars. At the end of the financial year his inventories include the following cars. What is the correct valuation to be recorded according to IAS 2, *Inventories*?

	Cost £	Net realisable value £
Vauxhall Corsa	2,800	3,500
Landrover Discovery	10,000	15,000
Nissan Primera	3,400	2,600
Ford Focus	6,000	7,500
Volkswagen Polo	1,200	500

(a)   £23,400

(b)   £21,900

(c)   £30,600

(d)   £29,100

4.3 The Betterland Company Limited purchased for its own use a freehold warehouse on 1st January 20-0 for £250,000. The directors decided to depreciate the warehouse over its estimated useful life of 50 years. At 1 January 20-5, the building is valued at £345,000, and the directors decide to incorporate this valuation into the books of account from this date.

1   What is the amount to be transferred to revaluation surplus?

    (a)   £120,000

    (b)   £100,000

    (c)   £125,000

    (d)   £250,000

2   Assuming that the asset's life still has 46 years to run as from the 1st January 20-5, what would be the depreciation charge from 31 December 20-5 onwards?

    (a)   £5,000

    (b)   £10,000

    (c)   £7,500

    (d)   £2,500

4.4 Which one of the following is an intangible asset?

(a)   short leaseholds

(b)   trademarks

(c)   trade receivables

(d)   investment properties

4.5 IAS 38, *Intangible Assets*, requires certain items of expenditure to be written off to the income statement in the year in which it is incurred. Which one of the following must be written off in this way?

(a)   research expenditure

(b)   development expenditure

(c)   internally generated goodwill

(d)   internally generated brands

4.6 (a) What are the points, all of which must be demonstrated, before development costs can be recognised in the balance sheet?

(b) Which costs can be included in the development of internally generated intangible assets, and which costs are excluded?

4.7 (a) Explain how an impairment review is carried out, and define the terms used.

(b) How is an impairment loss recorded in the financial statements?

4.8 Machin Limited has three assets in use

	carrying amount £	fair value less costs to sell £	value in use £
Compressor	8,000	12,000	10,000
Fork lift truck	20,000	18,000	19,000
Dumper truck	10,000	7,000	13,000

Which of the above assets is impaired and needs to be written down as indicated?

(a) compressor written down by £2,000

(b) fork lift truck written down by £2,000

(c) fork lift truck written down by £1,000

(d) dumper truck written down by £3,000

4.9 State *three* external sources of impairment and *three* internal sources of impairment.

4.10 What are the main differences between an operating lease and a finance lease, as defined by IAS 17, *Leases*? Summarise the accounting procedures for each by lessees.

4.11 Briefly explain the difference in accounting treatment, between an owner occupied freehold property, and that of a freehold investment property. You should make specific reference to IAS 16, *Property, Plant and Equipment*, and IAS 40, *Investment Property*.

4.12 On 1 January 20-0, Makeshift Enterprises plc purchased a freehold property, Castle Hamlets at a cost of £400,000, which it intended to hold as an investment property. The company adopts the fair value model for its investment property.

In subsequent years, the fair value of the property was as follows:

At 31 December	20-1	20-2	20-3
	£000	£000	£000
	440	460	380

Task 1
Show how the property and the changes in fair value will be recorded in the financial statements of Makeshift Enterprises for the years to 31 December 20-0 to 20-3.

Task 2
Show how the financial statements would differ if the property had been bought for the use of Makeshift Enterprises.

4.13 Chemco plc has its own research and development department, the breakdown of costs for the year to 31 December 20-3 are as follows:

(a) Project Xchem was started in July 20-3, researching into the possibility that an arm patch could be used to cure the common cold. Some minor testing had been completed but the results had proved to be disappointing and no real benefits recorded. It was unlikely that the project would continue in the foreseeable future and the costs to date amounted to £295,000.

(b) Project Zchem had also started this year, investigating the possibility of producing insulin in tablet form to help sufferers of diabetes. Results to date had proved to be most encouraging, and matters were progressing at a pace. Production is due to start next year (20-4) and demand for this type of product initially, is likely to be very high and lucrative. The product has already been patented and its planned selling price is likely to yield a high level of profit, until competition can enter the market in 20-9. Costs for the year to date amounted to £435,000.

Note: The company has sufficient finance and resources to complete both projects.

Task

How should the total research and development expenditure be dealt with in the financial statements for 20-3 and subsequent years (if appropriate)?

4.14 Answer the following questions which the directors of Poussin Limited have asked. Justify your answers, where appropriate, by reference to accounting concepts and international accounting standards.

(a) Why are we carrying forward development costs of £351,572 on the balance sheet? Should these costs be written off in the income statement in the year in which they are incurred? Under what circumstances can these costs be carried forward in the balance sheet and how will they be treated in the future?

(b) The auditors have asked us to reduce the value of some of our inventories – from cost of £147,213 to a net realisable value of £110,648. We take the view that it is only a temporary 'blip' in the market that has caused the fall – this time next year we are confident that we will be able to sell this inventory for over £200,000.

4.15 You have been assigned to assist in the preparation of the financial statements of Dowango Limited for the year ended 31 March 20-6. The company is a cash and carry operation that trades from a large warehouse on an industrial estate.

You have recently received a letter from the directors of Dowango Limited, the contents of which are listed below.

DOWANGO LIMITED

Dear AAT student,

In preparation for discussions about a possible loan to Dowango Limited, the bank has asked to see the latest financial statements of Dowango. We wish to ensure that the financial statements show the company in the best light. In particular, we wish to ensure that the assets of the business are shown at their proper value. We would like to discuss with you the following issues:

1   The non-current assets of our company are undervalued. We have received a professional valuation of the land and buildings which shows that they are worth more than is stated in our financial statements. The land has a current market value of £641,000 and the buildings are valued at £558,000.

2   The investments are recorded in our trial balance at cost. We realise that the market value of the investment is less than the cost, but since we have not yet sold it, we have not made a loss on it and so we should continue to show it at cost.

3   Inventories are recorded in our balance sheet at cost. Most of our inventories are worth more than this as we could sell them for more than we paid for them. Only a few items would sell for less than we paid for them. We have worked out the real value of our inventories as follows:

	Cost	Sales price
	£000	£000
Undervalued items	340	460
Overvalued items	25	15
Total	365	475

We have set out a number of questions we would like answered at our meeting in an appendix to this letter.

Yours sincerely

The Directors

Dowango Limited

Tasks

The questions from the appendix to the directors' letter are shown below. Write a memo to the directors answering these questions, which relate to the financial statements of Dowango Limited. Explain your answers, where relevant, by reference to company law, accounting concepts and applicable international accounting standards.

1   (a)   Can we show the land and buildings at valuation rather than cost?

   (b)   If we did so, how would the valuation of land and buildings be reflected in the financial statements?

   (c)   Would revaluing the land and buildings have any effect upon the gearing ratio of the company and would this assist us in our attempt to get a loan from the bank?

   (d)   What effect would a revaluation have upon the future results of the company?

2   Can we continue to show the investments at cost?

   The investments consist of shares in a retail company that were purchased with a view to resale at a profit. Dowango Limited owns 2 per cent of the share capital of the company. At the end of the year a valuation of the shares was obtained with a view to selling the shares in the forthcoming year. The shares were valued at £56,000, but originally cost Dowango £64,000.

3   What is the best value for inventories that we can show in our balance sheet in the light of the information we have given you about sales price?

Accounting for liabilities and the income statement

This chapter focuses on the international accounting standards that impact mainly on the way in which liabilities are accounted for in both the income statement and the balance sheet. We then turn our attention to those standards that affect principally the income statement.

For the liabilities side of the balance sheet we consider standards that cover:

- income taxes (IAS 12)
- leases (IAS 17)
- provisions, contingent liabilities and contingent assets (IAS 37)
- events after the balance sheet date (IAS 10)

Accounting standards which affect mainly the income statement include:

- property, plant and equipment (IAS 16)
- revenue (IAS 18)
- borrowing costs (IAS 23)
- earnings per share (IAS 33)
- segment reporting (IAS 14)

PERFORMANCE CRITERIA COVERED

unit 11: DRAFTING FINANCIAL STATEMENTS

element 11.1

draft limited company financial statements

A   draft limited company financial statements from the appropriate information

B   correctly identify and implement subsequent adjustments and ensure that discrepancies, unusual features or queries are identified and either resolved or referred to the appropriate person

C   ensure that limited company financial statements comply with relevant accounting standards and domestic legislation and with the organisation's policies, regulations and procedures

E   ensure that confidentiality procedures are followed at all times

ACCOUNTING FOR LIABILITIES

The first part of this chapter explains the accounting treatment of liabilities – non-current and current – as specified by the relevant international accounting standards. It is well worth going back to the *Framework* document for the definition of a liability (page 16) : *'a present obligation of the entity arising from past events, the settlement of which is expected to result in an outflow from the entity of resources embodying economic benefits.'*

Note the three key parts of the definition:

• a present obligation of the entity

• arising from past events

• the settlement of which is expected to result in an outflow from the entity

Thus a company which has bought goods or services on credit has a present obligation in the form of an amount owed to trade payables, which arises from past events such as a purchase order made last month, and which will result in settlement in the form of resources embodying economic benefits, ie payment will be made from the company's bank account.

In order to be recognised on the balance sheet, liabilities must be capable of being reliably measured. If the liability cannot be reliably measured then it will often be disclosed in the notes to the accounts, eg a contingent liability.

The international accounting standards which follow set out the recognition and measurement criteria of different liabilities: *Income Taxes* (IAS 12), *Leases* (IAS 17), *Provisions, Contingent Liabilities and Contingent Assets* (IAS 37) and *Events after the Balance Sheet Date* (IAS 10).

IAS 12 – INCOME TAXES

This standard sets out the accounting treatment for taxes on income – such as the corporation tax which is paid by UK companies and is based on their profits. In the UK, the chancellor of the Exchequer sets out, in budget announcements, the various rates of corporation tax. Most larger companies in the UK pay part of their tax due every three months, with some amounts due to be paid in the current accounting period and other amounts due in the following accounting period.

current tax

This is the amount of income taxes payable in respect of the taxable profit for the year. Note that taxable profit may well differ from the accounting profit shown by the income statement – this is because the tax authorities (in the UK, HM Revenue & Customs) determine the rules as to which expenses are allowable for tax purposes.

The tax expense for the year, from the ordinary activities of the entity, is recognised on the face of the income statement. The amount of unpaid current tax is recognised as a liability on the balance sheet, under the heading of current liabilities. If, by chance, an entity has overpaid tax, then the excess amount is recognised as an asset, under the heading of current assets.

The amount of current tax is to be measured in the financial statements using the tax rates applicable at the balance sheet date.

The amount of any current tax relating to items reported directly in equity – for example, through the reserves – is to be disclosed as a note to the financial statements.

deferred tax

Deferred tax liabilities are the amounts of income taxes payable in future periods in respect of taxable temporary differences. These temporary differences arise when the tax due for a particular accounting period is deferred because of the impact of capital allowances or other factors.

Deferred tax comes about because the taxable profit of a business is often different from the profit shown in the income statement. In the UK, this happens because HM Revenue & Customs disallows depreciation and amortisation shown in the income statement and, instead, allows a capital allowance against tax for the purchase of non-current assets.

An example of a capital allowance is 25 per cent reducing balance, which is allowed by the tax authorities on office equipment, machinery and most vehicles. For example, the capital allowances on a machine costing £10,000 will be:

	£
Cost price	10,000
Year 1 capital allowance at 25%	2,500
	7,500
Year 2 capital allowance at 25%	1,875
	5,625
Year 3 capital allowance at 25%	1,406
	4,219
	and so on . . .

If the company owning the machine had a profit of £15,000 in year 1 after allowing for depreciation on the machine of, say, £1,000, the taxable profit would be calculated as follows:

	£
Profit in year 1	15,000
Add back depreciation expense	1,000
	16,000
Less capital allowance	2,500
Taxable profit	13,500

Thus the company would pay tax on profits of £13,500 rather than £15,000. This is because the capital allowance is higher than the depreciation expense. As the tax benefit of the capital allowance has been received earlier than the depreciation expense, the company will make a transfer from the income statement to deferred tax account to record a possible liability to HM Revenue & Customs. The transfer will be for £2,500 – £1,000 = £1,500 x the company's tax rate. The possible liability to the tax authorities is that, if the machine was sold at the end of year 1 for £9,000 (ie cost, less depreciation to date), HM Revenue & Customs would claim for a balancing charge of £1,500, ie £9,000 – (£10,000 – £2,500 capital allowance) x the company's tax rate.

In the ordinary course of events, amounts transferred to deferred tax account will reverse (ie be transferred back to the income statement) over time – see Case Study below.

In the circumstances described above, the balance of deferred tax account is shown as a liability on the balance sheet, usually under the heading of non-current liabilities.

IAS 12 requires that deferred tax liabilities should be recognised for all taxable temporary differences, except those relating to goodwill where amortisation is not tax-deductible, and the initial recognition of certain assets and liabilities in transactions that effect neither accounting profit nor taxable profit.

The amount of any deferred tax relating to items reported directly in equity – for example, through the reserves – is to be disclosed as a note to the financial statements.

Case Study

RAVEN LIMITED:
ACCOUNTING FOR DEFERRED TAX

situation

Raven Limited buys a machine for £10,000. The machine is expected to last for ten years and have a nil residual value. The company uses straight-line depreciation.
HM Revenue & Customs gives a capital allowance of 25 per cent reducing balance on the machine.
Raven Limited pays corporation tax at the rate of 30 per cent.

solution

- Depreciation is at £1,000 per year (ie 10 per cent, using the straight-line method).
- Capital allowances are at 25 per cent reducing balance.
- The amounts are shown in the table below:

YEARS	1	2	3	4	5	6	7	8	9	10
	£	£	£	£	£	£	£	£	£	£
depreciation	1,000	1,000	1,000	1,000	1,000	1,000	1,000	1,000	1,000	1,000
capital allowance	2,500	1,875	1,406	1,054	791	593	445	334	250	188
difference	(1,500)	(875)	(406)	(54)	209	407	555	666	750	812

■ The difference multiplied by the tax rate is transferred (to) or from deferred tax account, as follows:

Dr	**Deferred tax account**	Cr
	Year 1 Transfer from income	
	statement	450*
	* £1,500 difference x 30% corporation tax	

■ The year 1 income statement will show a transfer to deferred tax of £450, as follows:

Income statement – year 1

	£
Profit before tax	x
Tax	(x)
Transfer to deferred tax account	(450)
Transfer from deferred tax account	x
Profit for the year	x

Note that, in practice, only the net figure for tax (ie current tax, together with transfers to or from deferred tax account) is shown in the income statement; the separate amounts are disclosed as a note to the accounts.

■ The balance sheet will show a potential liability to HM Revenue & Customs of £450, usually under the heading of non-current liabilities, as follows:

Balance sheet – year 1

	£
Non-current assets	x
Current assets	x
Current liabilities	(x)
Non-current liabilities	(x)
Deferred tax account	(450)
Net assets	x

■ In years 2, 3 and 4, further transfers will be debited to the income statement and credited to deferred tax account. From year 5 onwards, the capital allowances will begin to reverse by debiting deferred tax account with the difference multiplied by the tax rate, and crediting the income statement with a 'transfer from deferred tax account'.

■ When the machine is finally sold any small discrepancies between capital allowances and the sale proceeds will be resolved by means of a balancing charge or allowance.

Case Study

SANTA PLC:
SHOWING THE TAX LIABILITIES

situation
The following balances are taken from the accounting system of Santa plc as at 31 December 2006:

	£	£
Deferred tax		8,000
Inventories	51,200	
Property, plant and equipment at cost or revaluation	250,000	
Cash and cash equivalents	4,500	
Share capital		100,000
Share premium account		25,000
Trade payables		75,400
Trade receivables	92,800	
Revaluation reserve		50,000
Loan (repayable in 2011)		40,000
Profit for year before tax		68,300
Retained earnings at start of year		61,800
Dividends paid	30,000	
	428,500	428,500

Notes:

• Corporation tax liability on the profits for the year is £25,400

• £4,000 is to be transferred to deferred tax account

You are helping with the year end financial statements and are asked to prepare:

• income statement, starting with profit before tax

• balance sheet

for the year ended 31 December 2006.

solution

SANTA PLC
Income statement (extract) for the year ended 31 December 2006

	£
Profit for year before tax	68,300
Tax	(25,400)
Transfer to deferred tax account	(4,000)
Profit for year	38,900

Balance sheet as at 31 December 2006

	£	£
Non-current assets		
Property, plant and equipment at cost or revaluation		250,000
Current assets		
Inventories	51,200	
Trade receivables	92,800	
Cash and cash equivalents	4,500	
	148,500	
Current liabilities		
Trade payables	(75,400)	
Tax liabilities	(25,400)	
	(100,800)	
Net current assets		47,700
Total assets *less* current liabilities		297,700
Non-current liabilities		
Loan	(40,000)	
Deferred tax account	*(12,000)	
		(52,000)
Net assets		245,700

* £8,000 + £4,000 transfer = £12,000

EQUITY	£
Share capital	100,000
Share premium account	25,000
Revaluation reserve	50,000
Retained earnings	*70,700
Total equity	245,700

* £61,800 at start + £38,900 profit for year − £30,000 dividends paid

LIABILITIES SIDE OF BALANCE SHEET

Three further accounting standards impact mainly on the liabilities side of the balance sheet:

IAS 17 – Leases

IAS 37 – Provisions, contingent liabilities and contingent assets

IAS 10 – Events after the balance sheet date

Note that these standards often also have an effect on both the income statement and on the assets side of the balance sheet.

IAS 17 – Leases

This standard has already been looked at in detail in Chapter 4 (pages 120-127).

On the lessee's balance sheet, finance leases are recognised on the liabilities side at the lower of the fair value of the asset being leased and the present value of the minimum lease payments. The amount is to be split between non-current and current liabilities, as appropriate.

IAS 37 – Provisions, contingent liabilities and contingent assets

These three items – provisions, contingent liabilities, contingent assets – represent uncertainties that may have an effect on future financial statements. They need to be accounted for consistently so that users can have a fuller understanding of their effect on financial statements.

The objective of IAS 37 is to ensure that appropriate recognition criteria and measurement bases are applied to provisions, contingent liabilities and contingent assets and that sufficient information is disclosed in the notes to the financial statements to enable users to understand their nature, timing and amount.

provisions

A **provision** is a liability of uncertain timing or amount.

A **liability** is

– a present obligation as a result of past events

– where settlement is expected to result in an outflow of economic benefits (eg payment will be made)

An **obligating event** is an event that creates a legal or constructive obligation resulting in an entity having no realistic alternative to settling the obligation.

A **legal obligation** derives from a contract, legislation, or other operation of law.

A **constructive obligation** derives from an entity's actions such as an established pattern of past practice (eg to refund the difference if another local shop is currently selling the same goods at a lower price), or where the entity has created a valid expectation (eg to refund cash against returned goods without insisting on seeing the receipt).

A provision is to be recognised as a liability in the financial statements when:

– an entity has a present obligation as a result of a past event

– it is probable that an outflow of economic benefits will be required to settle the obligation

– a reliable estimate can be made of the amount of the obligation

Unless all of these conditions are met, no provision should be recognised (in which case the liability may be contingent – see next page).

IAS 37 uses the word 'probable', in connection with the outflow of economic benefits, as being more likely to occur than not, ie a more than 50% likelihood of its occurrence.

The 'reliable estimate' of the amount of the obligation should be the best estimate of the expenditure required to settle the present obligation at the balance sheet date. When the time value of money is material, present value techniques can be used to estimate the amount of the provision.

IAS 37 identifies and lists a number of specific classes of provision:

– future operating losses: provisions are not be recognised

– onerous contracts, where the unavoidable costs of meeting the obligations of the contract exceed the economic benefits expected to be received under it: provisions are to be recognised for the present obligation under the contract

– restructuring, such as the sale or termination of part of the business, and changes in the management structure; restructuring costs (direct costs) can only be recognised as a provision when the business has a constructive obligation to restructure, eg a formal plan to a definite timetable which identifies the part of the business affected, the number of employees to be compensated for losing their jobs, and the expenditure of the restructuring.

Notes:

- Provisions are different from other liabilities such as trade payables and accruals. This is because, with provisions, there is uncertainty as to the timing or amount of the future expenditure required to settle. Contrast this with trade payables where the goods or services have been received or supplied and the amount due has either been invoiced or agreed with the supplier. Similarly, with accruals there is a liability to pay and, even if the amount may have to be estimated, the uncertainty is usually much less than for provisions.

- All provisions are contingent (because they are uncertain in timing or amount) but the word 'contingent' is used for assets and liabilities that are not recognised in the financial statements because their existence will be confirmed only by uncertain future events, which may or may not occur.

The amount of the change in the provision is recognised as an expense in the income statement, and the total amount of the provision is shown as a liability on the balance sheet (under the heading long-term provisions). At each balance sheet date, the amount of provisions is to be reviewed and adjusted to reflect the current best estimate. If a provision is no longer required, it is to be reversed and shown as income in the income statement. Provisions are only to be used for the expenditure for which the provision was originally recognised – to do otherwise would be to conceal the impact of different events on the financial statements.

Disclosure in the notes to the financial statements requires:

- details of changes in the amount of provisions between the beginning and end of the year
- a description of the provision(s) and expected timings of any resulting transfers
- an indication of the uncertainties regarding the amount or timing of any resulting transfers

contingent liabilities

A **contingent liability** is either:

- a possible obligation arising from past events whose existence will be confirmed only by the occurrence or non-occurrence of one or more uncertain future events not wholly within the entity's control; or
- a present obligation that arises from past events but is not recognised because:

(a) it is not probable that an outflow of economic benefits will be required to settle the obligation; or

(b) the obligation cannot be measured with sufficient reliability

Note that a contingent liability is a *possible* obligation, ie less than 50% likelihood of its occurrence (contrast this with the *probable* obligation of a provision, ie more than 50% likelihood of its occurrence).

A contingent liability is not recognised in the financial statements; however, it should be disclosed as a note to the statements which includes:

– a brief description of the nature of the contingent liability

– an estimate of its financial effect

– an indication of the uncertainties relating to the amount or timing of any outflow

– the possibility of any re-imbursement

Note that where a contingent liability is considered to be remote (contrast with possible), then no disclosure is required in the notes to the statements.

contingent assets

A **contingent asset** is a possible asset arising from past events whose existence will be confirmed only by the occurrence or non-occurrence of one or more uncertain future events not wholly within the entity's control.

A business should not recognise a contingent asset in its financial statements (because it could result in the recognition of income that may never be realised). However, when the realisation of the profit is virtually certain, then the asset is no longer contingent and its recognition in the statements is appropriate.

A contingent asset is disclosed only where an inflow of economic benefits is probable; disclosure in the notes to the financial statements should include:

– a brief description of the nature of the contingent asset

– an estimate of its financial effect

Note that, where the asset is considered to be either possible or remote, then no disclosure is required in the notes to the statements.

summary

The following diagram summarises the ways in which provisions, contingent liabilities and contingent assets are to be handled in the financial statements.

PROVISIONS (more than 50% likelihood of occurrence)	**CONTINGENT LIABILITIES** (less than 50% likelihood of occurrence)	

Probable
• provision recognised in
  financial statements as a liability
• disclosure of provision in
  notes, giving details of the
  figure shown in the statements
	Possible
	• no liability recognised in
	  financial statements
	• disclosure of contingent
	  liability in notes
		Remote
		• no liability recognised in
		  financial statements
		• no disclosure of
		  contingent liability in
		  notes

CONTINGENT ASSETS		

Probable
• no asset recognised in
  financial statements
• disclosure of contingent
  asset in notes
	Possible
	• no asset recognised in
	  financial statements
	• no disclosure of
	  contingent asset in notes
		Remote
		• no asset recognised in
		  financial statements
		• no disclosure of
		  contingent asset in notes

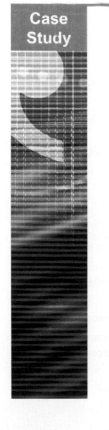

Case Study

WYVERN WATER: WHAT SHOULD BE SHOWN IN THE FINANCIAL STATEMENTS?

situation

Wyvern Water Limited is a producer of spa water which is bottled at source high in the Wyvern Hills. The company also produces a very successful high energy drink – with a secret mix of Wyvern Water, glucose, and vitamins – marketed under the 'Dr Wyvern' label to sports enthusiasts.

You are helping to prepare the year end financial statements and have been asked to decide how the following should be reported in the year to 31 December 2006.

1   Earlier in the year, a small batch of bottles of spa water was contaminated with oil from the bottling machinery. Although the problem was spotted by quality control checks, and most bottles were withdrawn from sale, some were sold to the public. In a few instances consumers of the water suffered severe stomach upsets and had to spend a night in hospital. These consumers are currently suing Wyvern Water for damages. The company's legal representatives consider that it is probable that the company will lose the case and that damages of £50,000 will be awarded against the company.

2   Wyvern Water holds worldwide patents and trademarks for the 'Dr Wyvern' energy drink. However, it has recently had letters from somebody claiming to be a Dr Wyvern who says that he devised the secret formula for the drink over fifty years ago. The mysterious Dr Wyvern is claiming royalties on sales of the drink for the

past fifty years and says he will sue the company for £10m if he is not paid. Wyvern Water has checked carefully and found that the formula for the high energy drink was devised ten years ago by its own development team and that all applicable patents and trademarks are held. The company has sought legal advice and been advised that it is extremely unlikely that the claimant's case, if it gets to court, will be successful.

3   During the year Wyvern Water Limited has formed a separate company, Wyvern Foods Limited, to manufacture 'homestyle' pies and cakes. Wyvern Water has given a guarantee to Mercia Bank plc in respect of bank overdraft facilities provided to Wyvern Foods. At 31 December 2006 it is considered possible (but not probable) that Wyvern Water will have to make payment under the guarantee.

solution

1   Court case for damages

- The present obligation is the potential liability to pay damages from a past event, ie the sale of contaminated bottled water.
- It is probable that the company will lose the case and have to pay damages.
- The amount of damages is reliably estimated at £50,000.
- The company will record a provision as an expense in its income statement and will record a liability in its balance sheet (under the heading long-term provisions).
- Details of the provision will be disclosed in the notes to the financial statements.

2   Claim for past royalties

- This is a possible obligation arising from past events, ie the sale of 'Dr Wyvern' energy drink.
- However, the possible obligation will be confirmed only by a future event – a court case.
- Legal advice considers the claimant's chances of success in a court case to be remote.
- This is a contingent liability, which will not be recognised in the accounts.
- Because the likelihood of losing the case is remote, there will be no disclosure of the contingent liability in the notes to the financial statements.

3   Bank guarantee

- The guarantee is a present obligation arising from a past event, ie the giving of the bank guarantee.
- However, at 31 December 2006, no transfer of economic benefits is probable to settle the obligation.
- This is a contingent liability, which will not be recognised in the accounts.
- Because the likelihood of having to meet the terms of the guarantee is possible (but not probable), details of the contingent liability will be disclosed in the notes to the financial statements.

IAS 10 – Events after the balance sheet date

Events after the balance sheet date are favourable or unfavourable events that occur between the balance sheet date and the date when the financial statements are authorised for issue.

This standard recognises that there may be events which occur, or information that becomes available after the end of the financial year that need to be reflected in the financial statements. For example, if a customer becomes insolvent after the year end and the amount of the receivable is material, it may be necessary to make changes in the financial statements for the year to reflect this.

Any such changes can only be made in the period

- after the end of the financial year, and
- before the financial statements are authorised for issue (usually by the board of directors)

Once the financial statements have been authorised for issue, they cannot be altered.

IAS 10 distinguishes between

- adjusting events, and
- non-adjusting events

Adjusting events provide evidence of conditions that existed at the balance sheet date. If material, changes should be made to the amounts shown in the financial statements. Examples of adjusting events include:

- the settlement after the balance sheet date of a court case which confirms that a present obligation existed at the balance sheet date
- non-current assets, the determination after the balance sheet date of the purchase price, or sale price, of assets bought or sold before the year end
- assets, where a valuation shows impairment
- inventories, where net realisable value falls below cost price
- trade receivables, where a customer has become insolvent
- the determination after the balance sheet date of the amount of profit-sharing or bonus payments
- the discovery of fraud or errors that show that the financial statements are incorrect

Non-adjusting events are indicative of conditions that arose after the balance sheet date. No adjustment is made to the financial statements; instead, if material, they are disclosed by way of notes which explain the nature of the event and, where possible, give an estimate of its financial effect. Examples of non-adjusting events include:

- business combinations (see Chapter 8)
- discontinuing a significant part of the business
- major purchase of assets
- losses of production capacity, eg caused by fire, flood or strikes
- announcing or commencing a major restructuring
- major share transactions
- large changes in asset prices or foreign exchange rates
- changes in tax rates
- entering into significant commitments or contingent liabilities
- commencing litigation based on events arising after the balance sheet date

Dividends declared or proposed on ordinary shares after the balance sheet date are not to be recognised as a liability on the balance sheet. Instead, they are non-adjusting events which are disclosed by way of a note – see also page 68 for more on the treatment of dividends in financial statements.

Going concern – an entity cannot prepare its financial statements on a going concern basis if, after the balance sheet date, management determines either that it intends to liquidate the business or to cease trading, or that there is no realistic alternative to these courses of action.

Date of authorisation for issue – entities must disclose the date when the financial statements were authorised for issue and who gave that authorisation. (If anyone has the power to amend the financial statements after issue, this fact must be disclosed.)

INCOME STATEMENT

In this section we look at accounting standards that affect mainly the income statement:

IAS 16   – Property, plant and equipment

IAS 18   – Revenue

IAS 23   – Borrowing costs

IAS 33   – Earnings per share

IAS 14   – Segment reporting

Note that these standards often also have an effect on the balance sheet – affecting either assets or liabilities.

IAS 16 – Property, plant and equipment

We have already seen – in Chapter 4 – how this standard sets out the principles of accounting for tangible non-current assets. Thus the standard affects both the balance sheet and the income statement.

The income statement is mainly affected by the depreciation expense, where the objective of depreciation is to allocate systematically the depreciable amount of an asset over its useful life.

All tangible non-current assets having a known useful life are to be depreciated (the usual exception is land).

Further details of IAS 16 are given on pages 98-107.

IAS 18 – Revenue

This standard sets out the accounting treatment to ensure that the revenue shown in the income statement is correctly stated.

Revenue is the gross inflow of economic benefits arising from the ordinary activities of an entity. Examples of revenue include sales of goods, rendering of services, interest, royalties and dividends.

Tutorial note: the term 'income' – which is defined in the *Framework* document (see page 16) – is a wider definition that includes both revenue from ordinary activities and gains from non-revenue activities (such as the disposal of non-current assets, or the revaluation of assets).

Fair value is the amount for which an asset could be exchanged, or a liability settled, between knowledgeable, willing parties in an arm's length transaction.

IAS 18 states that revenue is to be measured at the fair value of the consideration received or receivable. The standard then sets out the rules for the recognition of the three types of revenue:

- sale of goods
- rendering of services
- interest, royalties and dividends

sale of goods

Revenue from the sale of goods is to be recognised when all of the following criteria have been met:

- the seller of the goods has transferred to the buyer the significant risks and rewards of ownership
- the seller retains no continuing managerial involvement in the goods and no effective control over the goods
- the amount of revenue can be measured reliably

- it is probable that the economic benefits will flow to the seller
- the costs incurred, or to be incurred, in respect of the transaction can be measured reliably

rendering of services

For the sale of services, revenue is to be recognised by reference to the stage of completion (eg the percentage of completeness) of the transaction at the balance sheet date. All of the following criteria must be met:

- the amount of revenue can be measured reliably
- it is probable that the economic benefits will flow to the seller of the service
- at the balance sheet date, the stage of completion can be measured reliably
- the costs incurred, and the costs to complete, in respect of the transaction can be measured reliably

interest, royalties and dividends

Revenue for these items, provided that it is probable that the economic benefits will flow to the entity and that the amount of revenue can be measured reliably, is to be recognised in the following way:

- for interest – using a time basis to calculate the interest
- for royalties – on an accrual basis in accordance with the royalty agreement
- for dividends – when the shareholder's right to receive payment is established

IAS 23 – Borrowing costs

This standard sets out the standard – or 'benchmark' – accounting treatment for borrowing costs – eg interest on bank overdrafts – as being recognised as an expense in the income statement of the period in which they are incurred.

Borrowing costs are interest and other costs incurred by an entity in connection with the borrowing of funds.

A **qualifying asset** is an asset that takes a substantial period of time to get ready for its intended use or sale.

The benchmark treatment is that borrowing costs are to be recognised as an expense in the period in which they are incurred. The alternative treatment allowed by IAS 23 is that borrowing costs in relation to the acquisition, construction, or production of a qualifying asset can be capitalised as part of the cost of the asset. Note the following points which expand on the terms and use of this alternative treatment:

* when funds are borrowed specifically for the qualifying asset, the costs which may be capitalised are the actual borrowing costs incurred, less any investment income earned from the temporary investment of the borrowings

* when funds are borrowed generally, and include a qualifying asset, the borrowing costs which may be capitalised are calculated by reference to the expenditure on the qualifying asset and the weighted average of all the general borrowing costs of the entity (for example, total borrowing £100,000 including expenditure of £20,000 on a qualifying asset, borrowing costs for year are £10,000 = £2,000 of borrowing costs to be capitalised)

* capitalisation of borrowing costs starts when
  - expenditures for the asset are being incurred
  - borrowing costs are being incurred
  - activities that are necessary to prepare the asset for its intended use or sale are in progress

* capitalisation of borrowing costs ceases when substantially all the activities necessary to prepare the qualifying asset for its intended use or sale are complete

IAS 33 – Earnings per share — ordinary shares only

Earnings per share (EPS) is an accounting ratio that is widely used by investors and others to measure the performance of a company (see Chapter 7, page 206). EPS is presented on the face of the income statement of all public limited companies whose shares are publicly traded, for example, on a stock exchange; it is widely quoted in the financial press – the *Financial Times*, for example, gives the EPS figures for those companies listed on its share prices pages. Note that, in the UK, earnings per share is often stated as the number of pence per share.

EPS relates to ordinary shares – these are equity instruments that are subordinate to all other classes of equity instruments. This means that the holders of ordinary shares will be the last to receive their money in the event of the company winding up.

The main method of calculation of earnings per share allowed by IAS 33 is the *basic method*, which is calculated as follows:

$$\frac{\text{Profit after tax}}{\text{Number of issued ordinary shares}}$$

Note that the profit (or loss) used in the calculation is the amount that is attributable to ordinary equity holders, ie after allowing for:

- tax
- minority interests (see Chapter 8)
- dividends on preference shares

Two EPS calculations are required to be given:

- using the profit or loss attributable to ordinary equity holders
- using the profit or loss from continuing operations

Both of these are to be presented on the face of the income statement (in practice, they are usually shown after, or below, the income statement).

It is important to note that EPS is affected by the issue of additional ordinary shares during a financial year. When an issue has been made at full market price, EPS is calculated on the basis of the average number of shares in issue during the period, using the weighted average. For example:

start of financial year (1 January)	100,000	ordinary shares
new issue at full market price (1 July)	50,000	ordinary shares
average number of shares in issue	*125,000	

* 100,000 + (50,000 ÷ 2 [ie half a year])

Case Study

MARTLEY SERVICES:
CALCULATING EARNINGS PER SHARE

situation

The income statement (extract) of Martley Services plc for 2006 is as follows:

Income statement (extract) for the year ended 31 December 2006

Continuing Operations	£000
Profit before tax	820
Tax	(230)
Profit for the year from continuing operations	590
Discontinued Operations	
Profit for the year from discontinued operations	120
Profit for the year attributable to equity holders	710

The company's share capital at 31 December 2006 is £10m ordinary shares of £1 each. No new shares were issued during the year.

(a) You are asked to calculate the basic earnings per share of Martley Services plc for 2006.

(b) The company did consider making a new issue of £4m ordinary shares of £1 each at full market value on 1 October 2006. Although the issue did not go ahead, the finance director asks you to calculate what the EPS figure would have been for the year.

solution

(a) Basic earnings per share

profit for the year attributable to equity holders

$$\frac{\text{Profit after tax}}{\text{Number of issued ordinary shares}} = \frac{£710,000}{10,000,000} = 7.1\text{p per share}$$

profit for the year from continuing operations attributable to equity holders

$$\frac{\text{Profit after tax from continuing operations}}{\text{Number of issued ordinary shares}} = \frac{£590,000}{10,000,000} = 5.9\text{p per share}$$

Both of these EPS figures are to be presented on the face of the income statement.

(b) New issue of shares at full market value

EPS is calculated on the basis of the weighted number of shares in issue during the period. This would be:

10,000,000 + (4,000,000 ÷ 4 [a quarter of a year, ie three months]) = 11,000,000

EPS calculation would be:

profit for the year attributable to equity holders

$$\frac{£710,000}{11,000,000} = 6.45\text{p per share}$$

profit for the year from continuing operations attributable to equity holders

$$\frac{£590,000}{11,000,000} = 5.36\text{p per share}$$

IAS 14 – Segment reporting

Large companies often provide a range of products or services, in many parts of the world. Such a company will give financial information about its various activities in two main ways:

- by type of product or service (eg hotels, pubs, clubs)
- by geographical area (eg United Kingdom, European Union, North America)

Each segment – product or service, geographical area – may have different levels of profitability, growth or risk. Information about segments is therefore relevant to assessing the performance of an entity, but may not be available from the aggregated (combined) information given in the financial statements.

IAS 14 applies to all entities whose shares or debt are publicly traded, for example, on a stock exchange. Other companies can choose to disclose segment information voluntarily.

There are two types of segment identified by IAS 14:

- A **business segment**, which is a distinguishable component of an entity that
  - provides a single product or service, or a group of related products and services; and
  - is subject to risks and returns that are different from those of other business segments

  In determining whether products or services are related, an entity would consider factors such as the nature of the products or services, and the nature of the production processes.

- A **geographical segment**, which is a distinguishable component of an entity that
  - provides products and services within a particular economic environment; and
  - is subject to risks and returns that are different from those of components operating in other economic environments

  Factors to be considered when identifying geographical segments include the similarity of economic and political conditions, proximity of operations, and special risks of particular areas.

An entity has to decide which way round to present its segments:

- business as the primary source, with geographical as the secondary source; or
- geographical as the primary source, with business as the secondary source

The dominant source and nature of the entity's risks and returns will be the deciding factor. For example, a UK manufacturing company with a range of products which are sold in various world markets will most likely use business as its primary segment, with geographical as a secondary segment. By contrast, a company with manufacturing plants in countries throughout the world is likely to use geographical as its primary segment, with business as a secondary segment.

IAS 14 requires that segment information must conform to the accounting policies used for preparing and presenting the financial statements of the entity.

An extract from the segment reporting of InBev, a Belgian limited company, is shown below.

---

2. SEGMENT REPORTING

Segment information is presented in respect of the company's geographical segments based on location of customers. Segment results, assets and liabilities include items directly attributable to a segment as well as those that can be allocated on a reasonable basis.

Million euro	North America		Central & South America		Western Europe		Central & Eastern Europe		Asia Pacific		Holding companies and global export		Consolidated	
	2004	2003	2004	2003	2004	2003	2004	2003	2004	2003	2004	2003	2004	2003
Net turnover	1,852	1,849	1,205	-	3,464	3,523	1,253	1,022	642	496	152	154	8,568	7,044
EBITDA	810	387	476	-	646	685	259	232	162	145	(28)	49	2,325	1,498
Profit from operations	632	272	375	-	223	334	82	113	45	76	(47)	44	1,310	839

Note: EBITDA is Earnings Before Interest, Tax, Depreciation and Amortisation

---

> *Tutorial note*
>
> In the examination for *Drafting Financial Statements* there will be no assessment involving the preparation of segment information.

CONFIDENTIALITY PROCEDURES

It is a requirement of the Companies Act for directors of companies to disclose whether the financial statements have been prepared in accordance with accounting standards, particulars of any material departure from the standards and the reasons for the departure. Whilst this information is readily available to users, for those involved in the preparation of the financial statements, confidentiality procedures must be observed at all times:

- regarding any discussion about accounting standards with the directors

- regarding how the standards have been applied to a particular set of financial statements

- concerning any figures used but not disclosed in the financial statements; for example, the calculation of deferred tax, provisions, and events after the balance sheet

- concerning any investigations to determine whether to treat an item in one way rather than another; for example, whether to classify something as a provision to be recognised in the financial statements, or as a contingent liability to be disclosed as a note

Chapter Summary

- IAS 12, *Income Taxes*, requires that current tax is to be recognised on the face of the income statement. The amount of unpaid current tax is recognised as a liability on the balance sheet.

- For deferred tax, IAS 12 requires that liabilities should be recognised for all taxable temporary differences (except those relating to goodwill where amortisation is not tax-deductible, and the initial recognition of certain assets and liabilities in transactions that affect neither accounting profit nor taxable profit).

- IAS 17, *Leases*, requires that, on the lessor's balance sheet, finance leases are to be recognised on the liabilities side at the lower of the fair value of the asset being leased and the present value of the minimum lease payments. The amount is to be split between non-current and current liabilities, as appropriate. See also pages 120-127.

- IAS 37, *Provisions, Contingent Liabilities and Contingent Assets*, ensures that appropriate recognition criteria and measurement bases are applied to these three types of uncertainties. It requires that sufficient information is disclosed in the notes to the financial statements to enable users to understand their nature, timing and amount.

- IAS 10, *Events after the Balance Sheet Date*, allows for events which may occur, or information that becomes available, in the period between the end of the financial year and the date the financial statements are authorised for issue to be reflected in the financial statements. The standard distinguishes between adjusting events and non-adjusting events.

- IAS 16, *Property, Plant and Equipment*, requires that all tangible non-current assets having a known useful life are to be depreciated (the usual exception is land). See also pages 98-107.

- IAS 18, *Revenue*, sets out the accounting treatment to ensure that the revenue shown in the income statement is correctly stated. It covers the rules for the recognition of three types of revenue:
  - sale of goods
  - rendering of services
  - interest, royalties and dividends

- IAS 23, *Borrowing Costs*, sets out the 'benchmark' accounting treatment for borrowing costs as being recognised as an expense in the income statement of the period in which they are incurred. The alternative treatment is that borrowing costs in relation to the acquisition, construction or production of a qualifying asset can be capitalised as part of the cost of the asset.

- IAS 33, *Earnings per Share*, requires all listed companies to present the EPS figure on the face of the income statement. Two EPS calculations are required to be given:
  - using the profit or loss attributable to ordinary equity holders
  - using the profit or loss from continuing operations

- IAS 14, *Segment Reporting*, requires companies to give financial information about their activities in two main ways:
  - by business segment (type of product or service)
  - by geographical segment (area of the world in which they operate)

Key Terms		
	current tax	the amount of income taxes payable in respect of the taxable profit for the year
	deferred tax	the amounts of income taxes payable in future periods in respect of taxable temporary differences
	provision	a liability of uncertain timing or amount
	contingent liability	*either* a possible obligation arising from past events whose existence will be confirmed only by the occurrence or non-occurrence of one or more uncertain future events not wholly within the entity's control;

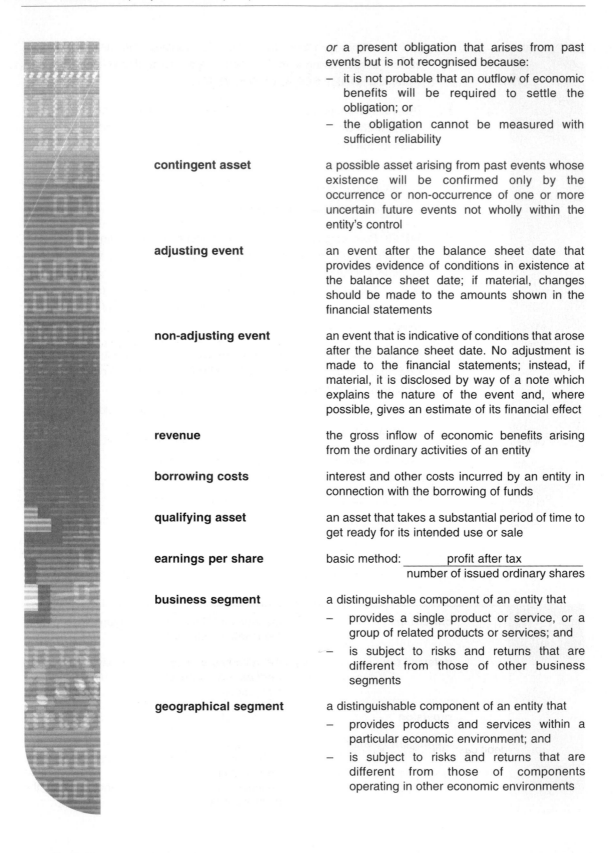

or a present obligation that arises from past events but is not recognised because:

- it is not probable that an outflow of economic benefits will be required to settle the obligation; or
- the obligation cannot be measured with sufficient reliability

contingent asset   a possible asset arising from past events whose existence will be confirmed only by the occurrence or non-occurrence of one or more uncertain future events not wholly within the entity's control

adjusting event   an event after the balance sheet date that provides evidence of conditions in existence at the balance sheet date; if material, changes should be made to the amounts shown in the financial statements

non-adjusting event   an event that is indicative of conditions that arose after the balance sheet date. No adjustment is made to the financial statements; instead, if material, it is disclosed by way of a note which explains the nature of the event and, where possible, gives an estimate of its financial effect

revenue   the gross inflow of economic benefits arising from the ordinary activities of an entity

borrowing costs   interest and other costs incurred by an entity in connection with the borrowing of funds

qualifying asset   an asset that takes a substantial period of time to get ready for its intended use or sale

earnings per share   basic method: $\dfrac{\text{profit after tax}}{\text{number of issued ordinary shares}}$

business segment   a distinguishable component of an entity that

- provides a single product or service, or a group of related products or services; and
- is subject to risks and returns that are different from those of other business segments

geographical segment   a distinguishable component of an entity that

- provides products and services within a particular economic environment; and
- is subject to risks and returns that are different from those of components operating in other economic environments

Student Activities

5.1   Which of the following could be recognised as an expense in the income statement?

(a)   a non-adjusting event after the balance sheet date

(b)   a possible contingent liability

(c)   internally generated goodwill

(d)   research and development expenditure

5.2   IAS 37, *Provisions, Contingent Liabilities and Contingent Assets*, states that a contingent liability at the balance sheet date should be disclosed in the financial statements for that year, if:

(a)   its occurrence is probable and the amount of the obligation can be estimated reliably

(b)   its occurrence is possible and the amount of the obligation can be estimated reliably

(c)   its occurrence is remote

(d)   its occurrence is virtually certain and the amount of the obligation can be estimated reliably

5.3   According to IAS 10, *Events after the Balance Sheet Date*, which one of the following is an adjusting event?

(a)   the closure of a major factory after the year end

(b)   the signing of a major export contract after the year end

(c)   a strike by the workforce after the year end, which threatens the profitability of the company

(d)   a customer who was forced into liquidation, after the year end, but the amount of the trade receivable is recorded in the balance sheet as at the actual year end

5.4   When dealing with current tax in accordance with IAS 12, *Income Taxes*, which one of the following best describes the amount due to be paid in the financial statements?

(a)   debit income statement   credit cash and cash equivalents

(b)   debit income statement   credit tax payable

(c)   debit cash and cash equivalents   credit tax payable

(d)   debit cash and cash equivalents   credit income statement

5.5   Which one of the following statements is correct when dealing with deferred taxation, according to IAS 12, *Income Taxes*?

(a)   the taxable profit and the profit shown by the income statement are one and the same, allowances being based upon depreciation

(b)   the taxable profit is the same as the balance of cash and cash equivalents, ensuring that there is enough cash to pay the tax payable

(c)   the taxable profit is the same as the net book value of the tangible non-current assets, after adjusting for depreciation

(d)   the taxable profit is different from the profit shown by the income statement due to the fact that depreciation is replaced by a system of capital allowances

5.6   According to IAS 18, *Revenue*, how is revenue to be measured?

(a)   at the fair value of the consideration received or receivable

(b)   at the lower of cost and net realisable value

(c)   at cost or revaluation, less impairment losses

(d)   at the amount of cash and cash equivalents received

5.7   In the rules for the recognition of revenue given in IAS 18, *Revenue*, which of the following are set out in detail?

1.   interest
2.   royalties
3.   sale of goods
4.   rendering of services
5.   dividends

(a)   3 and 4

(b)   2, 3 and 4

(c)   1, 2, 3 and 4

(d)   all of them

5.8   At the beginning of its financial year, on 1 April 20-6, Alexis Limited has 50m £1 ordinary shares in issue. On 1 July 20-6, the company issues a further 10m £1 ordinary shares at full market price. No further ordinary shares are issued during the financial year. What is the number of shares that is to be used in the calculation of basic earnings per share, for the financial year ended 31 March 20-7?

(a)   10m

(b)   50m

(c)   57.5m

(d)   60m

5.9   Define adjusting and non-adjusting events, giving an example of each.

5.10   State how a material provision and a material contingent liability should be treated and accounted for in financial statements.

5.11   (a)   Explain the 'benchmark' accounting treatment set out in IAS 23, *Borrowing Costs*. *as expenditure*

     (b)   What alternative treatment is allowed? *Can be capitalised*

5.12   The income statement (extract) of Wyvern Stores plc for 20-6 is as follows:

Income statement (extract) for the year ended 31 December 20-6

Continuing Operations	£000
Profit before tax	540
Tax	(150)
Profit for the year from continuing operations	390
Discontinued Operations	
Loss for the year from discontinued operations	(60)
Profit for the year attributable to equity holders	330

handwritten notes:
0.0195 $\frac{390,000}{20,000,000}$ or $2p$

$\frac{330,000}{20,000,000} = 0.0165$ or $2p$

The company's share capital at 31 December 20-6 is £20m ordinary shares of £1 each. No new shares were issued during the year.

Task 1

You are asked to calculate the basic earnings per share of Wyvern Stores plc for 20-6.

Task 2

The company did consider making a new issue of £5m ordinary shares of £1 each at full market value on 1 July 20-6. Although the issue did not go ahead, the finance director asks you to calculate what the EPS figure would have been for the year. *half/6 months 2.5m   20,000,000*

Note: calculate EPS in pence per share, to two decimal places. *390   22,500,000*

handwritten: $\frac{390}{22500} = 0.017 \times 100 = 1.7$

5.13   What is the main purpose of IAS 14, *Segment Reporting*? *handwritten:* $\frac{330}{22500} = 0.014 \times 100 = 1.4$

5.14   Answer the following questions which the directors of Gernroder Limited have asked concerning the financial statements for the year ended 30 September 20-6. Where appropriate, make reference to international accounting standards to justify your answers.

     (a)   The auditors have asked us to reduce the value of some of our inventory – from the cost of £156,590 to £101,640, which is the amount at which we sold the inventory after the year end. Why should something which happened after the year end be at all relevant to the balances at the year end? *IS10*

     (b)   Our accountant knows that, in early October, we announced our proposal to pay a final dividend of £75,000 for the year but she hasn't shown a liability for it in the financial statements.

     (c)   We had to dismiss an employee in early October. The former employee has now started legal proceedings for unfair dismissal. Our lawyers tell us that the company will probably lose the case and think that a reliable estimate of damages awarded against us is £20,000. As we employed this person at the financial year end we feel that we ought to show the estimated amount of damages as an expense in the income statement and as a liability on the balance sheet.

this chapter covers . . .

In this chapter we study the cash flow statement, which links profit from the income statement with changes in assets and liabilities in the balance sheet, and the effect on the cash of the company. We will cover:

- an appreciation of the need for a cash flow statement

- the cash flows for the sections of the statement

- how the cash flows relate to the areas of business activity

- the interpretation of cash flow statements

Tutorial note: In the layouts of cash flow statements in this chapter – and also in the examination – we use what is termed the 'indirect method'. Another method – the 'direct method' – is allowed by IAS 7, Cash Flow Statements; this method is discussed on page 186. However, as the AAT Examination assesses only the indirect method (although you should be aware of the direct method), this is the method we will study in detail in this chapter.

PERFORMANCE CRITERIA COVERED

unit 11: DRAFTING FINANCIAL STATEMENTS

element 11.1

draft limited company financial statements

A draft limited company financial statements from the appropriate information

B correctly identify and implement subsequent adjustments and ensure that discrepancies, unusual features or queries are identified and either resolved or referred to the appropriate person

C ensure that limited company financial statements comply with relevant accounting standards and domestic legislation and with the organisation's policies, regulations and procedures

D prepare and interpret a limited company cash flow statement

E ensure that confidentiality procedures are followed at all times

INTRODUCTION

The income statement shows profitability, and the balance sheet shows asset strength. While these two financial statements give us a great deal of information on the progress of a company during an accounting period, profit does not equal cash, and strength in assets does not necessarily mean a large bank balance.

The **cash flow statement** links profit with changes in assets and liabilities, and the effect on the cash of the company.

A cash flow statement uses information from the accounting records (including income statement and balance sheet) to show an overall view of money flowing in and out of a company during an accounting period.

Such a statement explains to the shareholders why, after a year of good profits for example, there is a reduced balance at the bank or a larger bank overdraft at the year-end than there was at the beginning of the year. The cash flow statement concentrates on the liquidity of the business: it is often a lack of cash (a lack of liquidity) that causes most businesses to fail.

Such is the importance of cash flow statements, that companies preparing and presenting accounts in accordance with international accounting standards are required to include a cash flow statement as an integral part of their financial statements.

FORMAT OF THE CASH FLOW STATEMENT

IAS 7, *Cash Flow Statements*, provides the guidelines for a format for cash flow statements, divided into three sections:

- **Operating activities** – the main revenue-producing activities of the business, together with the payment of interest and tax

- **Investing activities** – the acquisition and disposal of long-term assets, and other investments

- **Financing activities** – receipts from the issue of new shares, payments to repay shares, changes in long-term borrowings

The cash flows for the year affecting each of these areas of business activity are shown in the statement.

At the bottom of the cash flow statement is shown the net increase in cash and cash equivalents for the period, together with the cash and cash equivalents, both at the beginning and at the end of the period.

Note the following terms:

- *cash*, which comprises cash on hand and demand deposits

- *cash equivalents*, which are short-term, highly liquid investments that can easily be converted into cash (an example of a cash equivalent is money held in a term account, provided that the money can be withdrawn within three months from the date of deposit).

Bank overdrafts which are payable on demand are included as a part of cash and cash equivalents.

The diagram on the next page shows the main cash flows (inflows and outflows of cash and cash equivalents) under each heading, and indicates the content of the cash flow statement. The first section – operating activities – needs a word of further explanation, particularly as it is the main source of cash flow for most companies.

operating activities

The cash flow from operating activities is calculated by using figures from the income statement and balance sheet as follows:

	profit from operations (profit, before deduction of tax & interest)
add	depreciation charge for the year
add	loss on sale of non-current assets (or *deduct* gain on sale of non-current assets) – see page 176
deduct	investment income
add	decrease in inventories (or *deduct* increase in inventories)
add	decrease in trade receivables (or *deduct* increase in trade receivables)
add	increase in trade payables (or *deduct* decrease in trade payables)
equals	**cash (used in)/from operations**
deduct	interest paid in period
deduct	tax paid on income in period (eg corporation tax)
equals	**net cash (used in)/from operating activities**

Notes:

- Depreciation is added to profit because depreciation is a non-cash expense, that is, no money is paid out by the company in respect of depreciation charged to the income statement.

- Cash flows relating to the purchase and sale of non-current assets are shown in the investing activities section.

- The investment income deducted here will be shown in the investing activities section.

LAYOUT OF A CASH FLOW STATEMENT

A cash flow statement uses a common layout which can be amended to suit the particular needs of the company for which it is being prepared. The example layout shown on page 172 (with specimen figures included) is commonly used – see also the cash flow statement for InBev, a Belgian limited company, shown on page 72.

In the Examination for *Drafting Financial Statements*, a pro-forma for a cash flow statement will be provided.

CASH FLOW STATEMENT

Operating activities

- Profit from operations (ie profit, before deduction of tax and interest)
- Depreciation charge for the year (see page 176 for treatment of a gain or a loss on sale of non-current assets)
- Less investment income
- Changes in inventories, trade and other receivables and payables
- Less interest paid
- Less taxes paid on income (eg corporation tax)

Investing activities

- Inflows: sale proceeds from property, plant and equipment, intangibles, and other long-term (non-current) assets
- Outflows: purchase cost of property, plant and equipment, intangibles, and other long-term (non-current) assets
- Interest received
- Dividends received
- Inflows: the sale proceeds of investments in subsidiaries and other business units
- Outflows: the purchase cost of investments in subsidiaries and other business units

Financing activities

- Inflows: receipts from increase in share capital (note: no cash inflow from a bonus issue of shares – see page 76), raising/increase of loans
- Outflows: repayment of share capital/loans, and finance lease liabilities
- Dividends paid

Contents of a cash flow statement

ABC LIMITED
CASH FLOW STATEMENT FOR THE YEAR ENDED 31 DECEMBER 2006

	£	£
Net cash (used in)/from operating activities		78,000
Cash flows from investing activities		
Purchase of non-current assets	(125,000)	
Proceeds from sale of non-current assets	15,000	
Interest received	10,000	
Dividends received	–	
Sale of investments in subsidiaries, other business units	–	
Purchase of investments in subsidiaries, other business units	–	
Net cash (used in)/from investing activities		(100,000)
Cash flows from financing activities		
Proceeds from issue of share capital	275,000	
Repayment of share capital	(–)	
Proceeds from long-term borrowings	–	
Repayment of long-term borrowings	(140,000)	
Dividends paid (note: amount paid during year)	(22,000)	
Net cash (used in)/from financing activities		113,000
Net increase/(decrease) in cash and cash equivalents		91,000
Cash and cash equivalents at beginning of year		105,000
Cash and cash equivalents at end of year		196,000

Reconciliation of profit from operations to net cash flow from operating activities

	£
Profit from operations (note: before tax and interest)	75,000
Adjustments for:	
Depreciation for year	10,000
Decrease in inventories	2,000
Increase in trade receivables	(5,000)
Increase in trade payables	7,000
Cash (used in)/from operations	89,000
Interest paid (note: amount paid during year)	(5,000)
Income taxes paid (note: amount paid during year)	(6,000)
Net cash (used in)/from operating activities	78,000

notes on the cash flow statement

- The separate amounts shown for each section can, if preferred, be detailed in a note to the cash flow statement. The operating activities section is invariably set out in detail as a note below the cash flow statement, with just the figure for net cash from operating activities (see example opposite) being shown on the statement – see grey line. (Tutorial note: some examination questions ask only for this section to be completed.)

- Money amounts shown in brackets indicate a deduction or, where the figure is a sub-total, a negative figure.

- The changes in the main working capital items of inventories, receivables and payables have an effect on cash balances. For example, a decrease in inventory increases cash, while an increase in receivables reduces cash.

- IAS 7 allows some flexibility in the way in which companies present their cash flow statements. In particular, the cash flows from interest and dividends received and paid can be classified as operating or investing or financing activities – how they are classified should be applied consistently.

- Cash flows arising from taxes on income – eg corporation tax – are always classified as operating activities, unless they can be specifically identified with financing and investing activities.

- The cash flow statement concludes with a figure for the net increase or decrease in cash and cash equivalents for the year. This is calculated from the subtotals of each of the three sections of the statement. Added to this is the amount of cash and cash equivalents at the beginning of the year. Thus the final figure of the statement is that of cash and cash equivalents at the end of the year.

Case Study

NEWTOWN TRADING COMPANY LIMITED: CASH FLOW STATEMENT

situation

The balance sheets of Newtown Trading Company Limited for 2005 and 2006 are shown on the next page.

Prepare a cash flow statement for the year ended 31 December 2006 and comment on the main points highlighted by the statement. Note the following points:

- Extract from the income statement for 2006:

	£
Profit from operations	9,400
Interest paid	(400)
Profit before tax	9,000
Tax	(1,500)
Profit after tax	7,500

- Dividends of £1,500 were paid in 2005, and £2,000 in 2006.
- During 2006 the property was revalued at £125,000.

Tutorial note
When preparing a cash flow statement from financial statements, take a moment or two to establish which is the earlier year and which is the later year. In this Case Study they are set out from left to right, ie 2005 followed by 2006. In some Activities and Examinations, the later year is shown first, ie 2006 followed by 2005.

BALANCE SHEETS AS AT 31 DECEMBER

	2005			2006		
	£	£	£	£	£	£
	Cost	Dep'n	Net	Cost or reval'n	Dep'n	Net
Non-Current Assets						
Property	75,000	–	75,000	125,000	–	125,000
Plant and equipment	22,200	6,200	16,000	39,000	8,900	30,100
	97,200	6,200	91,000	164,000	8,900	155,100
Current Assets						
Inventories		7,000			11,000	
Trade receivables		5,000			3,700	
Cash and cash equivalents		1,000			500	
		13,000			15,200	
Current Liabilities						
Trade payables		(5,500)			(6,800)	
Tax liabilities		(1,000)			(1,500)	
		(6,500)			(8,300)	
Net Current Assets			6,500			6,900
			97,500			162,000
Non-Current Liabilities						
Debentures			(5,000)			(3,000)
NET ASSETS			92,500			159,000
EQUITY						
Ordinary share capital			80,000			90,000
Share premium account			1,500			2,500
Revaluation reserve			–			50,000
Retained earnings			11,000			16,500
TOTAL EQUITY			92,500			159,000

solution

NEWTOWN TRADING COMPANY LIMITED
CASH FLOW STATEMENT FOR THE YEAR ENDED 31 DECEMBER 2006

	£	£
Net cash (used in)/ from operating activities (see below)		9,300
Cash flows from investing activities		
Purchase of non-current assets (plant and equipment)	(16,800)	
Net cash (used in)/ from investing activities		(16,800)
Cash flows from financing activities		
Issue of ordinary shares at a premium		
ie £10,000 + £1,000 =	11,000	
Repayment of debentures	(2,000)	
Dividends paid	(2,000)	
Net cash (used in)/ from financing activities		7,000
Net increase/(decrease) in cash and cash equivalents		(500)
Cash and cash equivalents at beginning of year		1,000
Cash and cash equivalents at end of year		500

Reconciliation of profit from operations to net cash flow from operating activities	£
Profit from operations (before tax and interest)	9,400
Adjustments for:	
Depreciation for year*	2,700
Increase in inventories	(4,000)
Decrease in trade receivables	1,300
Increase in trade payables	1,300
Cash (used in)/from operations	10,700
Interest paid	(400)
Income taxes paid	(1,000)
Net cash (used in)/ from operating activities	9,300

notes on the cash flow statement

*   Depreciation charged: £8,900 – £6,200 = £2,700

The liability for tax – which is a current liability at 31 December 2005 – is paid in 2006. Likewise, the current liability for tax at 31 December 2006 will be paid in 2007 (and will appear on that year's cash flow statement).

The dividend is the amount *paid* during 2006, ie £2,000.

The revaluation of the property (increase in the value of the non-current asset, and revaluation reserve recorded in the equity section) does not feature in the cash flow statement because it is a non-cash transaction.

how useful is the cash flow statement?

The following points are highlighted by the statement on the previous page:

- cash generated from operations is £10,700 (this is before interest and tax is paid for the year)

- net cash from operating activities is £9,300

- a purchase of plant and equipment of £16,800 has been made, financed partly by operating activities, and partly by an issue of shares at a premium

- the bank balance during the year has fallen by £500, ie from £1,000 to £500

In conclusion, the picture shown by the cash flow statement is that of a business which is generating cash from its operating activities and using the cash to build for the future.

GAIN OR LOSS ON DISPOSAL OF NON-CURRENT ASSETS

a difference between book value and sale proceeds

When a company sells non-current assets it is most unlikely that the resultant sale proceeds will equal the carrying value (cost/revaluation less accumulated depreciation).

dealing with a gain or loss on disposal

The accounting solution is to transfer any small gain or loss on sale – non-cash items – to the income statement. However, such a gain or loss on sale must be handled with care when preparing a cash flow statement because, in such a statement we have to adjust for non-cash items when calculating the net cash from operating activities; at the same time we must separately identify the amount of the sale proceeds of non-current assets in the investing activities section.

Case Study

H & J WELLS LIMITED: GAIN OR LOSS ON DISPOSAL OF NON-CURRENT ASSETS

situation

H & J Wells Limited is an electrical contractor. For the year ended 30 June 2006 its income statement is as follows:

	£	£
Gross profit		37,500
Expenses:		
General expenses	(23,000)	
Provision for depreciation: plant	(2,000)	
equipment	(3,000)	
		(28,000)
Profit from operations		9,500

gain on sale

During the course of the year the company has sold the following non-current asset; the effects of the sale transaction have not yet been recorded in the income statement:

		£
Plant:	cost price	1,000
	depreciation to date	(750)
	net book value (carrying value)	250
	sale proceeds	350

As the plant has been sold for £100 more than book value, this sum is shown in the income statement, as follows:

	£	£
Gross profit		37,500
Gain on sale of non-current assets		100
		37,600
Expenses:		
General expenses	(23,000)	
Provision for depreciation: plant	(2,000)	
equipment	(3,000)	
		(28,000)
Profit from operations		9,600

The cash flow statement, based on the amended income statement, will include the following figures:

CASHFLOW STATEMENT (EXTRACT) OF H & J WELLS LIMITED
FOR THE YEAR ENDED 30 JUNE 2006

	£	£
Cash flows from operating activities		
Profit from operations	9,600	
Adjustments for:		
Depreciation for year	5,000	
Gain on sale of non-current assets	(100)	
(Increase)/decrease in inventories	. . .	
(Increase)/decrease in trade receivables	. . .	
Increase/(decrease) in trade payables	. . .	
Net cash (used in)/from operating activities		14,500
Cash flows from investing activities		
Purchase of non-current assets	(. . .)	
Proceeds from sale of non-current assets	350	
Net cash (used in)/from investing activities		350

Note that the gain on sale of non-current assets is deducted in the operating activities section because it is non-cash income. (Only the sections of the cash flow statement affected by the sale are shown above.)

loss on sale

If the plant in the Case Study had been sold for £150, this would have given a 'loss on sale' of £100. This amount would be debited to the income statement, to give an amended profit from operations of £9,400. The effect on the cash flow statement would be twofold:

1 In the operating activities section, loss on sale of non-current assets of £100 would be added; the net cash from operating activities remains at £14,500 (which proves that both gain and loss on sale of non-current assets are items which do not affect cash)

2 In the investing activities section, proceeds from sale of non-current assets would be £150

conclusion: gain or a loss on sale of non-current assets

The rule for dealing with a gain or a loss on sale of non-current assets in cash flow statements is:

• add the amount of the loss on sale, or deduct the amount of the gain on sale, to or from the profit from operations when calculating the net cash from operating activities

- show the total sale proceeds, ie the amount of the cheque received, as proceeds from sale of non-current assets in the investing activities section

The Case Study of Retail News Limited (see below) incorporates calculations for both a gain and a loss on sale of non-current assets.

REVALUATION OF NON-CURRENT ASSETS

From time-to-time some non-current assets are revalued upwards and the amount of the revaluation is recorded in the balance sheet. The most common asset to be treated in this way is property. The value of the non-current asset is increased and the amount of the revaluation is placed to a revaluation surplus in the equity section of the balance sheet where it increases the value of the shareholders' investment in the company. As a revaluation is purely a 'book' adjustment, ie no cash has changed hands, it does not feature in a cash flow statement – see the Case Study of Newtown Trading Company Limited on pages 173 to 176.

DISCONTINUED OPERATIONS

IFRS 5, *Non-current Assets Held for Sale and Discontinued Operations*, requires disclosure of the net cash flows from discontinued operations (see also page 61). The cash flows attributable to the operating, investing and financing activities are to be disclosed either on the face of the cash flow statement or in the notes to the financial statements.

Case Study

RETAIL NEWS LIMITED: PREPARING THE CASH FLOW STATEMENTS

Tutorial note

This is quite a complex example of cash flow statements which incorporates a number of points:

- gain on sale of non-current assets
- loss on sale of non-current assets
- issue of shares at a premium
- calculation of tax paid

As there are two years' cash flow statements to produce, it is suggested that you work through the Case Study seeing how the figures have been prepared for the first year (year ended 2005); then attempt the second year (year ended 2006) yourself, checking against the Case Study.

situation

Martin Jackson is a shareholder in Retail News Limited, a company that operates newsagent shops in the town of Wyvern. Martin comments that, whilst the company is making reasonable profits, the bank balance has fallen quite considerably. He provides you with the following information for Retail News Limited:

Balance sheet as at 31 December

	2004		2005		2006	
	£000	£000	£000	£000	£000	£000
Non-Current Assets at cost		274		298		324
Depreciation		(74)		(98)		(118)
		200		200		206
Current Assets						
Inventories	50		74		85	
Trade receivables	80		120		150	
Cash and cash equivalents	10		–		–	
	140		194		235	
Current Liabilities						
Trade payables	(72)		(89)		(95)	
Bank overdraft	–		(15)		(46)	
Tax liabilities	(4)		(5)		(8)	
	(76)		(109)		(149)	
Net Current Assets		64		85		86
NET ASSETS		264		285		292
EQUITY						
Ordinary share capital		200		210		210
Share premium account		–		5		5
Retained earnings		64		70		77
TOTAL EQUITY		264		285		292

Income statement extracts for the year ended 31 December

	2004 £000	2005 £000	2006 £000
Profit from operations	25	31	50
Interest paid	–	(3)	(15)
Profit before tax	25	28	35
Tax	(5)	(7)	(10)
Profit after tax	20	21	25

Notes

- Dividends paid were: £15,000 in 2005, and £18,000 in 2006.

- During the year to 31 December 2005, non-current assets were sold for £30,000, the cost of the assets sold was £40,000 and depreciation was £20,000.

- During the year to 31 December 2006, non-current assets with an original cost of £35,000 were sold at a loss on sale of £5,000 below net book value; the depreciation on these assets sold had amounted to £15,000.

REQUIRED: Prepare a cash flow statement for the years ended 2005 and 2006.

solution

RETAIL NEWS LIMITED
CASH FLOW STATEMENT FOR THE YEAR ENDED 31 DECEMBER

	2005 £000 £	2005 £000 £	2006 £000 £	2006 £000 £
Net cash (used in)/from operating activities (see below)		9		33
Cash flows from investing activities				
Purchase of non-current assets (see below)	(64)		(61)	
Proceeds from sale of non-current assets	30		15	
Net cash (used in)/from investing activities		(34)		(46)
Cash flows from financing activities				
Proceeds from issue of share capital at a premium (see below)	15		–	
Dividends paid	(15)		(18)	
Net cash (used in)/from financing activities		–		(18)
Net increase/(decrease) in cash and cash equivalents		(25)		(31)
Cash and cash equivalents at beginning of year		10		(15)
Cash and cash equivalents at end of year		(15)		(46)

Reconciliation of profit from operations to net cash flow from operating activities

	2005 £000	2006 £000
Profit from operations	31	50
Adjustments for:		
Depreciation for year	44	35
(Gain)/loss on sale of non-current assets (see below)	(10)	5
Increase in inventories	(24)	(11)
Increase in trade receivables	(40)	(30)
Increase in trade payables	17	6
Cash (used in)/from operations	18	55
Interest paid	(3)	(15)
Income taxes paid (see below)	(6)	(7)
Net cash (used in)/from operating activities	9	33

Points to note from the cash flow statement:

■ **Depreciation for year**

	2005 £000	2006 £000
Depreciation at start of year*	74	98
Depreciation on asset sold	(20)	(15)
	54	83
Depreciation at end of year*	98	118
Depreciation for year	44	35

* figures taken from balance sheet

■ **Gain/(loss) on sale of non-current assets**

	2005 £000	2006 £000
Cost price of assets sold	40	35
Depreciation to date	(20)	(15)
Net book value (carrying value)	20	20
Proceeds from sale	30	*15
Gain/(loss) on sale of non-current assets	10	(5)

* Proceeds from sale at £5,000 below net book value

Note that the gain on sale is *deducted from*, and loss on sale is *added to*, operating profit because they are non-cash income; the proceeds from sale are shown in the investing activities section

■ **Income taxes paid**

From the information available we can calculate the amount of tax paid in the year as follows:

Liability at start of year*	4	5
Income statement transfer	7	10
	11	15
Liability at end of year*	(5)	(8)
Amount of tax paid in year	6	7

* figures taken from balance sheet

■ **Payments to acquire non-current assets**

Non-current assets at cost at start of year	274	298
Cost price of asset sold	(40)	(35)
	234	263
Non-current assets at cost at end of year	298	324
Purchase of non-current assets	64	61

■ **Dividends paid**

From the information given, the amount of dividends paid were:

2005	£15,000
2006	£18,000

These amounts are shown in the financing activities section of the relevant year's cash flow statement.

■ **Issue of ordinary shares at a premium**

Ordinary share capital at start of year	200
Share premium account at start of year	–
	200
Ordinary share capital at end of year	210
Share premium account at end of year	5
	215
Issue of ordinary shares at a premium	15

conclusion: how useful is the cash flow statement?

The following points are highlighted by the cash flow statements of Retail News Limited for 2005 and 2006:

- a good cash flow generated from operations in both years – well above the amounts paid for corporation tax and dividends

- inventories, receivables and payables have increased each year – in particular the receivables have increased significantly

- interest paid in 2006 is high because of the increasing bank overdraft (and will, most probably, be even higher in 2007)

- new non-current assets have been bought each year – £64,000 in 2005 and £61,000 in 2006; apart from a share issue of £15,000 in 2005, these have been financed through the bank account

The company appears to be expanding quite rapidly, with large increases in non-current assets and the working capital items. As most of this expansion has been financed through the bank (apart from the share issue of £15,000 in 2005), there is much pressure on the bank account. It would be better to obtain long-term finance – either a loan or a new issue of shares – rather than using the bank overdraft.

LINKS TO OTHER FINANCIAL STATEMENTS

As the cash flow statement is one of the main financial statements prepared at the end of an accounting period, it needs to be read in conjunction with the income statement and balance sheet. In order to help the user of the cash flow statement, IAS 7 requires that there should be explanatory notes on:

- cash and cash equivalents
- segmental cash flows

cash and cash equivalents

Companies must disclose the components of cash and cash equivalents and reconcile the amounts shown in the cash flow statement with the figures from the balance sheet. Thus, for ABC Limited (see page 172) the reconciliation could be shown as follows, with specimen figures used:

Reconciliation of cash and cash equivalents

	31 December 2005	31 December 2006
	£	£
Cash	20,000	26,000
Overdraft	(45,000)	(20,000)
Short-term deposits	130,000	190,000
Cash and cash equivalents	105,000	196,000

segmental cash flows

IAS 7 encourages companies to present their cash flow statements using segmental analysis – for example, by business segment, by geographical segment. See also IAS 14 *Segment Reporting*, on page 159.

INTERPRETING THE CASH FLOW STATEMENT

The cash flow statement is important because it identifies the sources of cash flowing into the company and shows how they have been used. To get an overall view of the company, we need to read the statement in conjunction with the other main financial statements – income statement and balance sheet – and also in the context of the previous year's statements.

You could be asked to interpret a cash flow statement in the Examination. The following points should be borne in mind:

- Like the other financial statements, the cash flow statement uses the money measurement concept. This means that only items which can be recorded in money terms can be included; also we must be aware of the effect of inflation if comparing one year with the next.

- Look for positive cash flows from the operating activities section. In particular, look at the subtotal 'cash (used in)/from operations' – this shows the cash from revenue-producing activities before the payment of interest and tax.

- Make a comparison between the amount of profit and the amount of cash generated from operations. Identify the reasons for major differences between these figures – look at the changes in the working capital items of inventories, receivables and payables, and put them into context. For example, it would be a warning sign if there were large increases in these items in a company with falling profits, and such a trend would put a strain on the liquidity of the business. Also consider the company's policies on collecting receivables (and potential for bad debts), payment to payables (is the company paying too quickly?) and control of inventories (are surpluses building up?).

- Look at the figure for 'net cash (used in)/from operating activities', ie the cash from operations after interest and tax have been paid. If it is a positive figure, it shows that the company has been able to meet its interest and tax obligations to loan providers and the tax authorities.

- The investing activities section of the statement shows the amount of investment made during the year (eg the purchase of non-current assets). In general there should be a link between the cost of the investment and an increase in loans and/or share capital – it isn't usual to finance non-current assets from short-term sources, such as a bank overdraft.

- In the financing activities section of the statement, where there has been an increase in loans and/or share capital, look to see how the money has been used. Was it to buy non-current assets or other investments, or to finance inventory and receivables, or other purposes?

- Look at the amount of dividends paid – this is an outflow of cash that will directly affect the change in the bank balance. As a quick test, the amount of net cash from operating activities should, in theory, be sufficient to cover dividends paid; if it doesn't, then it is likely that the level of dividends will have to be reduced in future years.

- The cash flow statement, as a whole, links profit with changes in cash. Both of these are important: without profits the company cannot generate cash (unless it sells non-current assets), and without cash it cannot pay bills as they fall due.

CASH FLOW STATEMENTS: THE DIRECT METHOD

This chapter has focussed on preparing cash flow statements using the *indirect method*. Thus the operating activities section starts with the profit from operations. As an alternative, IAS 7 allows another method – the *direct method* – and, indeed, encourages companies to use it. For the operating activities section this method, instead of starting with profit, shows cash received from sales, less cash paid for purchases and overheads (excluding depreciation – a non-cash expense).

As an example of the direct method we will use the cash flow statement of ABC Limited shown on page 172. The cash (used in)/from operations is shown in the following way (with specimen figures included):

Cash flows from operating activities	£	£
Cash receipts from customers		759,000
Cash paid to suppliers and employees		(670,000)
Cash (used in)/from operations		89,000
Interest paid		(5,000)
Income taxes paid		(6,000)
Net cash (used in)/from operating activities		78,000

Note that the figure of £89,000 for cash (used in)/from operations is the same as that shown under the indirect method on page 172. The rest of the cash flow statement is presented in exactly the same way.

For *Drafting Financial Statements*, you should be aware of the direct method, but it will not be assessed.

CONFIDENTIALITY PROCEDURES

The accounting standard IAS 7 requires companies to produce a cash flow statement as a part of their financial statements. This means that cash flow statements are readily available to shareholders and interested parties either from Companies House (www.companieshouse.gov.uk) or from the company itself.

For those involved in the preparation of cash flow statements, confidentiality procedures must be observed at all times:

- during the preparation of published accounts

- during the period after the accounts have been prepared but before they are sent to shareholders, filed at Companies House, and disclosed to the public

- for detailed information that is needed in the preparation of cash flow statements (eg the calculation of profit or loss on sale of non-current assets, tax paid, dividends paid) but is not disclosed

Chapter Summary

- The objective of a cash flow statement is to show an overall view of money flowing in and out of a company during an accounting period

- IAS 7 is the accounting standard that sets out the requirements of cash flow statements.

- A cashflow statement is divided into three sections:

  1   operating activities – the main revenue-producing activities of the business, together with the payment of interest and tax

  2   investing activities – the acquisition and disposal of long-term assets, and some other investments

  3   financing activities – receipts from the issue of new shares, payments to cover the repayment of shares, changes in long-term borrowings

- There are two methods of setting out the operating activities section: the direct method and the indirect method. The examination for *Drafting Financial Statements* assesses only the indirect method (although you should be aware of the direct method).

- Limited companies are required to include a cash flow statement as a part of their financial statements.

- In the examination for *Drafting Financial Statements*, a pro-forma for a cash flow statement will be provided.

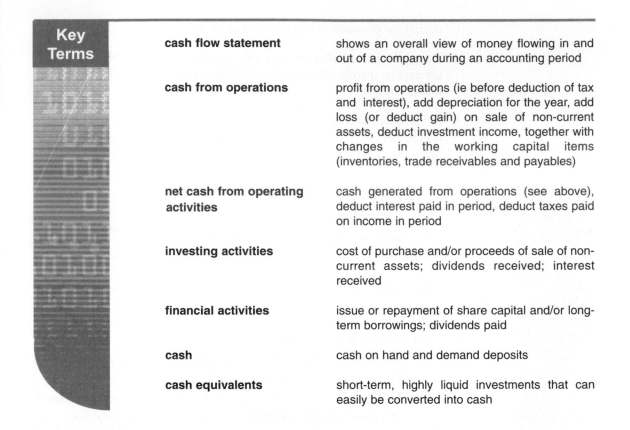

Student Activities

Osborne Books is grateful to the AAT for their kind permission to use past assessment material, which has been amended to incorporate the requirements of international accounting standards.
A blank photocopiable pro-forma of the cash flow statement is included in the Appendix – it is advisable to enlarge it to full A4 size.

6.1 Which of the following is **not** a section heading for cash flow statements?

(a) investing activities

(b) financing activities

(c) operating activities

(d) profit from operations

6.2 In the calculation of cash (used in)/from operating activities, depreciation is added back because:

(a) it is not allowable for taxation purposes

(b) it is a non-cash expense

(c) it appears under the heading of investing activities

(d) it is a financing activity

6.3   If a company's profit from operations is £50,000 and there were the following movements in the year:

depreciation charges	£7,500
increase in inventories	£5,000
decrease in trade receivables	£2,500
increase in trade payables	£4,000

What is the cash from operations for the year?
(a)   £59,000 inflow
(b)   £69,000 inflow
(c)   £36,000 inflow
(d)   £31,000 inflow

6.4   If a company's loss from operations is £6,000 and there were the following movements in the year:

depreciation charges	£10,000
decrease in inventories	£15,000
increase in trade receivables	£12,500
decrease in trade payables	£14,000

What is the cash from operations for the year?
(a)   £7,500 inflow
(b)   £1,500 outflow
(c)   £1,500 inflow
(d)   £7,500 outflow

6.5   What are the advantages to a company in producing a cash flow statement in accordance with IAS 7? Why might the users of a company's financial statements be interested in it?

6.6   The book-keeper of Cashedin Limited has asked for your assistance in producing a cash flow statement for the company for the year ended 30 September 20-5 in accordance with IAS 7.

He has derived the information which is required to be included in the cash flow statement, but is not sure of the format in which it should be presented. The information is set out below:

	£000s
Profit from operations (before interest and tax)	24
Depreciation charge for the year	318
Proceeds from sale of non-current assets	132
Issue of shares for cash	150
Cash received from new loan	200
Purchase of non-current assets for cash	358
Interest paid	218
Tax paid	75
Dividends paid	280
Increase in inventories	251
Increase in trade receivables	152
Increase in trade payables	165
Cash and cash equivalents at 1 October 20-4	395
Cash and cash equivalents at 30 September 20-5	50

REQUIRED

Using the information provided by the book-keeper, prepare a cash flow statement for Cashedin Limited for the year ended 30 September 20-5 in accordance with the requirements of IAS 7.

6.7   Radion plc's income statement for the year ended 31 December 20-3 and balance sheets for 20-2 and 20-3 were as follows:

Radion plc Income Statement for the year to 31 December 20-3

	£000	£000
Revenue		652
Cost of sales		(349)
GROSS PROFIT		303
Wages and salaries	(107)	
Depreciation charges	(30)	
Administrative expenses	(62)	(199)
PROFIT FROM OPERATIONS		104
Interest paid		(5)
PROFIT BEFORE TAX		99
Tax		(22)
PROFIT AFTER TAX		77

Radion plc Balance Sheets as at 31 December

	20-3		20-2	
	£000	£000	£000	£000
NON-CURRENT ASSETS				
Tangibles at net book value		570		600
CURRENT ASSETS				
Inventories	203		175	
Trade receivables	141		127	
Cash and cash equivalents	6			
	350		302	
CURRENT LIABILITIES				
Trade payables	(142)		(118)	
Tax liabilities	(22)		(19)	
Bank overdraft	–		(16)	
	(164)		(153)	
NET CURRENT ASSETS		186		149
		756		749
NON-CURRENT LIABILITIES				
Loans and debentures		–		(50)
		756		699
EQUITY				
Called up share capital		300		300
Share premium account		60		60
Retained earnings		396		339
TOTAL EQUITY		756		699

Notes to the accounts

- Dividends paid were: £25,000 in 20-2, and £20,000 in 20-3.
- During the year there were no purchases or sales of non-current assets.

REQUIRED

Prepare a cash flow statement for Radion plc for the year ended 31 December 20-3 in accordance with the requirements of IAS 7.

6.8 Pratt plc has supplied you with the following abridged income statement for the year to 31 October 20-3.

	£000
PROFIT FROM OPERATIONS	2,520
Interest paid	(168)
Profit before tax	2,352
Tax	(750)
Profit after tax	1,602

Balance Sheets as at 31 October

	20-3		20-2	
	£000	£000	£000	£000
NON-CURRENT ASSETS				
At cost	9,000		8,400	
Depreciation to date	(1,800)	7,200	(1,500)	6,900
CURRENT ASSETS				
Inventories	84		69	
Trade receivables	255		270	
Cash and cash equivalents	48		30	
	387		369	
CURRENT LIABILITIES				
Trade payables	(108)		(81)	
Tax liabilities	(291)		(285)	
	(399)		(366)	
NET CURRENT ASSETS (LIABILITIES)		(12)		3
		7,188		6,903
NON-CURRENT LIABILITIES				
Loans		(600)		(2,400)
		6,588		4,503
EQUITY				
Called up share capital		3,000		2,550
Share premium		177		–
Retained earnings		3,411		1,953
TOTAL EQUITY		6,588		4,503

Additional Information

- Dividends proposed were: £144,000 in 20-2, and £225,000 in 20-3. These dividends were paid in 20-3 and 20-4 respectively.
- During the year the company sold a non-current asset for £8,000 cash. The asset had originally cost £29,000 and had been depreciated by £18,000 at the time of sale.

REQUIRED

Task 1

Prepare a statement to show the reconciliation of profit from operations to net cash flow from operating activities for the year ended 31 October 20-3.

Task 2

Prepare a cash flow statement for the year ended 31 October 20-3 in accordance with the requirements of IAS 7.

6.9 Sadler plc's income statement for the year to 30 June 20-3 and balance sheets for 20-2 and 20-3 were as follows:

Sadler plc abridged Income Statement for the year to 30 June 20-3

	£000
PROFIT FROM OPERATIONS	1,100
Interest paid	(100)
PROFIT BEFORE TAX	1,000
Tax	(200)
PROFIT AFTER TAX	800

Sadler plc Balance Sheets as at 30 June

	20-2		20-3	
NON-CURRENT ASSETS	£000	£000	£000	£000
At cost	13,600		16,300	
Depreciation to date	(8,160)		(9,660)	
		5,440		6,640
CURRENT ASSETS				
Inventories	300		340	
Trade receivables	1,200		1,300	
Prepayments	100		80	
Cash and cash equivalents	40		20	
	1,640		1,740	
CURRENT LIABILITIES				
Trade payables	(660)		(800)	
Accruals	(60)		(120)	
Tax liabilities	(360)		(260)	
	(1,080)		(1,180)	
NET CURRENT ASSETS		560		560
		6,000		7,200

NON-CURRENT LIABILITIES

10% Debentures	–	(1,000)
	6,000	6,200

EQUITY

Called up share capital	4,000	4,000
Share premium account	600	600
Retained earnings	1,400	1,600
TOTAL EQUITY	6,000	6,200

Notes to the accounts

- Dividends proposed were: £600,000 in 20-2, and £500,000 in 20-3. These dividends were paid in 20-3 and 20-4 respectively.

- During the year the company sold some non-current assets, which had originally cost £1,600,000, on which there was accumulated depreciation totalling £400,000. The proceeds from the sale amounted to £1,400,000.

REQUIRED

Prepare a cash flow statement for Sadler plc for the year to 30 June 20-3 in accordance with the requirements of IAS 7.

6.10 You have been given the following information about George Limited for the year ending 31 March 20-5.

George Limited Income Statement for the year ended 31 March

	20-5		20-4	
	£000s	£000s	£000s	£000s
Revenue		2,500		1,775
Opening inventories	200		100	
Purchases	1,500		1,000	
Closing inventories	(210)		(200)	
Cost of sales		(1,490)		(900)
GROSS PROFIT		1,010		875
Depreciation		(275)		(250)
Other expenses		(500)		(425)
Gain on sale of fixed asset		2		–
PROFIT FROM OPERATIONS		237		200
Interest paid		(20)		(35)
PROFIT BEFORE TAX		217		165
Tax		(25)		(21)
PROFIT AFTER TAX		192		144

George Limited Balance sheet as at 31 March

	20-5		20-4	
	£000s	£000s	£000s	£000s
NON-CURRENT ASSETS		330		500
CURRENT ASSETS				
Inventories	210		200	
Trade receivables	390		250	
Cash and cash equivalents	–		10	
	600		460	
CURRENT LIABILITIES				
Trade payables	(150)		(160)	
Tax liabilities	(25)		(21)	
Bank overdraft	(199)		–	
	(374)		(181)	
NET CURRENT ASSETS		226		279
		556		779
NON-CURRENT LIABILITIES				
Debentures		–		(500)
Long-term loan		(200)		(100)
		356		179
EQUITY				
Called up share capital		40		25
Retained earnings		316		154
TOTAL EQUITY		356		179

Additional information

- Dividends proposed were: £30,000 in 20-4, and £35,000 in 20-5. These dividends were paid in 20-5 and 20-6 respectively.

- In May 20-4 a non-current asset was sold which originally cost £10,000 and was purchased in July 20-2. In June 20-4 a new asset was bought for £110,000. Non-current assets are depreciated at 25 per cent of cost. The policy is to charge a full year's depreciation in the year of purchase and none in the year of sale.

- Loan interest is charged at 10% p.a. The long-term loan was increased on 1 April 20-4.

- The 5% debentures were redeemed on 1 April 20-4.

- Sales and purchases were on credit. All other expenses, including interest due, were paid in cash.

- On 1 October 20-4 15,000 new ordinary £1 shares were issued at par.

REQUIRED

Task 1

Prepare a statement to show the reconciliation of profit from operations to net cash flow from operating activities for the year to 31 March 20-5.

Task 2

Prepare a cash flow statement for the year to 31 March 20-5 in accordance with the requirements of IAS 7

this chapter covers . . .

The income statements and balance sheets of limited companies are often interpreted by means of accounting ratios in order to assess strengths and weaknesses. Comparisons can be made between:

- *consecutive years for the same company*

- *similar companies in the same industry*

- *industry averages and the ratios for a particular company*

The accounts of a business can be interpreted in the areas of profitability, liquidity, efficient use of resources and financial position.

In this chapter we examine:

- *the importance of interpretation of financial statements*

- *the main accounting ratios and performance indicators*

- *a commentary on trends shown by the main accounting ratios*

- *how to report on the financial situation of a company*

- *limitations in the interpretation of accounts*

PERFORMANCE CRITERIA COVERED

unit 11: DRAFTING FINANCIAL STATEMENTS

element 11.2

interpret limited company financial statements

A   *identify the general purpose of financial statements used in limited companies*

B   *identify the elements of financial statements used in limited companies*

C   *identify the relationships between the elements within financial statements of limited companies*

D   *interpret the relationship between elements of limited company financial statements using ratio analysis*

E   *identify unusual features or significant issues within financial statements of limited companies*

F   *draw valid conclusions from the information contained within financial statements of limited companies*

G   *present issues, interpretations and conclusions clearly to the appropriate people*

INTERESTED PARTIES

Interpretation of financial statements is not always made by an accountant; interested parties – as we have seen in Chapter 1 (page 13) – include:

* **managers** of the company, who need to make financial decisions affecting the future development of the company

* **banks**, who are being asked to lend money to finance the company

* **suppliers**, who wish to assess the likelihood of receiving payment

* **customers**, who wish to be assured of continuity of supplies in the future

* **shareholders**, who wish to be assured that their investment is sound

* prospective **investors**, who wish to compare relative strengths and weaknesses

* **employees** and **trade unions**, who wish to check on the financial prospects of the company

* **government** and **government agencies**, eg HM Revenue & Customs, who wish to check they are receiving the amount due to them

We saw in Chapter 1 how the *Framework for the Preparation and Presentation of Financial Statements* requires that financial statements provide users with details of:

* financial position
* financial performance
* changes in financial position

From the financial statements the interested party will be able to calculate the main ratios, percentages and performance indicators. By doing this, the strengths and weaknesses of the company will be highlighted and appropriate conclusions can be drawn.

ACCOUNTING RATIOS AND THE ELEMENTS OF FINANCIAL STATEMENTS

The general term 'accounting ratios' is usually used to describe the calculations aspect of interpretation of financial statements. The term 'ratio' is, in fact, partly misleading because the performance indicators include percentages, time periods, as well as ratios in the strict sense of the word.

The main themes covered by the interpretation of accounts are:

- **profitability** – the relationship between profit and revenue, assets, equity and capital employed

- **liquidity** – the stability of the company on a short-term basis

- **use of resources** – the effective and efficient use of assets and liabilities

- **financial position** – the way in which the company has been financed

In Chapter 1 we saw how the elements of financial statements are the building blocks from which financial statements are constructed. The elements are defined by the *Framework for the Preparation and Presentation of Financial Statements* and comprise (see also page 16):

- assets
- liabilities
- equity
- income
- expenses

Accounting ratios make use of the elements in the interpretation of accounts – the relationship between elements is what we are measuring, together with any changes from one year to the next, or between different companies in the same industry, or an industry average. The main themes of interpretation of accounts use the elements as follows:

- **profitability** – measures the relationship between income and expenses; also the profits or losses measured against equity

- **liquidity** – focuses on the relationship between assets and liabilities

- **use of resources** – analyses the profits or losses in relation to the assets and the liabilities of the company

- **financial position** – compares the relationship between the equity and the liabilities of the company

For example, one measure of the profitability of a company is to compare the profits or losses with the equity, as follows:

To illustrate this, the first two years' financial statements of a company show the relationship to be:

Year 1		*Year 2*	
£100 profit		£200 profit	
÷	= 10%	÷	= 20%
£1,000 equity		£1,000 equity	

Thus it can be seen that an increase in the profit in year two has had an effect on the performance of the company because the relationship between profit and equity has changed from year 1.

MAKING USE OF ACCOUNTING RATIOS

It is important when examining a set of financial statements and calculating accounting ratios to relate them to reference points or standards. These points of reference might be to:

- establish trends from past years, to provide a standard of comparison
- benchmark against another similar company in the same industry
- compare against industry averages

Above all, it is important to understand the relationships between ratios: one ratio may give an indication of the state of the company, but this needs to be supported by other ratios. Ratios can indicate symptoms, but the cause will then need to be investigated.

Another use of ratios is to estimate forward the likely profit or balance sheet of a company. For example, it might be assumed that the same gross profit percentage as last year will also apply next year; thus, given an estimated increase in revenue, it is a simple matter to estimate gross profit. In a similar way, by making use of ratios, net profit (profit before tax) and the balance sheet can be forecast.

Whilst all of the ratios calculated in this chapter use figures from the income statement and balance sheet, the cash flow statement is important too. It assists in confirming the views shown by the accounting ratios and provides further evidence of the position.

---

tutorial note

ACCOUNTING RATIOS FOR PROFITABILITY

■ Study the table and financial statements on the next two pages. They show the ways in which the profitability of a company is assessed.

■ Then read the section entitled 'Profitability' which follows.

■ Note that the accounting ratios from the financial statements of Wyvern Trading Company Limited are calculated and discussed in the Case Study on pages 217-222.

PROFITABILITY

One of the main objectives of a company is to make a profit. Profitability ratios examine the relationship between profit and revenue, assets, equity and capital employed. Before calculating the profitability ratios, it is important to read the income statement in order to review the figures.

The key profitability ratios are illustrated on the next page. We will be calculating and discussing the accounting ratios from these figures in the Case Study on pages 217-222.

gross profit percentage

$$\frac{Gross\ profit}{Revenue} \quad x \ \frac{100}{1}$$

This expresses, as a percentage, the gross profit (revenue minus cost of sales) in relation to revenue. For example, a gross profit percentage of 20 per cent means that for every £100 of revenue, the gross profit is £20.

The gross profit percentage (or margin) should be similar from year-to-year for the same company. It will vary between companies in different areas of business, eg the gross profit percentage on jewellery is considerably higher than that on food. A significant change from one year to the next, particularly a fall in the percentage, requires investigation into the buying and selling prices.

continued on page 203

PROFITABILITY

Gross profit/revenue percentage $=$ $\dfrac{\text{Gross profit}}{\text{Revenue}} \times \dfrac{100}{1}$

Expense/revenue percentage $=$ $\dfrac{\text{Specified expense}}{\text{Revenue}} \times \dfrac{100}{1}$

Profit from operations/revenue percentage $=$ $\dfrac{\text{Profit from operations*}}{\text{Revenue}} \times \dfrac{100}{1}$

* profit before finance costs and tax

Net profit/revenue percentage $=$ $\dfrac{\text{Net profit*}}{\text{Revenue}} \times \dfrac{100}{1}$

* profit before tax

Return on capital employed $=$ $\dfrac{\text{Profit from operations}}{\text{Capital employed*}} \times \dfrac{100}{1}$

* share capital + reserves + non-current liabilities

Return on equity $=$ $\dfrac{\text{Profit after tax*}}{\text{Equity}} \times \dfrac{100}{1}$

* profit for the period

Earnings per share $=$ $\dfrac{\text{Profit after tax}}{\text{Number of issued ordinary shares}}$

Wyvern Trading Company Limited
INCOME STATEMENT
for the year ended 31 December 2006

	£000s	£000s
Revenue		1,430
Opening inventories	200	
Purchases	1,000	
	1,200	
Less Closing inventories	240	
Cost of sales		(960)
Gross profit		470
Overheads:		
Distribution costs	(150)	
Administrative expenses	(140)	
		(290)
Profit from operations		180
Finance costs		(10)
Profit before tax		170
Tax		(50)
Profit for the year		120

Statement of changes in equity (extract)

Retained earnings

Balance at 1 January 2006	180
Profit for the year	120
	300
Dividends paid	(100)
Balance at 31 December 2006	200

BALANCE SHEET (extract)

Capital employed (share capital + reserves +non-current liabilities)	1,550
Equity (ordinary share capital + reserves)	1,450
Number of issued ordinary shares (000s)	1,250

Note: Items used in the ratios on the previous page are shown in bold type on a grey background

Gross profit percentage, and also net profit percentage (see next page), need to be considered in context. For example, a supermarket may well have a lower gross profit percentage than a small corner shop but, because of the supermarket's much higher revenue, the amount of profit will be much higher. Whatever the type of business, gross profit – both as an amount and a percentage – needs to be sufficient to cover the overheads (expenses), and then to give an acceptable return on investment.

expense/revenue percentage

$$\frac{Specified\ expense}{Revenue} \quad x \quad \frac{100}{1}$$

A large expense or overhead item can be expressed as a percentage of revenue: for example, the relationship between advertising and revenue might be found to be 10 per cent in one year, but 20 per cent the next year. This could indicate that an increase in advertising had failed to produce a proportionate increase in revenue.

Note that each expense falls into one of three categories of cost:

1 fixed costs, or

2 variable costs, or

3 semi-variable costs

Fixed costs remain constant despite other changes. Variable costs alter with changed circumstances, such as increased output or revenue. Semi-variable costs combine both a fixed and a variable element, eg hire of a car at a basic (fixed) cost, with a (variable) cost per mile.

It is important to appreciate the nature of costs when interpreting accounts: for example, if revenue this year is twice last year's figure, not all expenses will have doubled.

profit from operations percentage

$$\frac{Profit\ from\ operations^*}{Revenue} \quad x \quad \frac{100}{1}$$

* profit before finance costs and tax

Net profit is calculated after finance costs – such as loan and bank interest – have been charged to the income statement. Thus it may be distorted when comparisons are made between two different companies where one is heavily financed by means of loans, and the other is financed entirely by ordinary share capital. The solution is to calculate the profit from operations percentage which uses profit before finance costs and tax. Note that, in accounting terminology, profit from operations is often referred to as 'net profit' – however, there is a difference between the two: 'profit from operations' is before finance costs, 'net profit' is after finance costs.

net profit percentage

$$\frac{Net\ profit^*}{Revenue} \times \frac{100}{1}$$

* profit before tax

As with gross profit percentage, the net profit percentage (or margin) should be similar from year-to-year for the same company, and should also be comparable with other companies in the same line of business. Net profit percentage should, ideally, increase from year-to-year, which indicates that the overhead costs are being kept under control. Any significant fall should be investigated to see if it has been caused by:

- a fall in gross profit percentage

- and/or an increase in one particular expense, eg wages and salaries, advertising, etc

Tutorial note: Net profit percentage is not as good an indicator of business performance as profit from operations percentage. This is because net profit may be distorted – as mentioned above – by finance costs. If there is a choice between the two ratios in *Drafting Financial Statements*, always calculate and comment upon profit from operations percentage rather than net profit percentage.

return on capital employed (ROCE)

Return on capital employed expresses the profit of a company in relation to the capital employed. The percentage return is best thought of in relation to other investments, eg a bank might offer a return of five per cent. A person setting up a company is investing a sum of money in that company, and the profit is the return that is achieved on that investment. However, it should be noted that the risks in running a company are considerably greater than depositing the money with a bank, and an additional return to allow for the extra risk is needed.

The calculation of return on capital employed for limited companies must take note of their different methods of financing. It is necessary to distinguish between the ordinary shareholders' investment (the equity) and the capital employed by the company, which includes preference shares and debentures/long-term loans.

The calculation for capital employed is:

	Ordinary share capital
add	Reserves (capital and revenue)
equals	Equity
add	Preference share capital
add	Debentures/long-term (non-current) loans
equals	Capital Employed

The reason for including preference shares and debentures/long-term loans in the capital employed is that the company has the use of the money from these contributors for the foreseeable future, or certainly for a fixed time period.

The calculation of return on capital employed is:

$$\frac{\textit{Profit from operations*}}{\textit{Capital employed**}} \quad x \quad \frac{100}{1}$$

* profit before finance costs

** ordinary share capital + reserves + preference share capital + debentures/long-term (non-current) loans

Return on capital employed is also known as the *primary ratio* – see page 213.

return on equity

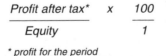

$$\frac{\textit{Profit after tax*}}{\textit{Equity}} \quad x \quad \frac{100}{1}$$

* profit for the period

Whilst return on capital employed looks at the overall return on the long-term sources of finance (the capital employed), return on equity focuses on the return for the ordinary shareholders. Return on equity indicates the return the company is making on their funds, ie ordinary shares and reserves. The economic decision as to whether they remain as ordinary shareholders is primarily whether they could get a better return elsewhere.

Note that, when calculating return on equity, use the profit for the period, ie after tax, which is the amount of profit available to the ordinary shareholders.

earnings per share

$$\frac{\textit{Profit after tax}}{\textit{Number of issued ordinary shares}}$$

Earnings per share (or EPS) measures the amount of profit (or loss) – usually expressed in pence – earned by each ordinary share, after tax. Comparisons can be made with previous years to provide a basis for assessing the company's performance.

See also IAS 33 *Earnings per Share*, on page 157.

---

tutorial note

ACCOUNTING RATIOS FOR LIQUIDITY, USE OF RESOURCES AND FINANCIAL POSITION

■ Study the ratios table and financial statements on the next two pages. They show the ways in which the liquidity, use of resources, and financial position of a company are assessed.

■ Then read the sections which follow.

■ Note that the accounting ratios from the financial statements of Wyvern Trading Company Limited are calculated and discussed in the Case Study on pages 217-222.

LIQUIDITY

Liquidity ratios measure the financial stability of a company, ie the ability of a company to pay its way on a short-term basis. Here we focus our attention on the current assets and current liabilities sections of the balance sheet.

The key liquidity ratios are shown on the next page; these are linked to the balance sheet of Wyvern Trading Company Limited. The ratios are calculated and discussed in the Case Study on pages 217-222.

continued on page 209

LIQUIDITY

Working capital ratio =
(or current ratio)

$$\frac{\text{Current assets}}{\text{Current liabilities}}$$

Liquid capital ratio =
(or quick ratio/acid test)

$$\frac{\text{Current assets} - \text{inventories}}{\text{Current liabilities}}$$

USE OF RESOURCES

Inventory turnover (days) =

$$\frac{\text{Inventories}}{\text{Cost of sales}} \times 365 \text{ days}$$

Receivables collection period (days) =

$$\frac{\text{Trade receivables}}{\text{Revenue}} \times 365 \text{ days}$$

Payables payment period (days) =

$$\frac{\text{Trade payables}}{\text{Purchases}} \times 365 \text{ days}$$

Asset turnover ratio =

$$\frac{\text{Revenue}}{\text{Net assets*}}$$

* non-current assets + current assets − current liabilities

FINANCIAL POSITION

Interest cover =

$$\frac{\text{Profit from operations}}{\text{Finance costs}}$$

Gearing =

$$\frac{\text{Debt (debentures/long-term loans, including preference shares)}}{\text{Capital employed*}} \times \frac{100}{1}$$

* ordinary share capital + reserves + preference share capital +debentures/ long-term (non-current) loans

alternative calculation:

$$\frac{\text{Debt}}{\text{Equity}} \times \frac{100}{1}$$

Wyvern Trading Company Limited
BALANCE SHEET
as at 31 December 2006

Non-current Assets	Cost	Dep'n to date	Net
	£000s	£000s	£000s
Property	1,100	250	850
Plant	300	120	180
Equipment	350	100	250
	1,750	470	1,280

Current Assets		
Inventories	240	
Trade receivables	150	
Cash and cash equivalents	135	
	525	

Current Liabilities		
Trade payables	(205)	
Tax liabilities	(50)	
	(255)	
Net Current Assets		270
		1,550
Non-current Liabilities		
10% Debentures		(100)
NET ASSETS		1,450

EQUITY	
Authorised and Issued Share Capital	
1,250,000 ordinary shares of £1 each, fully paid	1,250
Revenue Reserve	
Retained earnings	200
TOTAL EQUITY	1,450

INCOME STATEMENT (extract)

Cost of sales	960
Revenue	1,430
Purchases	1,000

Note: Items used in ratios are shown in bold type with a grey background.

working capital

Working capital = Current assets – Current liabilities

Working capital (often called *net current assets*) is needed by all companies in order to finance day-to-day trading activities. Sufficient working capital enables a company to hold adequate inventories, allow a measure of credit to its customers (receivables), and to pay its suppliers (payables) on the due date.

working capital ratio (or current ratio)

Working capital ratio = Current assets : Current liabilities

Working capital ratio uses figures from the balance sheet and measures the relationship between current assets and current liabilities. Although there is no ideal working capital ratio, an acceptable ratio is about 2:1, ie £2 of current assets to every £1 of current liabilities. However, a company in the retail trade may be able to work with a lower ratio, eg 1.5:1 or even less, because it deals mainly in cash and so does not have a large figure for receivables. A working capital ratio can be too high: if it is above 3:1 an investigation of the make-up of current assets and current liabilities is needed: eg the company may have too many inventories, too many receivables, or too much cash, or even too few payables.

Note that the current ratio can also be expressed as a percentage. For example, a current ratio of 2:1 is the same as 200 per cent.

liquid capital ratio (or quick ratio, or acid test)

Liquid capital ratio = $\dfrac{Current\ assets\ -\ inventories}{Current\ liabilities}$

The liquid capital ratio uses the current assets and current liabilities from the balance sheet, but inventories are omitted. This is because inventories are the least liquid current asset: they have to be sold, turned into receivables, and then the cash has to be collected. Thus the liquid ratio provides a direct comparison between receivables/cash and short-term liabilities. The balance between liquid assets, that is receivables and cash, and current liabilities should, ideally, be about 1:1, ie £1 of liquid assets to each £1 of current liabilities. At this ratio a company is expected to be able to pay its current liabilities from its liquid assets; a figure below 1:1, eg 0.75:1, indicates that the company would have difficulty in meeting the demands of payables. However, as with the working capital ratio, some companies are able to operate with a lower liquid ratio than others.

The liquid capital ratio can also be expressed as a percentage, eg 1:1 is the same as 100%.

USE OF RESOURCES

Use of resources measures how efficiently the management controls the current aspects of the company – principally inventories, trade receivables and trade payables. Like all accounting ratios, comparison needs to be made either with figures for the previous year, or with a similar company.

inventory turnover

$$\frac{Inventories}{Cost\ of\ sales} \quad x \quad 365\ days$$

Inventory turnover is the number of days' inventories held on average. This figure will depend on the type of goods sold by the company. For example, a market trader selling fresh flowers, who finishes each day when sold out, will have an inventory turnover of one day. By contrast, a jewellery shop – because it may hold large quantities of jewellery – will have a much slower inventory turnover, perhaps sixty or ninety days, or longer. Nevertheless, it is important for a company to keep its inventory days as short as possible, subject to being able to meet the needs of most of its customers. A company which is improving in efficiency will generally have a quicker inventory turnover comparing one year with the previous one, or with the inventory turnover of similar companies.

Inventory turnover can also be expressed as number of times per year:

$$Inventory\ turnover\ (times\ per\ year) \quad = \quad \frac{Cost\ of\ sales}{Inventories}$$

An inventory turnover of, say, twelve times a year means that about thirty days' inventories are held. Note that inventory turnover can only be calculated where a company buys and sells goods; it cannot be used for a company that provides a service.

receivables' collection period

$$\frac{Trade\ receivables}{Revenue} \quad x \quad 365\ days$$

This calculation shows how many days, on average, receivables take to pay for goods sold to them by the company. The collection time can be compared with that for the previous year, or with that of a similar company. In the UK, most trade receivables should make payment within about 30 days; however, with international trade, it will take longer for the proceeds to be received. A comparison from year-to-year of the collection period is a measure of the company's efficiency at collecting the money that is due to it and we are looking for some reduction in receivables' days over time. Ideally receivables' days should be shorter than payables' days (see the next page), thus indicating that money is being received from receivables before it is paid out to payables.

payables' payment period

$$\frac{Trade\ payables}{Purchases} \quad x \quad 365\ days$$

This calculation is the opposite aspect to that of receivables: here we are measuring the speed it takes to make payment to trade payables. While payables can be a useful temporary source of finance, delaying payment too long may cause problems. This ratio is most appropriate for companies that buy and sell goods; it cannot be used for a company that provides a service; it is also difficult to interpret when a company buys in some goods and, at the same time, provides a service, eg an hotel. Generally, though, we would expect to see the payables' days period longer than the receivables' days, ie money is being received from receivables before it is paid out to payables. We would also be looking for a similar figure for payables' days from one year to the next: this would indicate a stable company.

Note that there is invariably an inconsistency in calculating both receivables' collection and payables' payment periods: the figures for receivables and payables on the balance sheet include VAT, while revenue and purchases from the income statement exclude VAT. Strictly, therefore, we are not comparing like with like; however, the comparison should be made with reference to the previous year, or a similar company, calculated on the same basis from year-to-year.

asset turnover ratio

$$\frac{Revenue}{Net\ assets^*}$$

* non-current assets + current assets – current liabilities

This ratio measures the efficiency of the use of net assets in generating revenue. An increasing ratio from one year to the next indicates greater efficiency. A fall in the ratio may be caused either by a decrease in revenue, or an increase in net assets – perhaps caused by the purchase or revaluation of non-current assets, or increased inventories, or increased trade receivables as a result of poor credit control.

Different types of businesses will have very different asset turnover ratios. For example a supermarket, with high revenue and relatively few assets, will have a very high figure; by contrast, an engineering company, with lower revenue and a substantial investment in non-current and current assets, will have a much lower figure.

Note that for the purpose of ratio analysis in *Drafting Financial Statements*, net assets is defined as:

non-current assets + current assets – current liabilities

FINANCIAL POSITION

Financial position measures the strength and long-term financing of the company. Two ratios are calculated – interest cover and gearing. Interest cover considers the ability of the company to meet (or cover) its finance costs from its profit from operations; gearing focuses on the balance in the long-term funding of the company between monies from loan providers and monies from ordinary shareholders.

Both ratios look at aspects of loan finance and it is important to remember that both interest and loan repayments must be made on time; if they are not the loan provider may well be able to seek payment by forcing the company to sell assets and, in the worst case, may well be able to force the company into liquidation.

interest cover

$$\frac{\text{Profit from operations}}{\text{Finance costs}}$$

The interest cover ratio, linked closely to gearing, considers the safety margin (or cover) of profit over the finance costs of a company. For example, if the profit from operations was £10,000, and finance costs were £5,000, this would give interest cover of two times, which is a low figure. If the finance costs were £1,000, this would give interest cover of ten times which is a higher and much more acceptable figure. Thus, the conclusion to draw is that the higher the interest cover, the better (although there is an argument for having some debt).

gearing

$$\frac{\text{Debt (debentures/long-term loans, including preference shares)}}{\text{Capital employed*}} \quad x \quad \frac{100}{1}$$

* ordinary share capital + reserves + preference share capital + debentures/long-term (non-current) loans

Whilst the liquidity ratios seen earlier focus on whether the company can pay its way in the short-term, gearing is concerned with long-term financial stability. Here we measure how much of the company is financed by debt against capital employed (debt + equity), defined above. The higher the gearing percentage, the less secure will be the financing of the company and, therefore, the future of the company. This is because debt is costly in terms of finance costs (particularly if interest rates are variable). It is difficult to set a standard for an acceptable gearing ratio: in general terms, most investors (or lenders) would not wish to see a gearing percentage of greater than 50%.

Gearing can also be expressed as a ratio, ie debt:capital employed. Thus a gearing percentage of 50% is a ratio of 0.5:1.

An alternative calculation for gearing is to measure debt in relation to the equity of the company:

$$\frac{Debt}{Equity} \quad x \quad \frac{100}{1}$$

Usually in *Drafting Financial Statements*, either calculation is acceptable; both methods use similar components:

either $\dfrac{Debt}{Capital\ employed}$ or $\dfrac{Debt}{Equity}$

The first calculation will always give a lower gearing percentage than the second when using the same figures. For example:

$$\frac{£50,000\ (debt)}{£100,000\ (equity) + £50,000\ (debt)} \quad = \ 33\%$$

$$\frac{£50,000\ (debt)}{£100,000\ (equity)} \quad = \ 50\%$$

When making comparisons from one year to the next, or between different companies, it is important to be consistent in the way in which gearing is calculated in order for appropriate conclusions to be drawn.

USE OF THE PRIMARY RATIO

Return on capital employed (see page 204) is perhaps the most effective ratio used in the interpretation of accounts. This is because it expresses profit in relation to the capital employed and so is a direct measure of the efficiency of a company in using the capital available to it in order to generate profits.

Return on capital employed is often referred to as the primary ratio, since it can be broken down into the two secondary factors of:

- net profit percentage (see page 204)
- asset turnover ratio (see page 211)

The relationship between the three can be expressed in the form of a 'pyramid of ratios' (where the ratio at the top of the pyramid is formed from and relates arithmetically to the other two ratios):

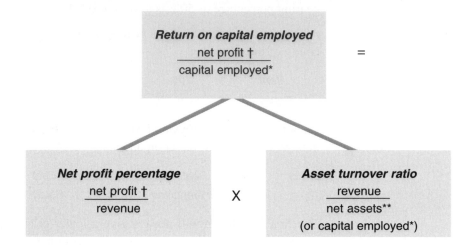

† net profit or, preferably, profit from operations (ie profit before finance costs)

* capital employed, ie share capital + reserves + long-term liabilities

** net assets, ie non-current assets + current assets − current liabilities

examples

- **Company Aye** has revenue of £500,000, a net profit of £50,000, and net assets/capital employed of £250,000. The pyramid of ratios is:

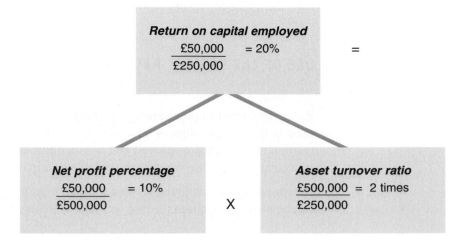

Thus it can be seen that, when the net profit percentage is multiplied by the asset turnover ratio, the answer is return on capital employed (the primary ratio):

10% x 2 times = 20% (primary ratio)

- **Company Bee** has revenue of £1,000,000, a net profit of £20,000, and net assets/capital employed of £100,000. The pyramid of ratios is:

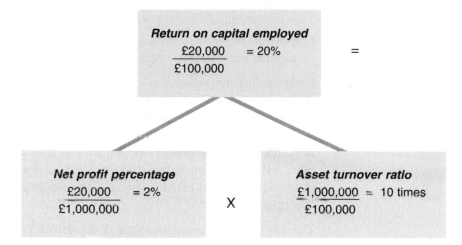

Here the primary ratio is made up of:

2% x 10 times = 20% (primary ratio)

By using the pyramid of ratios, we can get a better idea of how ratios relate one to another rather than considering them in isolation. Thus the primary ratio shows how the same return on capital employed can be achieved in different ways, depending on the type of business. It demonstrates the different ways of running a business – eg the supermarket (with low profit margins and high revenue) and the specialist shop (with higher profit margins, but lower revenue) – and how each achieves its return on capital employed.

INTERPRETATION OF ACCOUNTS

Interpretation of accounts is much more than a mechanical process of calculating a number of ratios. It involves the analysis of the relationships between the elements within financial statements and the presentation of the information gathered in a meaningful way to interested parties.

It is important that a logical approach is adopted to the process of interpreting accounts. The needs of the user – the person who has requested the information – must be the starting point. These needs are linked to the main themes of interpretation: profitability, liquidity, use of resources, and financial position. In recent examinations for *Drafting Financial Statements* the users have included:

- potential investors – mainly concerned about the profitability of an investment in a company
- potential lenders – concerned with a borrower's liquidity, use of resources, and financial position
- potential buyers – investigating financial statements to assess a proposed supplier's profitability, liquidity, and financial position

From the financial statements – usually income statement and balance sheet of a company – it is necessary to calculate a number of appropriate accounting ratios. In examinations, often you will be given two years' financial statements and will be told which ratios to calculate (but the formulae will not be given). Sometimes you may be asked to compare the ratios calculated with industry average figures (which will be given). In addition, you may be asked to indicate – but not required to calculate – other appropriate ratios.

The way in which the interpretation of accounts is presented to the user must be appropriate to the needs of the user. Thus a letter is most appropriate for a potential investor, a report for a potential lender, and a memorandum for a potential buyer (where both the buyer and the writer of the report work for the same company). Whichever form of presentation is used, take care over the layout and make sure that there are plenty of sub-sections to guide the user.

The form of the presentation to the user will usually include the following:

- calculation of ratios from financial statements (an examination question will normally state which ratios are to be calculated and for how many years)
- an explanation of the meaning of each ratio (try to use language that can be understood by users with a non-financial background)
- comment on the financial position of the company as shown by the ratios (making comparisons against guideline standards where applicable – eg 2:1 for the working capital ratio – and against industry averages, if they are given in the question); make use of the primary ratio (see pages 213-215), if appropriate.
- a statement of how the financial position of the company has changed over the period covered by the financial statements – usually two years (look for trends in the ratios and comment on what these mean and whether they show an improving or a worsening financial position; include comparisons against industry averages, if they are given in the question)

- a conclusion which links back to the needs of the user (to invest in, or to lend to, the company, or to use as a supplier) and summarises against the themes of interpretation relevant to the user: profitability, liquidity, use of resources, and financial position

Two Case Studies which now follow put into practice the analytical approach explained earlier in this chapter:

1   **Wyvern Trading Company Limited**

In the first we look at limited company financial statements from the point of view of a potential investor (for clarity, one year's statements are given although, in practice, more than one year would be used to establish a trend). The comments given indicate what should be looked for when analysing and interpreting a set of financial statements.

2   **Surgdressings Limited**

In the second we consider financial statements from the point of view of a potential buyer of products from the company. The interpretation seeks to assess the risk of switching to the supplier, and to make comparisons with industry average figures.

Case Study

WYVERN TRADING COMPANY LIMITED: ACCOUNTING RATIOS

situation

The following are the financial statements of Wyvern Trading Company Limited. The business trades in office supplies and sells to the public through its three retail shops in the Wyvern area; it also delivers direct to businesses in the area from its modern warehouse on a local business park.

The financial statements and accounting ratios are to be considered from the viewpoint of a potential investor.

solution

We will now analyse the accounts from the point of view of a potential investor. All figures shown are in £000s. The analysis starts on page 220.

Wyvern Trading Company Limited
INCOME STATEMENT
for the year ended 31 December 2006

	£000s	£000s
Revenue		1,430
Opening inventories	200	
Purchases	1,000	
	1,200	
Less Closing inventories	240	
Cost of sales		(960)
Gross profit		470
Overheads:		
Distribution costs	(150)	
Administrative expenses	(140)	
		(290)
Profit from operations		180
Finance costs		(10)
Profit before tax		170
Tax		(50)
Profit for the year		120

Statement of changes in equity (extract)

Retained earnings

Balance at 1 January 2006	180
Profit for the year	120
	300
Dividends paid	(100)
Balance at 31 December 2006	200

Wyvern Trading Company Limited
BALANCE SHEET as at 31 December 2006

Non-current Assets	Cost	Dep'n to date	Net
	£000s	£000s	£000s
Property	1,100	250	850
Plant	300	120	180
Equipment	350	100	250
	1,750	470	1,280

Current Assets

Inventories	240	
Trade receivables	150	
Cash and cash equivalents	135	
	525	

Current Liabilities

Trade payables	(205)	
Tax liabilities	(50)	
	(255)	

Net Current Assets		270
		1,550

Non-current Liabilities

10% debentures		(100)
NET ASSETS		1,450

EQUITY

Authorised and Issued Share Capital

1,250,000 ordinary shares of £1 each, fully paid	1,250

Revenue Reserve

Retained earnings	200
TOTAL EQUITY	1,450

PROFITABILITY

Gross profit/revenue percentage

$$\frac{£470}{£1,430} \quad \times \quad \frac{100}{1} \qquad = \ 32.87\%$$

Distribution costs to revenue

$$\frac{£150}{£1,430} \quad \times \quad \frac{100}{1} \qquad = \ 10.49\%$$

Profit from operations/revenue percentage

$$\frac{£180}{£1,430} \quad \times \quad \frac{100}{1} \qquad = \ 12.59\%$$

Net profit/revenue percentage

$$\frac{£170}{£1,430} \quad \times \quad \frac{100}{1} \qquad = \ 11.89\%$$

Return on capital employed

$$\frac{£180}{£1,250 + £200 + £100} \quad \times \quad \frac{100}{1} \qquad = \ 11.61\%$$

Return on equity

$$\frac{£120}{£1,250 + £200} \quad \times \quad \frac{100}{1} \qquad = \ 8.28\%$$

Earnings per share

$$\frac{£120}{1,250} \qquad\qquad\qquad = \ 9.6\text{p per ordinary share}$$

The gross and net profit percentages seem to be acceptable figures for the type of business, although comparisons should be made with those of the previous accounting period. A company should always aim at least to hold its percentages and, ideally, to make a small improvement. A significant fall in the percentages may indicate a poor buying policy, poor pricing (perhaps caused by competition), and the causes should be investigated.

Distribution costs seem to be quite a high percentage of revenue. Comparisons need to be made with previous years to see if these are increasing or decreasing. It may be possible for increases in revenue not to have a significant effect on this cost.

The small difference between net profit percentage and profit from operations percentage indicates that finance costs are relatively low.

Return on capital employed is satisfactory, but could be better. At 11.61% it is less than two percentage points above the ten per cent cost of the debentures (ignoring the tax advantages of issuing debentures). Return on equity is 8.28%, but a potential shareholder needs to compare this with the returns available elsewhere.

The figure for earnings per share indicates that the company is not highly profitable for its shareholders; potential shareholders will be looking for increases in this figure.

LIQUIDITY

Working capital (or current) ratio

$$\frac{£525}{£255} \qquad = 2.06:1$$

Liquid capital ratio (or quick ratio/acid test)

$$\frac{(£525 - £240)}{£255} \qquad = 1.12:1$$

The working capital and liquid capital ratios are excellent: they are slightly higher than the expected 'norms' of 2:1 and 1:1 respectively (although many companies operate successfully with lower ratios); however, they are not too high which would be an indication of inefficient use of assets.

These two ratios indicate that the company is very solvent, with no short-term liquidity problems.

USE OF RESOURCES

Inventory turnover

$$\frac{£240 \times 365}{£960} \qquad = \text{91 days (or 4 times per year)}$$

Receivables' collection period

$$\frac{£150 \times 365}{£1,430} \qquad = \text{38 days}$$

Payables' payment period

$$\frac{£205 \times 365}{£1,000} \qquad = \text{75 days}$$

Asset turnover ratio

$$\frac{£1,430}{£1,550*} \qquad = 0.92:1$$

* non-current assets + current assets − current liabilities

This group of ratios shows the main weakness of the company: not enough business is passing through for the size of the company.

Inventory turnover is very low for an office supplies business: the inventories are turning over only every 91 days − surely it should be faster than this?

Receivables' collection period is acceptable on the face of it − 30 days would be better − but quite a volume of the revenue will be made through the retail outlets in cash. This amount should, if known, be deducted from the revenue before calculating the receivables' collection period: thus the collection period is, in reality, longer than that calculated.

Payables' payment period is very slow for this type of business – long delays could cause problems with suppliers in the future.

The asset turnover ratio says it all: this type of business should be able to obtain a much better figure:

- either, revenue needs to be increased using the same net assets
- or, revenue needs to be maintained, but net assets reduced

FINANCIAL POSITION

Interest cover

$$\frac{£180}{£10} \qquad = \quad 18 \text{ times}$$

Gearing

$$\frac{£100}{£1,250 + £200 + £100} \quad \times \frac{100}{1} \quad = \quad 6.5\% \text{ or } 0.065:1$$

The interest cover figure of 18 is very high and shows that the company has no problems in paying interest.

The gearing percentage is very low: anything up to 50% (0.5:1) could be seen. A figure as low as 6.5% indicates that the company could borrow more money if it wished to finance, say, expansion plans (there are plenty of non-current assets for a lender – such as a bank – to take as security for a loan). At the present level of gearing there is a very low risk to potential investors.

Note that the alternative calculation for gearing is:

$$\frac{£100}{£1,250 + £200} \quad \times \frac{100}{1} \quad = \quad 6.9\% \text{ or } 0.069:1$$

CONCLUSION

This appears to be a profitable company, although there may be some scope for cutting down somewhat on the distribution costs (administrative expenses could be looked at too). The company offers a reasonable return on capital, although things could be improved.

The company is solvent and has good working capital and liquid capital ratios. Interest cover is high and gearing is very low – a good sign during times of variable interest rates.

The main area of weakness is in asset utilisation. It appears that the company could do much to reduce the days for inventory turnover and the receivables' collection period; at the same time payables could be paid faster. Asset turnover is very low for this type of business and it does seem that there is much scope for expansion within the structure of the existing company. As the benefits of expansion flow through to the financial statements, the earnings per share figure should show an improvement from its present modest amount. However, a potential investor will need to consider if the directors have the ability to focus on the weaknesses shown by the ratio analysis and to take steps to improve the company.

Case Study

ASSESSING A SUPPLIER – SURGDRESSINGS LIMITED: ACCOUNTING RATIOS

situation

You work for the Wyvern Private Hospital plc. The company has been approached by a supplier of surgical dressings, Surgdressings Limited, which is offering its products at advantageous prices.

The Surgical Director of Wyvern Private Hospital is satisfied with the quality and suitability of the products offered and the Finance Director, your boss, has obtained the latest financial statements from the company which are set out on the next page.

You have been asked to prepare a report for the Finance Director recommending whether or not to use Surgdressings Limited as a supplier of surgical dressings to the Hospital. You are to use the information contained in the financial statements of Surgdressings Limited and the Industry averages supplied. Included in your report should be:

- comments on the company's

  – profitability

  – liquidity

  – financial position

- consideration of how the company has changed over the two years

- comparison with the industry as a whole

The report should include calculation of the following ratios for the two years:

  – return on capital employed

  – net profit percentage

  – quick ratio/acid test

  – gearing

The relevant industry average ratios are as follows:

	2005	2004
Return on capital employed	11.3%	11.1%
Net profit percentage	16.4%	16.2%
Quick ratio/acid test	1.0:1	0.9:1
Gearing (debt/capital employed)	33%	35%

SURGDRESSINGS LIMITED
Summary income statements for the year ended 31 December

	2005	2004
	£000s	£000s
Revenue	4,600	4,300
Cost of sales	(2,245)	(2,135)
Gross profit	2,355	2,165
Overheads	(1,582)	(1,491)
Profit from operations	773	674

Summary balance sheets as at 31 December

	2005		2004	
	£000s	£000s	£000s	£000s
Non-current Assets		5,534		6,347
Current Assets				
Inventories	566		544	
Trade receivables	655		597	
Cash and cash equivalents	228		104	
	1,449		1,245	
Current Liabilities				
Trade payables	(572)		(504)	
Tax liabilities	(242)		(288)	
	(814)		(792)	
Net Current Assets		635		453
Long-term loan		(1,824)		(3,210)
NET ASSETS		4,345		3,590
EQUITY				
Share capital (ordinary shares)		2,300		2,000
Share premium		670		450
Retained earnings		1,375		1,140
TOTAL EQUITY		4,345		3,590

solution

REPORT

To: Finance Director, Wyvern Private Hospital plc

From: A Student

Date: today's date

Re: Analysis of Surgdressings Limited's financial statements 2004/2005

Introduction

The purpose of this report is to analyse the financial statements of Surgdressings Limited for 2004 and 2005 to determine whether the Hospital should use the company as a supplier of surgical dressings.

Calculation of ratios

The following ratios have been calculated:

	2005 company	2005 industry average	2004 company	2004 industry average
Return on capital employed	$\frac{773}{6,169}$ =12.5%	11.3%	$\frac{674}{6,800}$ = 9.9%	11.1%
Net profit percentage	$\frac{773}{4,600}$ =16.8%	16.4%	$\frac{674}{4,300}$ = 15.7%	16.2%
Quick ratio/acid test	$\frac{883}{814}$ = 1.1:1	1.0:1	$\frac{701}{792}$ = 0.9:1	0.9:1
Gearing	$\frac{1,824}{6,169}$ = 30%	33%	$\frac{3,210}{6,800}$ = 47%	35%

Comment and analysis

- In terms of profitability, the company has improved from 2004 to 2005.

- Return on capital employed has increased from 9.9% to 12.5% – this means that the company is generating more profit in 2005 from the available capital employed than it did in 2004. The company has gone from being below the industry average in 2004 to being better than the average in 2005.

- Net profit percentage has also improved, increasing from 15.7% in 2004 to 16.8% in 2005. This means that the company is generating more profit from revenue in 2005 than it did in the previous year. In 2004 the company was below the industry average but in 2005 it is better than the average. As it is now performing better than the average, this suggests that it may continue to be successful in the future.

- The liquidity of the company has improved during the year.

- The quick ratio (or acid test) has gone up from 0.9:1 to 1.1:1. This indicates that the liquid assets, ie receivables and cash, are greater than current liabilities in 2005. The company has gone from being the same as the industry average in 2004 to better than average in 2005. Thus, in 2005, Surgdressings Limited is more liquid than the average business in the industry.

- The financial position of the company has improved considerably during the year.

- In 2004 the gearing ratio was a high 47%. In 2005 the percentage of debt finance to capital employed declined to 30%. A high gearing ratio is often seen as a risk to a company's long-term survival: in times of economic downturn, when profits fall, a high-geared company will have increasing difficulty in meeting the finance costs of debt – in extreme cases, a company could be forced into liquidation. In 2004, the gearing ratio of Surgdressings Limited was much higher than the industry average, making it relatively more risky than the average of companies in the industry. The much improved ratio in 2005 is now below the industry average, making it less risky than the average of other companies in the industry.

CONCLUSION

- Based solely on the information provided in the financial statements of Surgdressings Limited and the ratios calculated, it is recommended that the company is used by Wyvern Private Hospital as a supplier of surgical dressings.

- The company has increasing profitability, liquidity and financial position in 2005 when compared with 2004. It also compares favourably with other companies in the same industry and appears to present a lower risk than the average of the sector.

LIMITATIONS IN THE INTERPRETATION OF ACCOUNTS

Although accounting ratios can usefully highlight strengths and weaknesses, they should always be considered as a part of the overall assessment of a company, rather than as a whole. We have already seen the need to place ratios in context and relate them to a reference point or standard. The limitations of ratio analysis should always be borne in mind.

retrospective nature of accounting ratios

Accounting ratios are usually retrospective, based on previous performance and conditions prevailing in the past. They may not necessarily be valid for making forward projections: for example, a large customer may become insolvent, so threatening the company with a bad debt, and also reducing revenue in the future.

differences in accounting policies

When the financial statements of a company are compared, either with previous years' figures, or with figures from a similar company, there is a danger that the comparative statements are not drawn up on the same basis as those currently being worked on. Different accounting policies, in respect of depreciation and inventory valuation for instance, may well result in distortion and invalid comparisons.

inflation

Inflation may prove a problem, as most financial statements are prepared on an historic cost basis, that is, assets and liabilities are recorded at their original cost. As a result, comparison of figures from one year to the next may be difficult. In countries where inflation is running at high levels any form of comparison becomes practically meaningless.

reliance on standards

We have already mentioned guideline standards for some accounting ratios, for instance 2:1 for the working capital ratio. There is a danger of relying too heavily on such suggested standards, and ignoring other factors in the balance sheet. An example of this would be to criticise a company for having a low current ratio when the company sells the majority of its goods for cash and consequently has a very low receivables figure: this would in fact be the case with many well-known and successful retail companies.

other considerations

Economic: The general economic climate and the effect this may have on the nature of the business, eg in an economic downturn retailers are usually the first to suffer, whereas manufacturers feel the effects later.

State of the business: The chairman's report of the company should be read in conjunction with the financial statements (including the cash flow statement) to ascertain an overall view of the state of the company. Of great importance are the products of the company and their stage in the product life cycle, eg is a car manufacturer relying on old models, or is there an up-to-date product range which appeals to buyers?

Comparing like with like: Before making comparisons between 'similar' companies, we need to ensure that we are comparing 'like with like'. Differences, such as the acquisition of assets – renting premises compared with ownership, leasing vehicles compared with ownership – will affect the profitability of the company and the structure of the balance sheet; likewise, the long-term financing of a company – the balance between debt finance and equity finance – will also have an effect.

Chapter Summary

- Accounting ratios are numerical values (percentages, time periods, ratios) extracted from the financial statements. They can be used to measure:
  - profitability
  - liquidity
  - use of resources
  - financial position

- Comparisons need to be made with previous financial statements, or those of similar companies.

- There are a number of limitations to be borne in mind when drawing conclusions from accounting ratios:
  - retrospective nature, based on past performance
  - differences in accounting policies
  - effects of inflation when comparing year-to-year
  - reliance on standards
  - economic and other factors

Key Terms

profitability	measures the relationship between profit and revenue, assets, equity and capital employed; ratios include:
	• gross profit percentage
	• expenses/revenue percentage
	• profit from operations percentage
	• net profit percentage
	• return on capital employed
	• return on equity
	• earnings per share
liquidity	measures the financial stability of a company, ie the ability of a company to pay its way on a short-term basis; ratios include:
	• working capital (current) ratio
	• liquid capital ratio (or quick ratio/acid test)
use of resources	measures how efficiently the management controls the current aspects of the company – principally inventories, trade receivables and trade payables; ratios include:
	• inventory turnover
	• receivables' collection period
	• payables' payment period
	• asset turnover ratio
financial position	measures the strength and long-term financing of the company; ratios include:
	• interest cover
	• gearing

Student Activities

Osborne Books is grateful to the AAT for their kind permission to use past assessment material, which has been amended to incorporate the requirements of international accounting standards.

7.1   The net profit/revenue percentage measures which one of the following?
    (a)   liquidity
    (b)   use of resources
    (c)   financial position
    (d)   profitability

7.2   The working capital ratio measures which one of the following?
    (a)   profitability
    (b)   financial position
    (c)   liquidity
    (d)   use of resources

7.3   Inventory turnover in an accounting period is best described by which one of the following definitions?
    (a)   value of inventories at the start of the period
    (b)   value of inventories at the end of the period
    (c)   number of times that the average level of inventory has been sold during the period
    (d)   average amount of time that inventory has been held throughout the period

7.4   Which one of the following headings best describes and measures gearing?
    (a)   financial position
    (b)   liquidity
    (c)   profitability
    (d)   use of resources

7.5   Below is the balance sheet of Matlock plc for the year ended 30 September 20-3

	£000	£000
NON-CURRENT ASSETS at net book value		500
CURRENT ASSETS		
Inventories	150	
Trade receivables	95	
Cash and cash equivalents	5	
	250	

CURRENT LIABILITIES

Trade payables	(175)
Bank overdraft	(25)
	(200)

NET CURRENT ASSETS	50
	550

NON-CURRENT LIABILITIES

Bank loan	(100)
	450

EQUITY

Called up ordinary share capital	300
Share premium account	50
Retained earnings	100
TOTAL EQUITY	450

1   What is the acid test ratio for Matlock plc?
    (a)   1.25:1
    (b)   0.5:1
    (c)   1:1
    (d)   5:1

2   The gearing ratio for Matlock plc should be calculated as follows:
    (a)   300/450 x 100
    (b)   350/450 x 100
    (c)   125/550 x 100
    (d)   100/550 x 100

3   If Matlock plc's revenue for the year (all on credit) was £405,000, what is the asset turnover ratio?
    (a)   0.9:1
    (b)   0.74:1
    (c)   0.81:1
    (d)   1.11:1

4   What is the receivables' collection period in days if the revenue (all on credit) of the business was £405,000 as in 3 above? (You will need to round up to whole days)
    (a)   86 days
    (b)   68 days
    (c)   158 days
    (d)   61 days

5   Which of the following is the correct calculation for interest cover?
    (a)   debt/finance costs
    (b)   finance costs/debt
    (c)   profit from operations/finance costs
    (d)   finance costs/profit from operations

7.6 Study the financial statements of the two public limited companies listed below and then calculate the accounting ratios in the questions which follow.

INCOME STATEMENTS	Hanadi plc		Abeer plc	
	£000	£000	£000	£000
Revenue		350		300
Cost of sales:				
Opening inventories	40		20	
Purchases	170		150	
	210		170	
Less Closing inventories	110	(100)	70	(100)
GROSS PROFIT		250		200
Expenses		(100)		(50)
PROFIT FROM OPERATIONS		150		150
Tax		(35)		(30)
PROFIT FOR THE YEAR		115		120

BALANCE SHEETS	Hanadi plc		Abeer plc	
	£000	£000	£000	£000
NON-CURRENT ASSETS AT NBV		465		325
CURRENT ASSETS				
Inventories	110		70	
Trade receivables	95		60	
Cash and cash equivalents	15		30	
	220		160	
CURRENT LIABILITIES				
Trade payables	(180)		(105)	
Tax liabilities	(35)		(30)	
	(215)		(135)	
NET CURRENT ASSETS		5		25
		470		350
EQUITY				
Ordinary shares £1 each		300		200
Share premium account		50		50
Retained earnings		120		100
TOTAL EQUITY		470		350

REQUIRED

Task 1

Calculate the following ratios for both businesses:

(a)   Gross profit as a percentage of revenue
(b)   Net profit as a percentage of revenue
(c)   Net profit as a percentage return on capital employed (ROCE)
(d)   Current ratio
(e)   Acid test ratio

Task 2

Comment upon what the ratios reveal, and make recommendations as to which business offers the better return from a profitability, efficiency and investment point of view.

7.7   Ratio analysis is a useful way for a business to compare one year's results with another and to highlight trends. It can also be a useful tool when comparing the results of a business with the results of a competitor. However the limitations of ratio analysis should always be kept in mind, when making any realistic judgement concerning the overall performance of any business.

REQUIRED

Discuss the limitations of ratio analysis when assessing and comparing company performance.

7.8   Jake Matease plans to invest in Fauve Limited. This is a chain of retail outlets. He is going to meet the Managing Director of Fauve Limited to discuss the profitability of the company. To prepare for the meeting he has asked you to comment on the change in profitability and the return on capital of the company. He has given you the profit and loss accounts of Fauve Limited and the summarised balance sheets for the last two years. These are set out below:

Fauve Limited
Summary income statements for the year ended 30 September

	20-1	20-0
	£000	£000
Revenue	4,315	2,973
Cost of sales	(1,510)	(1,189)
Gross profit	2,805	1,784
Distribution costs	(983)	(780)
Administrative expenses	(571)	(380)
Profit from operations	1,251	624
Finance costs	(45)	(27)
Profit before tax	1,206	597
Tax	(338)	(167)
Profit for the year	868	430

Note: A dividend of £300,000 was paid in 20-0, and of £340,000 in 20-1.

Fauve Limited
Balance sheets as at 30 September

	20-1		20-0	
	£000	£000	£000	£000
Non-current assets		6,663		4,761
Current assets	3,503		2,031	
Current liabilities	(1,736)		(1,387)	
Net current assets		1,767		644
		8,430		5,405
Equity:				
ordinary shares of £1 each		4,000		1,703
retained earnings		3,930		3,402
Long-term loan		500		300
		8,430		5,405

REQUIRED

Prepare a report for Jake Matease that includes the following:

(a)   a calculation of the following ratios of Fauve Limited for each of the two years:
* return on capital employed
* net profit percentage
* gross profit percentage
* asset turnover

(b)   an explanation of the meaning of each ratio and a comment on the performance of Fauve Limited as shown by each of the ratios

(c)   a conclusion on how the overall performance has changed over the two years

7.9   The directors of Dowango Ltd have asked to have a meeting with you. They are intending to ask the bank for a further long-term loan to enable them to purchase a company which has retail outlets. The directors have identified two possible companies to take over and they intend to purchase the whole of the share capital of one of the two targeted companies.

The directors have obtained the latest financial statements of the two companies, in summary form and these are set out below:

Summary income statements

	Company A	Company B
	£000	£000
Revenue	800	2,100
Cost of sales	(440)	(1,050)
Gross profit	360	1,050
Expenses	(160)	(630)
Profit from operations	200	420

Summary balance sheets

	Company A	Company B
	£000	£000
Non-current assets	620	1,640
Net current assets	380	1,160
Long-term loan	(400)	(1,100)
	600	1,700
Equity	600	1,700

REQUIRED

Advise the directors as to which of the two companies targeted for takeover is the more profitable and which one provides the higher return on capital. Your answer should include calculation of the following ratios:

- return on capital employed
- net profit margin
- asset turnover

You should also calculate and comment on at least *one* further ratio of your choice, for which you have sufficient information, which would be relevant to determining which of the companies is more profitable or provides the greater return on capital.

7.10 Rowan Healthcare plc is a private hospital group which has just lost its supplier of bandages. The company that has been supplying it for the last five years has gone into liquidation. The directors of Rowan Healthcare are concerned to select a new supplier which can be relied upon to supply the group with its needs for the foreseeable future. You have been asked by the finance director to analyse the financial statements of a potential supplier of bandages. You have obtained the latest financial statements of the company, in summary form, which are set out below.

Patch Limited
Summary income statements for the year ended 30 September

	20-8	20-7
	£000	£000
Revenue	2,300	2,100
Cost of sales	(1,035)	(945)
Gross profit	1,265	1,155
Expenses	(713)	(693)
Profit from operations	552	462

Patch Limited
Summary Balance sheets as at 30 September

	20-8		20-7	
	£000	£000	£000	£000
Non-current assets		4,764		5,418

continued on next page

Current assets

Inventories	522	419
Trade receivables	406	356
Cash and cash equivalents	117	62
	1,045	837

Current liabilities

Trade payables	(305)	(254)
Tax liabilities	(170)	(211)
	(475)	(465)

Net current assets	570	372
Long-term loan	(1,654)	(2,490)
	3,680	3,300

Share capital	1,100	1,000
Share premium	282	227
Retained earnings	2,298	2,073
	3,680	3,300

You have also obtained the relevant industry average ratios which are as follows:

	20-8	20-7
Return on capital employed	9.6%	9.4%
Net profit percentage	21.4%	21.3%
Quick ratio/acid test	1.0:1	0.9:1
Gearing (Debt/Capital Employed)	36%	37%

REQUIRED

Prepare a report for the finance director of Rowan Healthcare plc recommending whether or not to use Patch Ltd as a supplier of bandages. Use the information contained in the financial statements of Patch Ltd and the industry averages supplied.

Your answer should:

•   comment on the company's profitability, liquidity and financial position;

•   consider how the company has changed over the two years;

•   include a comparison with the industry as a whole.

The report should include calculation of the following ratios for the two years:

(a)   Return on capital employed

(b)   Net profit percentage

(c)   Quick ratio/acid test

(d)   Gearing

8 Consolidated accounts

This chapter examines the financial statements of groups of companies. The statements for a group include a consolidated income statement and a consolidated balance sheet. Such consolidated accounts show the position of the group as if it was a single economic entity. The chapter covers:

- definitions of parent and subsidiary companies, and the group
- accounting for goodwill, post-acquisition profits, and minority interest when using the purchase method for preparing consolidated balance sheets
- the use of fair values in consolidated accounts
- inter-company adjustments and profits
- consolidated income statements

Towards the end of the chapter we look at incorporating the results of associated companies – where fewer than half of the shares are owned – into the financial statements of the investor company.

PERFORMANCE CRITERIA COVERED

unit 11: DRAFTING FINANCIAL STATEMENTS

element 11.1

draft limited company financial statements

A   draft limited company financial statements from the appropriate information

B   correctly identify and implement subsequent adjustments and ensure that discrepancies, unusual features or queries are identified and either resolved or referred to the appropriate person

C   ensure that limited company financial statements comply with relevant accounting standards and domestic legislation and with the organisation's policies, regulations and procedures

E   ensure that confidentiality procedures are followed at all times

THE ACCOUNTING SYSTEMS OF AN ORGANISATION

Throughout your earlier studies of accounting you will have been aware of how a business must adapt the accounting system to suit its particular needs. In the same way, in *Drafting Financial Statements* a company's accounting systems are affected by a number of factors – these include the role of the company, its organisational structure, its administrative systems and procedures, and the nature of its business transactions. Provided that a company complies with the requirements of international accounting standards and the Companies Act, it can arrange its accounting systems to suit its needs.

Up until now we have studied and prepared the financial statements of individual companies, eg Wyvern Trading Company Limited. Such financial statements are often referred to as *unitary* accounts – because they relate to one company only. In this chapter we will study the accounts of groups of companies known as *consolidated* accounts – where one company (the parent company) owns or controls one or more other companies (subsidiary companies).

Before commencing our studies of consolidated accounts we will look at a Case Study which demonstrates two different ways of organising the accounting systems of large companies.

Case Study

CHOCOLAT LIMITED AND CHOC CABIN LIMITED: DIVISIONAL OR CONSOLIDATED?

situation

Both of these companies – Chocolat Limited and Choc Cabin Limited – manufacture high-quality chocolates and other confectionery which are sold through their own retail chains – shops on high streets and in shopping centres, and franchises located within department stores. Both companies also sell wholesale to major store chains, where the chocolates are boxed and branded under the name of the retailer.

The two companies are direct competitors, chasing the same market – their shops are to be found close to one another on many a high street or shopping centre. Despite their similarities, however, the way in which they organise their accounting systems is very different.

solution

Chocolat Limited – divisional accounting

This company uses a divisional approach to its accounting system, with a separate division for each of its main activities – manufacture, retail, and own-brand wholesale – illustrated as follows:

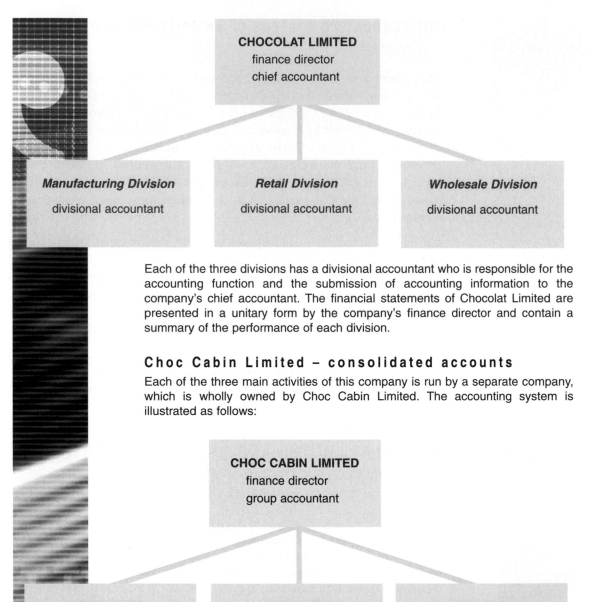

Each of the three divisions has a divisional accountant who is responsible for the accounting function and the submission of accounting information to the company's chief accountant. The financial statements of Chocolat Limited are presented in a unitary form by the company's finance director and contain a summary of the performance of each division.

Choc Cabin Limited – consolidated accounts

Each of the three main activities of this company is run by a separate company, which is wholly owned by Choc Cabin Limited. The accounting system is illustrated as follows:

Here, each company running one of the main activities maintains its own accounting system and is required to produce its own financial statements in accordance with the Companies Act and accounting standards – each has a company accountant to enable it to do so. As each company is wholly owned, it is a subsidiary company of Choc Cabin Limited, the parent company. In these circumstances, consolidated – or group – accounts are produced as the financial statements, in order to show a complete picture of the group. The parent company's group accountant will prepare the consolidated accounts for presentation by the company's finance director.

conclusion

This Case Study shows two different accounting systems – unitary financial statements with the reporting of divisional performance, and consolidated financial statements with subsidiary companies.

As an organisation grows, it must adapt its accounting systems to suit its needs – no one system is correct in all circumstances.

The divisional method often suits a company that grows organically where new divisions are set up to meet the requirements of the business, eg "we will set up a wholesale division". By contrast, subsidiary companies are often acquired as going concern businesses in order to expand rapidly, eg "we need to expand, let us buy an existing wholesale business".

While subsidiary companies often have more autonomy than divisions, the preparation of consolidated accounts is more complex – as we will see in this chapter – than that of unitary companies.

INTRODUCTION TO CONSOLIDATED ACCOUNTS

In recent years many companies have been taken over by other companies to form groups. Each company within a group maintains its separate legal entity, and so a group of companies may take the following form:

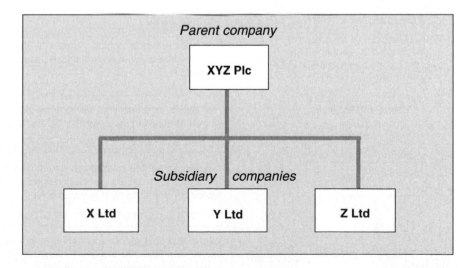

Two international accounting standards give guidance as to the accounting treatment for consolidated accounts:

- IFRS 3, *Business Combinations*
- IAS 27, *Consolidated and Separate Financial Statements*

IFRS 3 identifies a business combination as 'the bringing together of separate entities or businesses into one reporting entity.' A feature of most business combinations is that one business, the acquirer, obtains control over another business (or businesses), the acquiree. Control is defined by IFRS 3 as 'the power to govern the financial and operating policies of an entity or business so as to obtain benefits from its activities.' Both IFRS 3 and IAS 27 state that control is assumed when the acquirer owns more than 50 per cent of the voting shares of the acquiree. Where there is an ownership of 50% or less of the voting shares, control can still be obtained if the acquirer has:

- power over more than 50 per cent of the voting rights of the other company as a result of an agreement with other investors

- power to govern the financial and operating policies of the other company as a result of legislation or an agreement

- power to appoint or remove the directors of the other company

- power to cast the majority of votes at a board meeting of the other company

Although there are a variety of ways in which a business combination can be structured, we shall be studying the parent-subsidiary relationship in which the acquirer is the parent and the acquiree is the subsidiary. The key features of IFRS 3 are set out in the following diagram (the terms and techniques will be described in more detail later on).

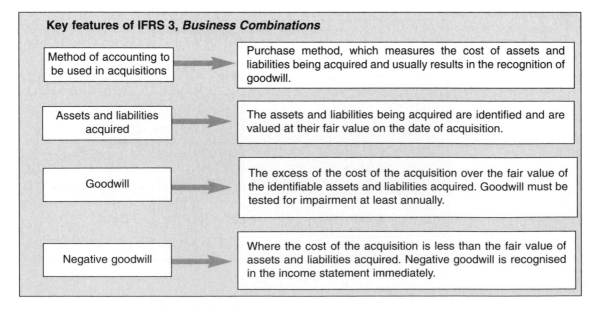

Key features of IFRS 3, *Business Combinations*

Method of accounting to be used in acquisitions	Purchase method, which measures the cost of assets and liabilities being acquired and usually results in the recognition of goodwill.
Assets and liabilities acquired	The assets and liabilities being acquired are identified and are valued at their fair value on the date of acquisition.
Goodwill	The excess of the cost of the acquisition over the fair value of the identifiable assets and liabilities acquired. Goodwill must be tested for impairment at least annually.
Negative goodwill	Where the cost of the acquisition is less than the fair value of assets and liabilities acquired. Negative goodwill is recognised in the income statement immediately.

PARENT AND SUBSIDIARY COMPANIES DEFINED

IAS 27 states that a group exists where one company (the parent) controls, either directly or indirectly, another company (the subsidiary). The definitions are:

* parent – a company that has one or more subsidiaries
* subsidiary – a company that is controlled by another company (the parent)
* group – a parent and all its subsidiaries

IAS 27 requires that consolidated financial statements are to be prepared for a group. Such financial statements include a consolidated income statement and a consolidated balance sheet – these are designed to show the position of the group as if it was a single economic entity.

When a parent company does not own 100 per cent of the shares of a subsidiary company, then there will be some shares owned by outsiders, who are termed the minority interest. For example, Adel Limited owns 75 per cent of the shares of Sade Limited – this creates a parent-subsidiary relationship, even though 25 per cent of Sade's shares are owned by outsiders, the minority interest. IAS 27 defines minority interest as 'that portion of the profit or loss and net assets of a subsidiary attributable to equity interests that are not owned, directly or indirectly through subsidiaries, by the parent.' On a consolidated balance sheet, the value of the minority interest is shown within equity, but separately from the parent shareholders' equity (see page 248).

CONSOLIDATION PROCEDURES

To prepare consolidated financial statements, items from both the parent and the subsidiary's financial statements are combined by adding together assets, liabilities, income and expenses. The following steps are taken to present the information of the group as that of a single economic entity:

* the carrying amount of the parent's investment in the subsidiary and the parent's portion of equity in the subsidiary are eliminated or cancelled out against each other – this usually results in the recognition of goodwill
* minority interest in the profit or loss of the subsidiary is identified
* minority interest in the net assets of the subsidiary is identified and shown separately from the parent shareholders' equity; there are two elements of minority interest:
  - the value at the date of acquisition

– the share of changes in equity since the date of acquisition

As well as dealing with the above, any intragroup balances, transactions, income and expenses need to be eliminated in full. Such transactions take place between the parent and subsidiary companies, eg one company sells goods to another, both within the same group.

When preparing consolidated financial statements, uniform accounting policies should be used by the group.

We shall now study the three major calculations used in the preparation of a consolidated balance sheet, each having a different relevant date:

1 goodwill – as at the date of acquisition of the subsidiary

2 post-acquisition profits – since the date of acquisition of the shares in the subsidiary

3 minority interest (or interests) – the stake of the other shareholders in the subsidiary at the date of the consolidated balance sheet

In the Case Studies which follow, we look at the preparation of consolidated balance sheets – starting with simple groups, and then incorporating calculations for goodwill, post-acquisition profits and minority interest. Included in the Case Studies are tutorial notes which explain the calculations.

Case Study

ACCOUNTING FOR SIMPLE GROUPS OF COMPANIES

situation

The summary balance sheets of Pam Limited, a parent company, and Sam Limited, the subsidiary of Pam, are shown below as at 31 December 2006. Sam Limited was acquired by Pam Limited as a subsidiary company on 31 December 2006.

	Pam Ltd £000	Sam Ltd £000
Investment in Sam:		
20,000 £1 ordinary shares at cost	40	–
Other net assets	40	40
	80	40
Share capital (£1 ordinary shares)	60	20
Retained earnings	20	20
	80	40

solution

The first thing to look at is the percentage of shares owned in the subsidiary by the parent company. Here Pam Limited owns all 20,000 shares of Sam Limited, so the subsidiary is 100 per cent owned. Note that the shares have been bought at the financial year-end, ie the date of the consolidated balance sheet.

The method of preparing the consolidated balance sheet of Pam Limited and its subsidiary Sam Limited is as follows:

1   the £40,000 cost of the investment in Sam (shown on Pam's balance sheet) cancels out directly against the share capital (£20,000) and retained earnings (£20,000) of Sam and is not shown on the consolidated balance sheet

2   add together the net assets of the two companies

3   show only the share capital and retained earnings of the parent company

The consolidated balance sheet (CBS) is shown in the far right column:

	Pam Ltd £000	Sam Ltd £000	CBS £000
Investment in Sam:			
20,000 £1 ordinary shares at cost	40	–	
Other net assets	40	40	80
	80	40	80
Share capital (£1 ordinary shares)	60	20	60
Retained earnings	20	20	20
	80	40	80

Tutorial Note

The reason for cancelling out the amount of the investment against the share capital and retained earnings of the subsidiary is because the amounts record a transaction that has taken place within the group. It does not need reporting because the balance sheet shows the group as if it was a single economic entity.

Case Study

GOODWILL – POSITIVE AND NEGATIVE

situation

The summary balance sheets of Peeble Limited, a parent company, and Singh Limited and Salvo Limited, its two subsidiaries, as at 31 December 2006 appear below. The investments in Singh Limited and Salvo Limited were bought on 31 December 2006.

	Peeble Ltd £000	Singh Ltd £000	Salvo Ltd £000
Non-current assets	30	25	20
Investment in Singh:			
20,000 £1 ordinary shares at cost	50		
Investment in Salvo:			
24,000 £1 ordinary shares at cost	25		
Net current assets	10	15	10
	115	40	30
Share capital (£1 ordinary shares)	70	20	24
Retained earnings	45	20	6
	115	40	30

solution

Peeble Limited owns all the shares of Singh Limited and Salvo Limited – the subsidiaries are 100 per cent owned. The acquisitions have been bought at the financial year-end – the date of the consolidated balance sheet.

As the cost price of the investment in the subsidiaries does not cancel out directly against the share capital and reserves, the difference represents goodwill:

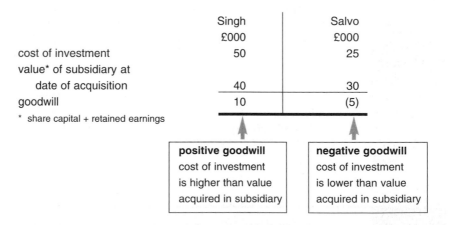

	Singh £000	Salvo £000
cost of investment	50	25
value* of subsidiary at date of acquisition	40	30
goodwill	10	(5)

* share capital + retained earnings

positive goodwill	**negative goodwill**
cost of investment is higher than value acquired in subsidiary	cost of investment is lower than value acquired in subsidiary

The consolidated balance sheet of Peeble Limited and its subsidiaries can now be prepared following the principles outlined in the previous Case Study. Positive goodwill is shown on the assets side of the consolidated balance sheet, with negative goodwill added to the income statement, thus increasing the figure for retained earnings. (Note, however, that IFRS 3 does say that, where negative goodwill is indicated, the first step should be to check the values used to ensure that they are correct in arriving at negative goodwill.)

PEEBLE LIMITED AND ITS SUBSIDIARIES
Consolidated balance sheet as at 31 December 2006

	£000
Goodwill	10
Other non-current assets 30 + 25 + 20	75
Net current assets 10 + 15 + 10	35
	120
Share capital	70
Retained earnings 45 + 5 (negative goodwill)	50
	120

Tutorial Note

In future years, positive goodwill must be subject to an impairment test at least annually – see IAS 36, *Impairment of Assets* (pages 112-117).

Case Study

PRE-ACQUISITION AND POST-ACQUISITION PROFITS

situation

The summarised balance sheets of Peat Limited, a parent company, and Stone Limited, its subsidiary, as at 31 December 2006 appear as follows:

	Peat Ltd	Stone Ltd
	£000	£000
Non-current assets	80	25
Investment in Stone:		
20,000 £1 ordinary shares at cost	35	
Current assets	25	10
Current liabilities	(10)	(8)
	130	27
Share capital (£1 ordinary shares)	100	20
Retained earnings	30	7
	130	27

Stone Limited was bought by Peat Ltd on 31 December 2005, when Stone's retained earnings were £5,000 (note that Stone has earned £2,000 since the date of acquisition).

Ten per cent of the goodwill is to be written off as an impairment loss.

> **Tutorial Note**
>
> The retained earnings of the subsidiary at the date of acquisition are those that have been earned pre-acquisition: they are included in the goodwill calculation.
>
> The retained earnings of the subsidiary after acquisition – post-acquisition profits – are earned while it is part of the group and are, therefore, part of the consolidated retained earnings shown on the consolidated balance sheet. Such consolidated retained earnings are available for distribution as dividends to shareholders – provided that there is sufficient cash in the bank to pay the dividends.

solution

1   Peat Limited owns all the shares of Stone Limited, ie the subsidiary is 100% owned.

2   The calculation of goodwill in Stone is as follows:

	£000
cost of investment	35
value of subsidiary at date of acquisition 20 + 5	*25
positive goodwill	10

* £20,000 of share capital, plus £5,000 of retained earnings at date of acquisition (ie pre-acquisition profits)

3   As ten per cent of the goodwill is to be written off as an impairment loss, £1,000 will be written off to the income statement in 2006, leaving £9,000 of goodwill to be shown in the balance sheet.

4   The post-acquisition retained earnings of Stone for the consolidated balance sheet are:

	£000
retained earnings at date of consolidated balance sheet	7
retained earnings at date of acquisition of Stone	5
post-acquisition retained earnings	2

PEAT LIMITED AND ITS SUBSIDIARY
Consolidated balance sheet as at 31 December 2006

	£000
Goodwill 10 – 1	9
Other non-current assets 80 + 25	105
Current assets 25 + 10	35
Current liabilities (10) + (8)	(18)
	131
Share capital	100
Retained earnings 30 + 2 – 1*	31
	131

* goodwill written off to the income statement

Case Study

MINORITY INTEREST

Tutorial Note

As noted earlier (page 241), minority interest occurs where the parent company does not own all the shares in the subsidiary company, eg a subsidiary is 75 per cent owned by a parent company; the 25 per cent of shares not owned by the parent is the minority interest.

The amount shown for minority interest on the consolidated balance sheet reflects the value of the subsidiary held by the minority shareholders, and is shown on the equity side (share capital and retained earnings) of the consolidated balance sheet, and identified separately.

situation

The summarised balance sheets of Pine Limited, a parent company, and Spruce Limited, its subsidiary, as at 31 December 2006 are shown below.

The investment in Spruce was bought on 31 December 2005, when Spruce's retained profit was £8,000.

Twenty per cent of the goodwill is to be written off as an impairment loss.

	Pine Ltd £000	Spruce Ltd £000
Non current assets	80	25
Investment in Spruce:		
15,000 £1 ordinary shares at cost	26	
Current assets	25	12
Current liabilities	(10)	(5)
	121	32
Share capital (£1 ordinary shares)	100	20
Retained earnings	21	12
	121	32

solution

1   Pine Limited owns 75 per cent of the shares of Spruce Limited, ie 15,000 shares out of 20,000 shares. Thus minority shareholders own 25 per cent of Spruce.

2   The calculation of goodwill in Spruce is as follows:

	£000
cost of investment	26
value of subsidiary at date of acquisition	
20 + 8 = 28 x 75% owned =	21
positive goodwill	5

Note that, for the goodwill calculation, the value of the subsidiary at date of acquisition is reduced to the percentage of shares owned, here 75 per cent.

3   As twenty per cent of the goodwill is to be written off as an impairment loss, £1,000 will be written off to the income statement in 2006, leaving £4,000 of goodwill to be shown in the balance sheet.

4   The post-acquisition profits of Spruce for the consolidated balance sheet are:

	£000
retained earnings at date of consolidated balance sheet	12
retained earnings at date of acquisition of Spruce	8
post-acquisition retained earnings	4
75% owned	3

Note that, for the calculation of post-acquisition retained earnings, the amount is reduced to the percentage of shares owned, here 75 per cent.

5   The minority interest in Spruce is:

	£000
value at date of consolidated balance sheet	32
25% minority interest	8

Note that, for the calculation of minority interest, the amount is reduced to the percentage of shares owned by the minority shareholders, here 25 per cent.

PINE LIMITED AND ITS SUBSIDIARY
Consolidated balance sheet as at 31 December 2006

	£000
Goodwill 5 – 1	4
Other non-current assets 80 + 25	105
Current assets 25 + 12	37
Current liabilities (10) + (5)	(15)
	131
Share capital	100
Retained earnings 21 + 3 – 1*	23
	123
Minority interest	8
	131

* goodwill written off to the income statement

Tutorial Note

When there is a minority interest, note that we do not reduce the value of the subsidiary's assets and liabilities in the consolidated balance sheet to allow for minority shareholders – what we are saying is that the parent company has *control* over the subsidiary's assets and liabilities.

The amount shown for the minority interest on the consolidated balance sheet is the value of the subsidiary held *at the date of the consolidated balance sheet.*

Minority interest is identified separately on the equity side (share capital and retained earnings) of the consolidated balance sheet in order to show the overall view of the group.

FAIR VALUES IN CONSOLIDATED ACCOUNTS

When a parent company acquires a majority holding of shares in a subsidiary company, it acquires both control of the subsidiary and also control of the subsidiary's assets and liabilities. IFRS 3 requires that the cost of the business acquired is to be measured at the total of:

- the fair values of all the assets and liabilities that existed at the date of acquisition
- any costs directly attributable to the business combination

Fair value is the amount for which an asset could be exchanged between knowledgeable, willing parties in an arm's length transaction (IAS 16, *Property, Plant and Equipment*). For example, the fair value of land and buildings would be the market value, for plant and equipment it would also be the market value, for raw materials it would be the current replacement cost.

Fair value has an effect on the calculations for goodwill, minority interest (where applicable), and sometimes on post-acquisition profits:

- goodwill is the excess of the cost of the acquisition over the fair value of the identifiable assets and liabilities acquired
- minority interest is the proportion of the subsidiary owned, based on the fair value of the subsidiary's identifiable assets and liabilities
- post-acquisition profits will be affected where the use of fair value for non-current assets leads to a different depreciation charge from that based on historic costs

The procedure for dealing with fair values is to restate the subsidiary's balance sheet using fair values. Increases in the valuation of assets are credited to revaluation reserve; decreases are debited to revaluation reserve. Any changes to the value of liabilities are also passed through revaluation reserve. Note that, to be dealt with in this way, the fair value of identifiable assets and liabilities must be capable of being measured reliably.

The Case Study which follows shows how fair values affect the calculations for the consolidated balance sheet.

Case Study

FAIR VALUES IN CONSOLIDATED ACCOUNTS

situation

On 31 December 2006, Pipe Limited bought 75 per cent of the share capital of Soil Limited at a cost of £37,000. At that date the two companies' balance sheets were as follows:

	Pipe Ltd £000	Soil Ltd £000
Non-current assets	60	18
Investment in Soil:		
9,000 £1 ordinary shares at cost	37	
Current assets	20	16
Current liabilities	(13)	(6)
	104	28
Share capital (£1 ordinary shares)	80	12
Retained earnings	24	16
	104	28

At the date of acquisition

– the fair value of Soil's non-current assets was £30,000

– the fair value of Soil's current assets was £12,000

solution

1 We must incorporate the fair values into Soil's balance sheet as follows:

	£000	£000
Non-current assets (increase in value)		
debit non-current assets account	12	
credit revaluation reserve		12
Current assets (reduction in value)		
debit revaluation reserve	4	
credit current assets		4

2 Thus Soil's balance sheet is:

	before £000	adjustment £000	after £000
Non-current assets	18	+ 12	30
Current assets	16	– 4	12
Current liabilities	(6)	–	(6)
	28	+ 8	36
Share capital	12	–	12
Revaluation reserve	–	+ 12 – 4 }	8
Retained earnings	16	–	16
	28	+ 8	36

3 Goodwill is:

	£000
cost of investment	37
value of subsidiary at date of acquisition	
fair value of 36 (see above) x 75% owned	27
positive goodwill	10

4 Minority interest is:

	£000
value at date of consolidated balance sheet	36
25% minority interest	9

5 There will be no post-acquisition profits at 31 December 2006, as this is the date at which the investment in the subsidiary is being made.

PIPE LIMITED AND ITS SUBSIDIARY
Consolidated balance sheet as at 31 December 2006

	£000
Goodwill	10
Other non-current assets 60 + 30 (at fair value)	90
Current assets 20 + 12 (at fair value)	32
Current liabilities (13) + (6)	(19)
	113
Share capital	80
Retained earnings	24
	104
Minority interest	9
	113

Tutorial Note

Goodwill will be tested for impairment at least annually.

There may be an adjustment each year to post-acquisition profits if the use of fair values leads to an additional depreciation charge.

INTER-COMPANY ADJUSTMENTS

We have already seen the need to cancel out the inter-company balances of investment in the subsidiary company (shown in the parent company's balance sheet) against the share capital and reserves (shown in the subsidiary company's balance sheet). Other inter-company amounts also have to be cancelled out or adjusted against each other when preparing consolidated balance sheets.

receivables, payables and loans

Where there are receivables, payables and loans between companies that are part of the same group, they cancel out against each other and do not show on the consolidated balance sheet.

Example 1

Beech Limited has sold goods to Cedar Limited for £5,000. Both Beech and Cedar are subsidiaries of Ash Limited. At the date of the consolidated balance sheet Cedar has not yet paid Beech for the goods, so:

- Beech has an asset of receivables, including the £5,000 due from Cedar
- Cedar has a liability of payables, including the £5,000 due to Beech

For the consolidated balance sheet of Ash Limited and its subsidiaries, the inter-company balance of receivables and payables will not be shown because it is between group companies.

Example 2

Ash Limited has made a loan to Beech Limited of £10,000. The loan shows:

- as an asset on Ash's balance sheet
- as a liability on Beech's balance sheet

For the consolidated balance sheet, the loan will not be shown because it is an inter-company balance within the group.

inter-company profits

Inter-company profits occur when one group company sells goods to another company within the group. If the goods have then been sold to buyers outside the group, then no adjustment to the consolidated balance sheet is necessary as the profit has been realised. However, when some or all of the goods remain in the inventory of a group company at the date of the consolidated balance sheet, then an adjustment for unrealised inter-company profits must be made.

For example, Able Limited and Baker Limited are parent company and subsidiary company respectively. Able sells goods which cost it £1,000 to Baker for £1,500. A consolidated balance sheet is prepared before Baker sells any of the goods. The £500 profit made by Able is included in its income statement, whilst the value of the inventory held by Baker includes Able's profit. For the consolidated balance sheet:

- the income statement of Able is reduced by £500
- the inventory of Baker is reduced by £500

This accounting adjustment ensures that the inventory of the group is stated in the consolidated balance sheet at cost to the group (or net realisable value, if lower) and that no unrealised profit is shown in the group accounts. Note that, if some of the goods had been sold by Baker, then only the profit on the proportion remaining in the group would be adjusted.

When a partly-owned subsidiary has sold goods to another group company and there are unrealised inter-company profits at the date of the consolidated balance sheet, minority interest needs to be adjusted for its share of the unrealised profits. This is illustrated in the Case Study which follows.

Case Study

INTER-COMPANY ADJUSTMENTS

situation

The summary balance sheets of Pearl Limited, a parent company, and Sea Limited, its subsidiary, as at 31 December 2006 are shown below.

The investment in Sea Limited was bought on 31 December 2005, when Sea's retained earnings were £10,000. At that date there were no material differences between the book value and fair value of any of the assets of Sea.

In 2006 Pearl writes off ten per cent of the goodwill on the acquisition of Sea as an impairment loss.

In November 2006, Sea sold goods costing £5,000 to Pearl at a price of £7,000. At 31 December 2006 half of those goods were unsold by Pearl.

	Pearl Ltd £000	Sea Ltd £000
Investment in Sea:		
12,000 £1 ordinary shares at cost	28	
Loan to Sea	10	
Net current assets	42	46
Loan from Pearl		(10)
	80	36
Share capital (£1 ordinary shares)	60	20
Retained earnings	20	16
	80	36

solution

1   Pearl Limited owns 60 per cent of the shares in Sea Limited, ie 12,000 shares out of 20,000 shares.

2 The calculation of goodwill is as follows:

	£000
cost of investment	28
value of subsidiary at date of acquisition	
20 + 10 = 30 x 60% owned =	18
positive goodwill	10

As ten per cent of the goodwill is to be written off as an impairment loss, £1,000 will be written off to the income statement in 2006, leaving £9,000 of goodwill to be shown in the balance sheet.

3 *Inter-company adjustments:*

Loan

The £10,000 loan from Pearl to Sea cancels out for the consolidated balance sheet, ie the asset on Pearl's balance sheet cancels out against the liability on Sea's balance sheet.

Inter-company profits:

Of the £2,000 profit made when Sea sold goods to Pearl at the date of the consolidated balance sheet, £1,000 is unrealised (because the goods remain in Pearl's inventory). For the consolidated balance sheet:

– the income statement of Sea is reduced by £1,000

– the inventory of Pearl is reduced by £1,000

Tutorial note

It is always advisable to make the inter-company adjustments before calculating post-acquisition profits and the minority interest. By doing this, minority shareholders (if any) will be charged or credited with their share of adjustments which affect the subsidiary company.

4 The post-acquisition profits of Sea are:

	£000
retained earnings at date of consolidated balance sheet:	
16 – 1 unrealised profit	15
retained earnings at date of acquisition	10
post-acquisition profits	5
60% owned	3

5 The minority interest in Sea is:

	£000
value at date of consolidated balance sheet:	
36 – 1 unrealised profit	35
40% minority interest	14

PEARL LIMITED AND ITS SUBSIDIARY
Consolidated balance sheet as at 31 December 2006

	£000
Goodwill 10 – 1 (impairment loss)	9
Net current assets 42 – 1 (inventory) + 46	87
	96
Share capital	60
Retained earnings 20 – 1 (impairment loss) + 3	22
	82
Minority interest	14
	96

Case Study

PREPARING FOR ASSESSMENT:
THE CONSOLIDATED BALANCE SHEET

Tutorial note

The task which follows is taken from the December 2004 AAT Examination; it is reproduced by kind permission of AAT. We will use it to demonstrate how the calculations for goodwill, post-acquisition profits and minority interest can be presented in a tabular format. The task has been amended to incorporate the requirements of international accounting standards.

situation

Alasmith plc has one subsidiary undertaking, Jones Limited, which it acquired on 1 October 2003. The balance sheets of Alasmith plc and Jones Limited as at 30 September 2004 are set out below.

Balance sheets as at 30 September 2004				
	Alasmith plc		**Jones Ltd**	
	£000	£000	£000	£000
Tangible non-current assets		56,320		39,320
Investment in Jones Limited		26,680		
Current assets				
Inventories	13,638		5,470	
Trade receivables	7,839		3,218	
Cash and cash equivalents	1,013		1,184	
	22,490		9,872	

continued on next page

Current liabilities			
Trade payables	(8,733)		(4,288)
Accruals	(450)		(543)
Tax liabilities	(1,059)		(311)
	(10,242)		(5,142)
Net current assets		12,248	4,730
Long-term loan		(20,000)	(8,850)
		75,248	35,200
Equity			
Called up share capital		25,000	6,000
Share premium account		10,000	4,000
Retained earnings		40,248	25,200
		75,248	35,200

You have been given the following information:

- The share capital of Jones Limited consists of ordinary shares of £1 each. There have been no changes to the balances of share capital and share premium during the year. No dividends were paid by Jones Limited during the year.

- Alasmith plc acquired 3,600,000 shares in Jones Limited on 1 October 2003.

- At 1 October 2003 the balance of retained earnings of Jones Limited was £19,800,000.

- The fair value of the non-current assets of Jones Limited at 1 October 2003 was £43,470,000. The book value of the non-current assets at 1 October 2003 was £35,470,000. The revaluation has not been recorded in the books of Jones Limited (ignore any effect on the depreciation for the year).

- For the year to 30 September 2004, Alasmith plc has written off ten per cent of the goodwill on the acquisition of Jones Limited as an impairment loss.

You are to prepare the consolidated balance sheet of Alasmith plc and its subsidiary undertaking as at 30 September 2004.

(Note: an AAT Examination always supplies a sample layout for this purpose).

solution

1   The percentage of shares owned by Alasmith plc in Jones Limited is:

$$\frac{3,600,000 \text{ shares}}{6,000,000 \text{ shares}} = \underline{60 \text{ per cent}}$$

2   The minority interest in Jones is, therefore, 100% – 60% = <u>40 per cent</u>

3   At the date of acquisition (1 October 2003), the non-current assets of Jones had the following values:

	£000
fair value	43,470
book value	35,470
difference	<u>8,000</u>

4   As fair value is higher than book value, this increase must be recorded in Jones' accounts:

	£000	£000
debit non-current assets account	8,000	
credit revaluation reserve		8,000

5   Goodwill on consolidation, post-acquisition profits, and minority interest are now calculated using a tabular layout. (Author's note: each of these figures can be calculated separately as demonstrated on previous pages; the answers will, of course, be the same!)

	equity	attributable to Alasmith		minority interest
		at acquisition	since acquisition	
	100%	60%	60%	40%
	£000	£000	£000	£000
share capital	6,000	3,600		2,400
share premium	4,000	2,400		1,600
revaluation reserve				
(see above)	8,000	4,800		3,200
retained earnings*				
at acquisition	19,800	11,880		7,920
since acquisition	5,400		3,240	2,160
	†43,200	22,680	3,240	17,280
price paid by Jake		26,680		
∴ positive goodwill		4,000		

* and † – see notes below

Notes on the calculations

	£000	
* retained earnings:	19,800	at date of acquisition
	5,400	post-acquisition profits
	25,200	as shown by Jones' balance sheet
† equity:	35,200	as shown by Jones' balance sheet
	8,000	revaluation reserve (to increase non-current assets to fair value)
	43,200	as shown above

Further calculations

6   Ten per cent of the goodwill is to be written off as an impairment loss:

4,000	goodwill on consolidation
400	impairment loss for year to 30 September 2004 (ie date of consolidated balance sheet)
3,600	goodwill as at 30 September 2004

7   The amount of goodwill written off is debited to the income statement and affects consolidated retained earnings as follows:

40,248	Alasmith's retained earnings
3,240	post-acquisition profits of Jones attributable to Alasmith (see above)
43,488	
400	less goodwill written off to income statement
43,088	consolidated retained earnings

8   The consolidated balance sheet can now be prepared as shown on the next page. Note that the workings figures (in £000s) are for guidance only and need not be detailed in the balance sheet.

ALASMITH PLC AND ITS SUBSIDIARY
Consolidated Balance Sheet as at 30 September 2004

	£000	£000
Non-current Assets		
Goodwill 4,000 – 400 written off	3,600	
Tangible assets 56,320 + 39,320 + 8,000 increase to fair value	103,640	
Investments	–	
		107,240
Current Assets		
Inventories 13,638 + 5,470	19,108	
Trade receivables 7,839 + 3,218	11,057	
Investments	–	
Cash and cash equivalents 1,013 + 1,184	2,197	
	32,362	
Total assets		**139,602**
Current Liabilities		
Trade payables 8,733 + 4,288	(13,021)	
Accruals 450 + 543	(993)	
Tax liabilities 1,059 + 311	(1,370)	
	(15,384)	
Net Current Assets		16,978
		124,218
Non-current Liabilities		
Long-term loan 20,000 + 8,850		(28,850)
Total liabilities		**44,234**
		95,368
Equity		
Share capital		25,000
Share premium account		10,000
Retained earnings (see workings on page 258)		43,088
Equity attributable to equity holders of the parent		78,088
Minority interest (see tabulation on page 257)		17,280
TOTAL EQUITY		95,368

CONSOLIDATED INCOME STATEMENTS

The consolidated income statement, like the consolidated balance sheet, is intended to show the position of the group as if it was a single economic entity. The consolidated income statement shows the shareholders of the parent company how much profit has been earned by the parent company and the subsidiaries, with a deduction for the proportion of profit due to minority interests. The diagram below shows the format of a consolidated income statement; as the diagram demonstrates, the figures are merged from the income statements of the parent company and the subsidiaries.

Format of consolidated income statement

Continuing Operations

Revenue	parent + subsidiaries – inter-company sales
Cost of sales*	see below
Gross profit	parent + subsidiaries – inter-company unrealised profit
Distribution costs	parent + subsidiaries
Administrative expenses	parent + subsidiaries
Profit from operations	parent + subsidiaries
Finance costs	parent + subsidiaries
Profit before tax	parent + subsidiaries
Tax	parent + subsidiaries
Profit for the period from continuing operations	parent + subsidiaries

Discontinued Operations

Profit/(loss) for the period from discontinued operations	parent + subsidiaries
Profit for the period	parent + subsidiaries

Attributable to:	
Equity holders of the parent	parent + profit of wholly-owned subsidiaries + parent's share of profit of partly-owned subsidiaries
Minority interest	minority interest's share of subsidiaries' profit

* Cost of sales:	
opening inventories	parent + subsidiaries
+ purchases	parent + subsidiaries – inter-company purchases
– closing inventories	parent + subsidiaries – inter-company unrealised profit

notes on the income statement format

- the full profit of subsidiaries is shown, with a separate note of the proportion of the profit due to the minority interest

- inter-company transactions are deducted for
    - inter-company sales
    - inter-company purchases
    - inter-company unrealised profit

Two Case Studies follow which demonstrate the preparation of consolidated income statements – firstly for a simple group, secondly incorporating inter-company transactions. The layout follows that shown in the diagram.

Case Study

INCOME STATEMENT FOR SIMPLE GROUPS

situation

The summary income statements of Pack Limited, a parent company, and Sack Limited, its subsidiary, for the year-ended 31 December 2006 are shown below.

Pack Limited bought 80 per cent of the ordinary shares of Sack Limited on 1 January 2006.

	Pack Ltd	Sack Ltd
Continuing Operations	£000	£000
Revenue	115	60
Cost of sales	(65)	(28)
Gross profit	50	32
Distribution costs	(5)	(8)
Administrative expenses	(15)	(12)
Profit before tax	30	12
Tax	(8)	(2)
Profit for the year	22	10

Notes:

- There were no discontinued operations during the year.
- There were no impairment losses on goodwill during the year.

solution

1. The figures from the income statements are merged.
2. The after-tax profit for the year of Sack is £10,000; of this 20 per cent, ie £2,000 is due to the minority interest.

PACK LIMITED AND ITS SUBSIDIARY

Consolidated Income Statement for the year ended 31 December 2006

Continuing Operations		£000
Revenue	115 + 60	175
Cost of sales	65 + 28	(93)
Gross profit	50 + 32	82
Distribution costs	5 + 8	(13)
Administrative expenses	15 + 12	(27)
Profit from operations	30 + 12	42
Finance costs		–
Profit before tax		42
Tax	8 + 2	(10)
Profit for the year		32
Attributable to:		
Equity holders of the parent	22 + (80% x 10*)	30
Minority interest	20% x 10*	2
		32

* Sack's after-tax profit for the year

Case Study

GROUP INCOME STATEMENT WITH ADJUSTMENTS

situation

The summary income statements of Perch Limited, a parent company, and Sole Limited and Skate Limited, its subsidiaries for the year-ended 31 December 2006 are shown on the next page.

Perch Limited bought all of the shares of Sole Limited on 1 January 2004, and 75 per cent of the shares of Skate Limited on 1 January 2006.

During the year to 31 December 2006 the following inter-company trading took place:

– Perch sold goods costing £6,000 to Sole at a price of £10,000; all of these goods had been sold by the year-end for £12,000

– Perch sold goods costing £20,000 to Skate at a price of £40,000; at the year-end half of these goods were unsold by Skate

Notes:

- There were no discontinued operations during the year.
- Dividends paid during the year were:

  Perch Limited, £50,000

  Sole Limited, £20,000

  Skate Limited, £12,000

- There were no impairment losses on goodwill during the year.

	Perch Ltd	Sole Ltd	Skate Ltd
Continuing Operations	£000	£000	£000
Revenue	400	200	150
Opening inventories	100	75	50
+ Purchases	300	150	100
– Closing inventories	150	100	40
Cost of sales	(250)	(125)	(110)
Gross profit	150	75	40
Distribution costs	(40)	(25)	(10)
Administrative expenses	(50)	(15)	(10)
Dividends from subsidiaries:			
Sole	20		
Skate	9		
Profit before tax	89	35	20
Tax	(20)	(10)	(4)
Profit for the year	69	25	16

solution

Tutorial Note

Inter-company revenue, purchases and unrealised profit are deducted from revenue, purchases and closing inventories respectively before the figures are shown in the consolidated income statement.

The dividends of subsidiary companies have been correctly recorded by Perch to show the proportion paid to the parent company – these will not be shown on the consolidated income statement because they are inter-company transactions.

The after-tax profit for the year of Sole is £25,000; as this subsidiary is wholly owned, all is due to the parent.

The after-tax profit of Skate is £16,000; of this 25 per cent, ie £4,000, is due to the minority interest.

PERCH LIMITED AND ITS SUBSIDIARIES

Consolidated Income Statement for the year ended 31 December 2006

Continuing Operations		£000
Revenue	400 + 200 + 150 – 10 – 40	700
Cost of sales*		(445)
Gross profit		255
Distribution costs	40 + 25 + 10	(75)
Administrative expenses	50 + 15 + 10	(75)
Profit from operations		105
Finance costs		–
Profit before tax		105
Tax	20 + 10 + 4	(34)
Profit for the year		71
Attributable to:		
Equity holders of the parent	71 – 4 (minority interest)	67
Minority interest	25% x 16 (Skate's after-tax profit for the year)	4
		71

* cost of sales:		
opening inventories	100 + 75 + 50	225
+ purchases	300 + 150 + 100 – 10 – 40	500
– closing inventories	150 + 100 + 40 – 10 (unrealised profit)	280
		445

STATEMENT OF CHANGES IN EQUITY

The consolidated financial statements include a statement of changes in equity. As we have already seen with published accounts (page 62) this shows:

- profit or loss for the period
- items of income and expense for the period that are recognised directly in equity (eg gains on the revaluation of property)
- the total of income and expense for the period (the sum of the first two items), split between the amounts attributable to the equity holders of the parent and the minority interest

IAS 1, *Presentation of Financial Statements*, allows alternative set-outs for the statement of changes in equity. The required information can be given in the form of a statement of recognised income and expense which, for consolidated accounts is as follows (with sample figures):

**Consolidated Statement of Recognised Income and Expense
for the year ended 31 December 2006**

	£000
Gains/(losses) on revaluation of properties	500
Tax on items taken directly to equity	(150)
Net income recognised directly in equity	350
Transfers	
eg the transfer to gain or loss on the sale	
of some types of assets	
Profit/(loss) for the year	3,325
Total recognised income and expense for the year	3,675
Attributable to.	
Equity holders of the parent	2,940
Minority Interest	735
	3,675

For *Drafting Financial Statements*, a pro-forma of this statement will always be given in the examination when it is required.

Note that, in practice, when using the statement of recognised income and expense, it is also necessary to give, as notes to the accounts, a reconciliation of opening and closing balances of share capital, reserves and retained earnings.

CASH FLOW STATEMENT

Included in the consolidated financial statements is a cash flow statement. This follows the same layout that we have seen in Chapter 6. A recent consolidated cash flow statement for InBev is shown on page 72.

ASSOCIATED COMPANIES

participating interest and significant influence

An associated company is defined by IAS 28, *Investments in Associates*, as 'an entity over which the investor has significant influence and that is neither a subsidiary nor an interest in a joint venture'. The relationship is that of investor and investee (the associated company).

The exercise of **significant influence** is where the investor takes part in the financial and operating policy decisions – such as the expansion or contraction of the business, changes in products, markets, activities – but is not in control over those policies.

As a general guideline, an associated company is where an investor owns between 20 per cent and 50 per cent of the ordinary shares of another company. However, ownership of shares by itself is not enough to establish an associated company relationship: ownership must be accompanied by the exercise of significant influence.

IAS 28 suggests that the existence of significant influence by an investor is indicated by one or more of the following:

• representation on the board of directors of the investee (the associated company)

• participation in policy-making processes

• material transactions between the investor and the investee

• interchange of managerial personnel

• provision of essential technical information

As we have seen earlier in this chapter, an ordinary share ownership above 50 per cent usually indicates a subsidiary company relationship; below 20 per cent is classed as a trade investment (see page 271). Thus an investment in an associated company is a substantial investment which is greater than a trade investment, but which is not as significant as a subsidiary company.

equity method of accounting

The equity method is the usual way of accounting for the results of associated companies. By this method we mean that the investor values its investment so as to reflect its interest in the net assets of the associated company. Initially the associated company is shown on the investor's balance sheet at cost (contrast this with subsidiary companies where assets and liabilities are included with those of the parent); the investor's share of subsequent profits or losses of the associated company are added to, or deducted from, the cost of the investment.

In the investor's financial statements, the key features of the equity method are:

- in the **income statement** (see diagram below) show the investor's share of the associated company's:

    - profit after tax (on the line above profit before tax)

- in the **balance sheet**

    - the investor's share of the net assets of the associated company is be included and separately disclosed as a non-current asset

    - goodwill arising on the investor's acquisition of its associate is included in the carrying amount of the associate (note that, as goodwill of associated companies is not shown separately in the investor's balance sheet, the entire carrying value is tested for impairment – see IAS 36, *Impairment of Assets*, pages 112-117)

    - any dividends received from the investee are used to reduce the carrying amount of the investment

---

**Format of consolidated income statement,
incorporating share of associated companies**

Note: this format is used for a group, ie parent + subsidiaries, together with associated companies
Continuing Operations

Group revenue	
Cost of sales	
Gross profit	
Distribution costs	no change to these figures: see page 260
Administrative expenses	
Group profit from operations	
Finance costs	
Share of after tax profit of associates	share of associates – inter-company unrealised profit
Profit before tax	group + share of after tax profit of associates
Tax	group
Profit for the period	group + share of after tax profit of associates
Attributable to:	
Equity holders of the parent	parent + subsidiaries + share of associates
Minority interest	minority interest's share of subsidiaries' profit

The equity method applies when investments in associates are held for the long-term. If investments are classified as being held for sale, they are to be accounted for in accordance with IFRS 5, *Non-current Assets Held for Sale and Discontinued Operations,* (see page 66).

The accounting policies of the investor are to be applied consistently and, if there are differences between those of investor and investee, adjustments are to be made when the associate's financial statements are used by the investor.

Case Study

ASSOCIATED COMPANIES

situation

On 31 December 2005, Icod Limited bought 25 per cent of the share capital of Arona Limited, its associated company, at a cost of £15,000. At that date the balance sheet of Arona was as follows:

	Arona Ltd
	£000
Non-current assets	28
Current assets	20
Current liabilities	(8)
	40
Share capital (£1 ordinary shares)	30
Retained earnings	10
	40

At 31 December 2006, before including the results of Arona, the balance sheets of Icod and Arona were as follows:

	Icod Ltd	Arona Ltd
	£000	£000
Non-current assets	100	35
Investment in associate at cost	15	–
Current assets	45	45
Current liabilities	(10)	(20)
	150	60
Share capital (£1 ordinary shares)	100	30
Retained earnings: at start of year	30	10
profits for 2006	20	20
	150	60

An extract from the income statements of Icod and Arona for 2006 showed the following:

	Icod Ltd £000	Arona Ltd £000
Profit from operations	75	28
Finance costs	(5)	(4)
Profit before tax	70	24
Tax	(20)	(4)
Profit for the year	50	20

Notes:

• At the date of acquisition there were no material differences between the book value and fair value of any of the assets of Arona.

• During the year, Icod paid a dividend of £30,000; Arona did not pay any dividends.

solution

Goodwill on acquisition

	£000
The calculation of goodwill in Arona is as follows:	
cost of investment	15
value of associate at date of acquisition	
40 (net assets) x 25% owned	10
goodwill	5

Tutorial note

For the goodwill calculation, the value of the associate – using net assets – at the date of acquisition is reduced to the percentage of shares owned, here 25 per cent.

Where fair values are different from book values, fair values are used in the calculation of goodwill.

Income statement for 2006

Icod reports its share of the associated company's profits as follows:

	£000	
Profit from operations	75	
Finance costs	(5)	
	70	
Share of after tax profit of associate	5	20 x 25%
Profit before tax	75	
Tax	(20)	
Profit for the year	55	

Tutorial note

The share of the after tax profit of the associate has been shown separately in the income statement of the investing company on the line above profit before tax.

Balance sheet as at 31 December 2006

The value of Arona, the associated company, is calculated as:

					£000
net assets of associated company	x	investor's share			
£60,000	x	25%		=	15
plus goodwill				=	5
					20

The balance sheet of Icod, incorporating the results of Arona, is as follows (£000):

Non-current assets	100
Investment in associate	20
Current assets	45
Current liabilities	(10)
	155
Share capital (£1 ordinary shares)	100
Retained earnings: 30 + 25 (see below)	55
	155

Tutorial note

An alternative way to calculate the value of Arona is:	£000
cost of investment	15
+ share of retained profits for year 20 x 25%	5
	20
Retained earnings for 2006 are:	
Icod, the investing company	50
– dividend paid by Icod	30
+ share of Arona, the associate	5
	25

TRADE INVESTMENTS

A trade investment is where a company holds shares in another company – either for its investment potential, or so as to take an interest in a major supplier or customer. Generally a trade investment is where the investor owns below 20 per cent of the ordinary shares of another company. At this level the percentage owned is not sufficient to make the investee an associated or subsidiary company – usually because the investor does not have significant influence.

The accounting treatment for trade investments is very simple. The investor records the investment as either a non-current or a current asset – depending on how long the shares are to be held: if more than twelve months from the balance sheet date, the investment is a non-current asset; if less, it is a current asset. Non-current asset trade investments are valued at either cost or valuation; if there is impairment, the non-current asset should be written down to its recoverable amount. Current asset trade investments are valued at the lower of cost and net realisable value.

Income from trade investments – usually in the form of dividends received – is credited in the income statement as 'income from investments', while the dividend cheque is debited to bank account.

DISCLOSURE AND CONFIDENTIALITY

the extent of disclosure

The international accounting standards IFRS 3, *Business Combinations*, and IAS 27, *Consolidated and Separate Financial Statements*, cover the techniques of consolidated accounting for parent and subsidiary companies and set out the detailed disclosures required in group accounts. IAS 28, *Investments in Associates*, deals with accounting for associated companies.

The published accounts of limited companies – which are readily available to shareholders and interested parties – include, where appropriate, group financial statements (including income statement, balance sheet and cash flow statement) which disclose the consolidated financial performance and financial position of the parent company and its subsidiary companies; the accounts also incorporate the results of associated companies. Thus the user is assured that the financial statements have been prepared in accordance with international accounting standards.

confidentiality procedures

For those involved in the preparation of the accounts, confidentiality procedures must be observed at all times:

- with the detailed financial statements of subsidiary and associated companies

- during the preparation of published accounts which incorporate the figures from subsidiary and associated companies

- for detailed information that is needed in the preparation of the accounts but is not required to be disclosed under international accounting standards

Chapter Summary

- Companies adapt their accounting systems to suit the needs of the organisation.

- Consolidated accounts are designed to show the position of a group – parent company and subsidiary companies – as if it was a single economic entity.

- There are three major calculations in the preparation of a consolidated balance sheet:
  - goodwill, calculated as at the date of acquisition of the subsidiary
  - post-acquisition profits, calculated since the date of acquisition of the shares in the subsidiary
  - minority interest, calculated at the date of the consolidated balance sheet

- The use of fair values affects:
  - goodwill, which is calculated as the cost of the investment in the subsidiary, less the fair value of the subsidiary's identifiable assets and liabilities
  - minority interest, which is the proportion of the subsidiary, based on the fair value of the subsidiary's identifiable assets and liabilities
  - post-acquisition profits, which will be affected where the use of fair value for non-current assets leads to a different depreciation charge from that based on historic costs

- Inter-company adjustments may have to be made when preparing consolidated balance sheets for:

  - receivables, payables and loans, which cancel out between companies within the group

  - inter-company profits, eg on sale of goods, which are unrealised at the date of the consolidated balance sheet

- When preparing a consolidated income statement:

  - the full profit of subsidiaries is shown, with a separate deduction for the proportion of the profit due to the minority interest

  - inter-company transactions are deducted for inter-company sales, inter-company purchases, and inter-company unrealised profit

- The consolidated financial statements include a statement of changes in equity – which is often given in the form of a statement of recognised income and expense. This shows:

  - profit or loss for the period

  - items of income and expense for the period that are recognised directly in equity

  - total income and expense for the period

- An associated company is where an investor owns generally between 20 per cent and 50 per cent of the ordinary shares of another company and exercises significant influence over its financial and operating policies.

- The equity method is the usual way of accounting for the results of associated companies:

  - initially the investment in the associated company is shown at cost on the investor's balance sheet

  - the investor's share of subsequent profits or losses are added to, or deducted from, the cost of the investment

  - the investor's income statement includes the share of the after tax profit of the associated company.

Key Terms

parent	a company that has one or more subsidiaries
subsidiary	a company that is controlled by another company
group	a parent and all its subsidiaries
parent company/ subsidiary company	a parent company has a subsidiary where any of the following apply:

- holds a majority of voting rights
- has power over more than 50 per cent of voting rights
- has power to govern the financial and operating policies
- has power to appoint or remove directors
- has power to cast the majority of votes at a board meeting

purchase method — method of accounting used in acquisitions which measures the cost of assets and liabilities being acquired and usually results in the recognition of goodwill

goodwill — the excess of the cost of the acquisition over the fair value of the identifiable assets and liabilities acquired

fair value — the amount for which an asset could be exchanged between knowledgeable, willing parties in an arm's length transaction' (IAS 16, *Property, Plant and Equipment*)

post-acquisition profits — profits earned by a subsidiary since the date of acquisition

minority interest — the owners of shares which are not owned by the parent company

statement of changes in equity — often represented by a statement of recognised income and expense which shows:

- profit or loss for period
- items of income and expense for period that are recognised directly in equity
- total income and expense for period

associated company — 'an entity over which the investor has significant influence and that is neither a subsidiary nor an interest in a joint venture' (IAS 28, *Investments in Associates*)

significant influence — where the investor takes part in the financial and operating policy decisions but is not in control over those policies

equity method — method of accounting for associated companies by which the investing company values its investment so as to reflect its interest in the net assets of the associated company

Student Activities

Osborne Books is grateful to the AAT for their kind permission to use past assessment material, which has been amended to incorporate the requirements of international accounting standards.

Blank photocopiable pro-formas of the consolidated income statement and consolidated balance sheet are included in the Appendix – it is advisable to enlarge them to full A4 size.

8.1 Sidney plc acquires 60% of the ordinary shares in Kidney Ltd on the 1 January 20-3. Kidney Ltd's net profit after tax for the year to 31 December 20-3 is £10,000.

What is the minority interest in the consolidated income statement for the year ended 31 December 20-3?

(a)   £6,000

(b)   £4,000

(c)   £2,000

(d)   £10,000

8.2 The Takeover plc invested £305,000 in 800,000 ordinary shares of 10 pence each in the Subsidiary Co Ltd. The Subsidiary Co Ltd's issued share capital and reserves at the date of acquisition were £100,000 in shares and £200,000 in reserves (£300,000 in total).

What is the value for goodwill arising on the acquisition?

(a)   £20,000

(b)   £5,000

(c)   £65,000

(d)   £6,500

8.3 The issued share capital of the Landmark Co Ltd consists of 400,000 ordinary shares of 25 pence each. The reserves of the company currently total £120,000. Seaside plc currently owns 300,000 ordinary shares in Landmark.

What is the total value for minority interest?

(a)   £55,000

(b)   £130,000

(c)   £165,000

(d)   £25,000

8.4 Walkingman Ltd is a subsidiary company which is 80% owned. Its profits for the year after tax to 31 December 20-3 are £200,000. During the year it has paid its shareholders dividends of £60,000.

What figure will appear in the consolidated income statement for minority interest?

(a) £160,000

(b) £40,000

(c) £28,000

(d) £52,000

8.5 What are group profits commonly referred to when they are earned and generated whilst under the parent company's control?

(a) pre-acquisition profits

(b) post-acquisition profits

(c) ex-acquisition profits

(d) minority interest

8.6 As at 31 December 20-3 the parent company has on its balance sheet trade receivables totalling £85,000. Its subsidiary company on the same day shows trade receivables of £40,000, of which £10,000 is an inter-group debt due from the parent company.

On the consolidated balance sheet for the group what is the correct valuation for trade receivables?

(a) £125,000

(b) £45,000

(c) £135,000

(d) £115,000

8.7 According to IFRS 3, *Business Combinations*, under what circumstances does an acquirer obtain control over another company?

8.8 The directors of Phantom plc have been in negotiation with the directors/ shareholders of another company, Roover plc with regard to the purchasing of 80% of the share capital from them. Phantom will pay £2,900,000 for the shares based on the valuation of the company at 30 April 20-3, this being the agreed date for acquisition.

The fair value of the non-current assets in Roover plc at 30 April 20-3 is £4,200,000. All the other assets and liabilities of the company are stated at fair value (ie balance sheet valuation)

Roover plc's balance sheet as at 30 April 20-3 is as follows:

	£000	£000
NON-CURRENT ASSETS AT NBV		3,500
CURRENT ASSETS		
Inventories	450	
Trade receivables	300	
Cash and cash equivalents	100	
	850	
CURRENT LIABILITIES		
Trade payables	(400)	
Tax liabilities	(200)	
	(600)	
NET CURRENT ASSETS		250
		3,750
NON-CURRENT LIABILITIES		
10% Debentures		(1,000)
		2,750
EQUITY		
Called up share capital		800
Share premium account		200
Retained earnings		1,750
		2,750

REQUIRED

Calculate the goodwill on consolidation that would arise on acquisition if Phantom plc purchased an 80% stakeholding in Roover plc on 30 April 20-3.

What figure for minority interest would appear in the consolidated balance sheet of Phantom plc as at 30 April 20-3?

8.9 You have been asked to assist in the preparation of the consolidated accounts of the Ringer Group of companies. Set out below are the balance sheets of Ringer plc and its subsidiary Sterling Ltd, as at 30 April 20-3.

	Ringer plc		Sterling Ltd	
	£000	£000	£000	£000
Non-current Assets at nbv		6,000		1,600
Investment in Sterling Limited		2,000		
Current Assets				
Inventories	1,900		800	
Trade receivables	1,500		500	
Cash and cash equivalents	600		100	
	4,000		1,400	

Current Liabilities				
Trade payables	(2,500)		(400)	
Tax liabilities	(400)		(100)	
	(2,900)		(500)	
Net Current Assets		(1,100)		(900)
		9,100		2,500
Non-current Liabilities				
Long-term loans		(2,000)		(500)
		7,100		2,000
Equity				
Called up share capital		2,000		1,000
Share premium account		1,000		500
Retained earnings		4,100		500
		7,100		2,000

Additional information

The share capital of both companies consists of ordinary shares of £1 denomination.

Ringer plc acquired 600,000 shares in Sterling Ltd on 30 April 20-3.

The fair value of the non-current assets of Sterling Ltd at 30 April 20-3 was £1,900,000.

REQUIRED

Prepare a consolidated balance sheet for Ringer plc as at 30 April 20-3. Any goodwill arising on consolidation should be shown as a non-current asset.

8.10 Crispin plc purchased 25% of the ordinary share capital in Kingston Ltd for £320,000 on 1 April 20-2. Kingston Ltd is an associate company and the directors would like to know how Kingston Ltd would be included in the results of the Crispin group. Extracts from Kingston Ltd's accounts are listed below:

Income statement for the year to 31 March 20-3

	£000
Profit before tax	420
Tax	(120)
Profit for the year	300

Balance sheet as at 31 March 20-3	£000
Non-current Assets	900
Net Current Assets	200
	1,100
10% Debentures	(100)
	1,000
Equity	
Called up share capital	400
Share premium account	100
Retained earnings	500
	1,000

Additional Information

Any goodwill is deemed not to be subject to impairment.

REQUIRED

What figures would appear in the consolidated income statement and consolidated balance sheet of the Crispin Group for the year to 31 March 20-3 to account for the results of Kingston Ltd?

8.11 The following summarised balance sheets relate to the Winston group of companies as at 30 November 20-3.

	Winston plc £000		Churchill Ltd £000
Non-current Assets at NBV		5,000	600
Investment in Churchill Limited		900	
Current Assets			
Inventories	150		30
Trade receivables	80		35
Cash and cash equivalents	10	240	5	70
Current Liabilities			
Trade payables		(160)	(120)
		5,980	550
Equity			
£1 Ordinary shares		4,000	400
Retained earnings		1,980	150
		5,980	550

Additional Information

Winston plc purchased a 90% holding in Churchill Ltd on 1 December 20-1 when Churchill's retained earnings balance was £50,000

During the year to 30 November 20-3 Churchill purchased goods from Winston for £60,000. Winston had invoiced these goods at cost plus 33.3%. A third of these goods were still held as inventories at the year end.

At 30 November 20-3 the following inter-group debt was still outstanding: Churchill owed Winston £10,000.

Ten per cent of any goodwill arising upon consolidation is to be written off as an impairment loss each year.

REQUIRED

Prepare the Winston group of companies consolidated balance sheet as at 30 November 20-3.

8.12 The summary income statements of Tom Limited, a parent company, and Ben Limited and Sarah Limited, its subsidiaries for the year ended 31 December 20-2 are as follows:

	Tom Ltd	Ben Ltd	Sarah Ltd
Continuing Operations	£000	£000	£000
Revenue	800	400	300
Opening inventories	200	150	100
+ Purchases	600	300	200
– Closing inventories	300	200	80
Cost of sales	(500)	(250)	(220)
Gross profit	300	150	80
Distribution costs	(80)	(50)	(20)
Administrative expenses	(100)	(30)	(20)
Dividends from subsidiaries:			
Ben	40		
Sarah	18		
Profit before tax	178	70	40
Tax	(40)	(20)	(8)
Profit for the year	138	50	32

Additional information
- Tom Limited bought all of the shares of Ben Limited on 1 January 20-0, and 75 per cent of the shares of Sarah Limited on 1 January 20-2.
- During the year to 31 December 20-2 the following inter-company trading took place:
  - Tom sold goods costing £12,000 to Ben at a price of £20,000; Ben had sold all of these goods by the year end for £24,000.
  - Tom sold goods costing £40,000 to Sarah at a price of £80,000; by the year end half of these goods were unsold by Sarah.
- There were no discontinued operations during the year.
- Dividends paid during the year were:
    Tom Limited, £100,000
    Ben Limited, £40,000
    Sarah Limited, £24,000
- There were no impairment losses on goodwill during the year.

REQUIRED

Prepare the consolidated income statement of Tom Limited and its subsidiaries for the year ended 31 December 20-2.

8.13 The managing director of Perran plc has asked you to prepare the consolidated income statement for the group. The company has one subsidiary undertaking, Porth Limited. The income statements for the two companies for the year ended 31 March 2006 are as follows:

Profit and loss accounts for the year ended 31 March 2006

	Perran plc	Porth Limited
Continuing Operations	*£000*	*£000*
Revenue	36,450	10,200
Cost of sales	(18,210)	(5,630)
Gross profit	18,240	4,570
Distribution costs	(5,735)	(1,210)
Administrative expenses	(4,295)	(450)
Dividends received from Porth Limited	750	–
Profit from operations	8,960	2,910
Finance costs	(1,720)	(300)
Profit before tax	7,240	2,610
Tax	(1,950)	(530)
Profit for the year	5,290	2,080

Additional information

- Perran plc acquired 75% of the ordinary share capital of Porth Ltd on 1 April 2005.

- During the year Porth Limited sold goods which had cost £500,000 to Perran plc for £750,000. All of the goods had been sold by Perran plc by the end of the year.

- There were no discontinued operations during the year.

- Dividends paid during the year were:

    Perran plc, £2,500,000

    Porth Limited, £1,000,000

- There were no impairment losses on goodwill during the year.

REQUIRED

Draft the consolidated income statement for Perran plc and its subsidiary undertaking for the year ended 31 March 2006.

ANSWERS TO STUDENT ACTIVITIES

CHAPTER 1: PURPOSE OF FINANCIAL STATEMENTS

1.1 (a) **1.2** (c)

1.3 Students should list any three of the following:

Existing and potential investors who are interested in:
- Profit
- Liquidity and cash flow
- Annual revenue (sales turnover)

Lenders who are interested in:
- Profit
- Loan capital and risk
- Asset and balance sheet value
- Liquidity and cash flow

Suppliers who are interested in
- Cash flow and liquidity
- The value of assets and liabilities

Employees who are interested in
- Profit
- Liquidity and cash flow

Customers who are interested in
- Profit
- The value of assets and liabilities
- Liquidity and cash flow

The government which is interested in
- Profit
- Annual revenue (sales turnover)

The public which is interested in:
- Profit
- Liquidity and cash flow

1.4 (a) Going concern
This presumes that the business will continue to trade for the foreseeable future and there is no intention to downscale or sell off key operations of the business.

(b) Prudence
This concept requires that financial statements should always, where there is any doubt, report a conservative figure for profit or the valuation of assets. Thus profits are not to be anticipated and should only be recognised when they can be measured reliably.

(c) Business entity
All financial statements should report and record on its business activities only. Therefore personal transactions are not part of this reporting and recording process and should be kept separate.

(d)   Accruals
This means that income and expenses are matched to the accounting period to which they relate. Thus income and expenses incurred are recognised in the income statement rather than the amounts received and paid (which is referred to as cash accounting).

1.5   (a)   Business entity concept
The private transactions of the managing director are his own affairs and nothing to with the business. Therefore the payment of his daughters' school fees should be charged to him and should not be an expense of the company.

(b)   Materiality Concept
A box of pencils in the stationery cupboard is not a material amount and will not have any real significance in the preparation of the financial statements. Therefore it should not be treated as part of closing inventories but recognised as an expense in the income statement.

(c)   Going concern concept.
If HH Limited is not likely to continue in the near future then different accounting rules would need to be adopted to reflect this; for example, non-current (fixed) assets would need to be measured at their net realisable value rather than at their net book values. Such a break up approach is in contrast to the going concern concept, which presumes that an entity will continue in the foreseeable future.

(d)   Accruals concept
Here income and expenses must be matched so that they relate to the same goods and time period. Rent clearly overlaps two accounting periods, the years ending 20-2 and 20-3, part being paid in advance (£1,000) which is carried forward as an asset on the balance sheet.

(e)   Prudence concept.
If the debt is irrecoverable then the £500 should be written off as a bad debt and charged against this year's profit. If there is any doubt to the liquidation question then the £500 should appear as part of the provision for doubtful receivables (bad debts).

(f)   Consistency concept
The inventories should continue to be valued on a FIFO basis unless there are any genuine reasons for adopting another method of valuation, which will give a more true and fair view of the company's accounts. The manipulation of tax payments does not fall within this category. Note that International Accounting Standard No 2, *Inventories*, does not permit the use of the LIFO basis for valuing inventories (see page 127).

1.6   (a)   There is a conflict here between the accruals concept and the prudence concept. The accruals concept states that expenses should be matched against income which they generate. Thus it might be argued that, since half the income expected to result from the advertising campaign will be achieved in 20-6, it might be appropriate to defer half the expense of the advertising campaign until 20-6. However, the concept of prudence states that profits are not to be anticipated and should only be recognised when they can be measured reliably. As accruals is an underlying assumption in the preparation of financial statements (see *Framework* on page 21) it is likely to prevail over prudence, which is part of the characteristic of reliability.

The most likely treatment in the financial statements is that half of the cost of the advertising campaign will be recognised as an expense in the 20-5 accounts, with the other half carried forward in the balance sheet as a prepayment to be recognised as an expense in the 20-6 accounts.

(b)   The managing director has taken inventories for his own use; the cost of the inventories should be charged to him, and the value of closing inventories reduced accordingly.

(c)   Under the business entity concept the company is separate from Jonathan Brown. As the loan was made to the company it should be disclosed in the financial statements.

1.7   Task 1

(a)   The objective of financial statements is to 'provide information about the financial position, performance and changes in financial position of an entity that is useful to a wide range of users in making economic decisions'.

(b)   In a limited company, financial statements provide information to shareholders to enable them to assess the performance of management, for example in generating profits for the period or in improving the financial position of the company. It may also assist them in deciding whether to continue holding their shares in the company, to acquire more shares or to dispose of all or part of their holding.

Task 2

(a)   The elements of financial statements are:

- assets
- liabilities
- equity
- income
- expenses

(b)   The accounting equation that underlies the balance sheet relates to the following elements:

Assets – Liabilities = Equity

The change in equity in the period is equal to the capital contributed from owners plus profits in the form of income, and losses in the form of expenses. Income – Expenses = Profit. Thus the income statement explains how the change in equity arising from sources other than contributions from owners came about (note that items of income and expenses that do not arise from ordinary activities are reported separately within the income statement).

1.8   (a)   *Assets* are resources controlled by an entity as a result of past events and from which future economic benefits are expected to flow to the entity.

Liabilities are present obligations of an entity arising from past events, the settlement of which is expected to result in an outflow from the entity of resources embodying economic benefits.

Equity is the residual interest in the assets of the entity after deducting all its liabilities.

(b)   In the equity section of the balance sheet of a limited company capital balances would appear. These include funds contributed by shareholders, retained earnings, and other gains and losses.

1.9 NOTES FOR THE DIRECTORS

(a) The elements in a balance sheet and the balances in Machier Limited which fall under those elements are as follows:

Elements	Balances
Assets	Non-current assets, current assets
Liabilities	Current liabilities, non-current loan
Equity	Share capital, share premium, retained earnings

(b) The accounting equation is as follows:
(figures in £000)

Assets		Liabilities	= Equity
(£4,282 + £975)	–	(£749 + £2,800)	= £1,708
£5,257	–	£3,549	= £1,708

1.10 (c)

1.11 (a) materiality

(b) business entity

(c) accruals

(d) going concern

1.12 (a) • **Financial position** is reported through a balance sheet.

• **Financial performance** is reported through an income statement.

• **Changes in financial position** are reported through a cash flow statement.

(b) An **entity** is an organisation, such as a limited company, whose activities and resources are kept separate from those of the owner(s).

(c)

Four examples of users	Economic decisions
• existing and potential investors	• whether to continue to hold, sell or buy shares in the company
• lenders	• whether to make a loan to the company
• suppliers	• whether to supply the company with goods or services
• employees	• whether to continue working for the company

Other users of financial statements include customers, governments and government agencies, the public and managers.

CHAPTER 2: INTRODUCTION TO LIMITED COMPANY ACCOUNTS

2.1 (b)

2.2 (c)

2.3 (b)

2.4 Preference shares have a fixed rate of return and this is the maximum dividend that any such shareholder can receive on their investment.

Preference shares rank above ordinary shares in the case of a winding up or liquidation order. This means that if there are any surplus funds left after paying all the liabilities, preference shareholders will receive their money before ordinary shareholders.

Ordinary shares are often referred to as equity shares as they are the primary risk takers who are rewarded with dividends. The dividend payable tends to vary from year to year based upon the profits generated, the higher the profit then the more likelihood of an increased dividend.

Ordinary shareholders are the only type of share normally to receive a vote at the annual general meeting. Therefore as owners they can vote on company policy and the election of directors.

In the event of the company becoming insolvent, ordinary shareholders will be the last to receive any repayment of their investment.

2.5
- Directors' salaries/remuneration
- Debenture interest payable
- Tax

2.6 **Income statement for Gretton plc for the year to 31 March 20-2**

	£000	£000
Revenue		2,350
Opening inventories	140	
Purchases	960	
	1,100	
Closing inventories	(180)	
Cost of sales		(920)
GROSS PROFIT		1,430
Overheads:		
Administrative expenses	(210)	
Distribution costs	(420)	
Rent, rates and insurance	(487)	
Depreciation (non-current assets)	(95)	
		(1,212)
PROFIT BEFORE TAX		218
Tax		(32)
PROFIT FOR THE YEAR		186

Statement of changes in equity (extract)

Retained earnings

Balance at 1 April 20-1	242
Profit for the year	186
	428
Dividends paid	(60)
Balance at 31 March 20-2	368

Balance sheet of Gretton plc as at 31 March 20-2

	Cost £000	Dep'n £000	Net £000
NON-CURRENT ASSETS	950	315	635
CURRENT ASSETS			
Inventories		180	
Trade receivables		670	
Cash and cash equivalents		15	
		865	
Total assets			**1,500**
CURRENT LIABILITIES			
Trade payables		(260)	
Tax liabilities		(32)	
		(292)	
NET CURRENT ASSETS			573
Total liabilities			**292**
NET ASSETS			1,208
EQUITY			
Ordinary shares			600
Share premium account			240
Retained earnings (see above)			368
TOTAL EQUITY			1,208

Note (amounts in £000): assets £1,500 – liabilities £292 = equity £1,208

Working notes:

Journal

		Dr £000	Cr £000
1	Inventories – Balance sheet	180	
	Inventories – Income statement		180
2	Tax – Income statement	32	
	Tax payable – Balance sheet		32
3.	Depreciation – Income statement	95	
	Accumulated depreciation – Balance sheet		95

2.7 **Income statement of Hickson plc for the year to 30 September 20-2**

	£	£
Revenue		280,000
Opening inventories	25,000	
Purchases	125,000	
	150,000	
Closing inventories	(49,000)	
Cost of sales		(101,000)
GROSS PROFIT		179,000
Overheads:		
Wages and salaries	(40,000)	
Directors fees	(29,000)	
Printing, telephone & stationery	(7,000)	
General expenses	(6,000)	
Rent, rates and insurance	(11,000)	
Depreciation:		
– Equipment	(14,000)	
– Fixtures and fittings	(6,000)	
– Motor vehicles	(12,500)	
		(125,500)
PROFIT FROM OPERATIONS		53,500
Finance costs (debenture interest)		(4,000)
PROFIT BEFORE TAX		49,500
Tax		(8,000)
PROFIT FOR THE YEAR		41,500

Statement of changes in equity (extract)

Retained earnings

Balance at 1 October 20-1	21,400
Profit for the year	41,500
	62,900
Dividends paid	(6,400)
Balance at 30 September 20-2	56,500

Balance sheet of Hickson plc as at 30 September 20-2

NON-CURRENT ASSETS	Cost	Dep'n	Net
	£	£	£
Equipment	140,000	34,000	106,000
Fixtures and fittings	40,000	16,000	24,000
Vehicles	80,000	42,500	37,500
	260,000	92,500	167,500
CURRENT ASSETS			
Inventories		49,000	
Trade receivables		26,000	
Cash and cash equivalents		6,000	
		81,000	
Total assets			*248,500*
CURRENT LIABILITIES			
Trade payables		(14,000)	
Tax liabilities		(8,000)	
Accruals		(4,000)	
		(26,000)	
NET CURRENT ASSETS			55,000
			222,500
NON-CURRENT LIABILITIES			
8% Debenture loan			(50,000)
Total liabilities			*76,000*
NET ASSETS			172,500
EQUITY			
Ordinary shares of 25p each			80,000
Share premium account			36,000
Retained earnings			56,500
TOTAL EQUITY			172,500

Note: assets £248,500 – liabilities £76,000 = equity £172,500

Working notes
Journal

		Dr	Cr
		£	£
1	Inventories – Balance sheet	49,000	
	Inventories – Income statement		49,000
2.	Debenture interest payable – Income statement	4,000	
	Accruals – Balance sheet		4,000
3	Depreciation: Equipment – Income statement	14,000	
	Accum depreciation: Equipment – Balance sheet		14,000
	Depreciation: Fixtures – Income statement	6,000	
	Accum depreciation: Fixtures – Balance sheet		6,000
	Depreciation: Vehicles – Income statement	12,500	
	Accum depreciation: Vehicles – Balance sheet		12,500
4	Tax – Income statement	8,000	
	Tax payable – Balance sheet		8,000

2.8 **Income statement of Grayson plc for the year to 31 December 20-2**

	£	£
Revenue		2,640,300
Opening inventories	318,500	
Purchases	2,089,600	
	2,408,100	
Closing inventories	(340,600)	
Cost of sales		(2,067,500)
GROSS PROFIT		572,800
Overheads:		
Administrative expenses (120,180 – 12,200)	(107,980)	
Distribution costs (116, 320 + 21,300)	(137,620)	
Wages and salaries	(112,800)	
Directors' salaries	(87,200)	
Postage and telephone	(7,900)	
Bad debts	(8,900)	
Motor expenses	(12,280)	
Increase in provision for doubtful receivables	(2,400)	
		(477,080)
PROFIT FROM OPERATIONS		95,720
Finance costs:		
Loan stock interest (10,000 + 10,000)	(20,000)	
Bank interest	(7,720)	
		(27,720)
PROFIT BEFORE TAX		68,000
Tax		(45,000)
PROFIT FOR THE YEAR		23,000

Statement of changes in equity (extract)

Retained earnings

Balance at 1 January 20-2	144,276
Profit for the year	23,000
	167,276
Dividends paid	(60,000)
Balance at 31 December 20-2	107,276

Balance sheet of Grayson PLC as at 31 December 20-2

NON-CURRENT ASSETS	£	£	£
Office equipment at net book value			110,060
Vehicles at net book value			235,000
			345,060
CURRENT ASSETS			
Inventories		340,600	
Trade receivables	415,800		
Provision for doubtful receivables	(12,474)	403,326	
Prepayments		12,200	
Cash and cash equivalents		20,640	
		776,766	
Total assets			**1,121,826**

CURRENT LIABILITIES
Trade payables	(428,250)	
Tax liabilities	(45,000)	
Accruals (21,300 + 10,000)	(31,300)	
	(504,550)	
NET CURRENT ASSETS		272,216
		617,276

NON-CURRENT LIABILITIES
10% Loan stock	(200,000)	
Bank loan account	(50,000)	
		(250,000)
Total liabilities		**754,550**
NET ASSETS		367,276

EQUITY
Ordinary shares of 50p each	260,000
Retained earnings (see above)	107,276
TOTAL EQUITY	367,276

Note: assets £1,121,826 – liabilities £754,550 = equity £367,276

Working notes
Journal

		Dr £	Cr £
1	Interest payable – Income statement	10,000	
	Accruals – Balance sheet		10,000
2	Payments in advance – Balance sheet	12,200	
	Administrative expenses – Income statement		12,200
	Distribution costs – Income statement	21,300	
	Accruals – Balance sheet		21,300
3	Increase in provision for doubtful receivables – Income statement	2,400	
	Provision for doubtful receivables – Balance sheet		2,400
4	Inventories – Balance sheet	340,600	
	Inventories – Income statement		340,600
5	Tax – Income statement	45,000	
	Tax payable – Balance sheet		45,000

Increase in provision for doubtful receivables:

	£
New provision (3% x £415,800)	12,474
Less already provided	10,074
Net increase in provision	2,400

CHAPTER 3: PUBLISHED ACCOUNTS OF LIMITED COMPANIES

3.1   (d)

3.2   IAS 1, *Presentation of Financial Statements*, states that a complete set of financial statements comprises:
- balance sheet
- income statement
- statement of changes in equity
- cash flow statement
- accounting policies and explanatory notes

3.3   (b)

3.4   (a)

3.5   A statement of changes in equity is important to shareholders because it shows the changes that have taken place to their stake in the company. It includes not only the *realised* profit or loss from the income statement, but also *unrealised* profits (such as the revaluation of property) which are taken directly to reserves.

The information given in the statement of changes in equity is:
- profit or loss for the period
- items of income and expense for the period that are recognised directly in equity (eg gains or losses on the revaluation of property)
- the total of income and expense for the period (the sum of the first two items)
- the effects on equity of any changes in accounting policies and correction of errors

IAS 1, *Presentation of Financial Statements*, allows alternative set-outs for the statement of changes in equity. The required information can be given in the form of a 'statement of recognised income and expense'. When this is used, shareholders will also need to refer to notes to the accounts which give a reconciliation of opening and closing balances of share capital, reserves and retained earnings.

3.6   Items that are included in a Directors Report include any four of the following:
- a statement of the principal activities of the company
- directors' names and their shareholdings
- proposed dividends
- a review of the previous 12 months' activities
- future developments
- significant differences between the book value and market value of land and buildings
- political and charitable contributions
- policy on the employment of disabled people
- health and safety at work of employees
- action taken on employee involvement and consultation
- policy on the payment of suppliers

3.7 **Task 1**

Journal	Debit	Credit
	£000	£000
Inventories – Balance sheet	180	
Inventories – Income statement		180
Tax – Income statement	65	
Tax payable – Balance sheet		65

Task 2

Proudlock plc: Income statement for the year ended 31 March 20-2

Continuing Operations	£000
Revenue	2,295
Cost of sales [1]	(1,180)
GROSS PROFIT	1,115
Distribution costs	(500)
Administrative expenses	(240)
PROFIT FROM OPERATIONS	375
Income from non-current asset investments	75
PROFIT BEFORE TAX	450
Tax	(65)
PROFIT FOR THE YEAR	385

Statement of changes in equity (extract)

Retained earnings	
Balance at 1 April 20-1	350
Profit for the year	385
	735
Dividends paid	(140)
Balance at 31 March 20-2	595

Proudlock plc:
Balance Sheet as at 31 March 20-2

NON-CURRENT ASSETS	£000	£000
Property, plant and equipment (1,000–500)		500
Investments		600
		1,100
CURRENT ASSETS		
Inventories	180	
Trade receivables	600	
Cash and cash equivalents	75	
	855	
Total assets		**1,955**
CURRENT LIABILITIES		
Trade and other payables [2]	(395)	
Tax liabilities	(65)	
	(460)	
NET CURRENT ASSETS		395
Total liabilities		**460**
NET ASSETS		1,495

EQUITY
Share capital	700
Share premium	200
Retained earnings	595
TOTAL EQUITY	1,495

Working notes

1	Cost of sales	£
	Opening inventories	160
	Purchases	1,200
		1,360
	Closing inventories	(180)
		1,180

2	Trade and other payables	
	Trade payables	300
	Other payables	80
	Accruals	15
		395

3.8   **Task 1**

Journal	*Debit*	*Credit*
	£000	*£000*
Inventories – Balance sheet	250	
Inventories – Income statement		250
Depreciation: Buildings (210 – 110 x 5%) – Income statement	5	
Accum Depreciation: Buildings – Balance sheet		5
Depreciation: Plant (125 x 20%) – Income statement	25	
Accum Depreciation: Plant – Balance sheet		25
Tax – Income statement	135	
Tax payable – Balance sheet		135

Task 2
Broadfoot plc: Income statement for the year ended 31 March 20-2

Continuing Operations	*£000*
Revenue	1,300
Cost of sales[1]	(388)
GROSS PROFIT	912
Distribution costs (240 + 6)	(246)
Administrative expenses (185 + 6)	(191)
PROFIT FROM OPERATIONS	475
Tax	(135)
PROFIT FOR THE YEAR	340

Statement of changes in equity (extract)

Retained earnings

Balance at 1 April 20-1	350
Profit for the year	340
	690
Dividends paid	(100)
Balance at 31 March 20-2	590

Broadfoot plc: Balance Sheet as at 31 March 20-2

NON-CURRENT ASSETS	£000	£000
Property, plant and equipment[3]		182
CURRENT ASSETS		
Inventories	250	
Trade receivables	628	
Cash and cash equivalents	15	
	893	
Total assets		**1,075**
CURRENT LIABILITIES		
Trade and other payables (60 + accruals 90)	(150)	
Tax liabilities	(135)	
	(285)	
NET CURRENT ASSETS		608
Total liabilities		**285**
NET ASSETS		790
EQUITY		
Share capital		200
Retained earnings		590
TOTAL EQUITY		790

Working notes

1	**Cost of sales**	£
	Opening inventories	150
	Depreciation[2]	18
	Purchases	470
		638
	Closing inventories	(250)
	Cost of sales	388

2   **Depreciation**

	Total	Cost of sales 60%	Dist'n 20%	Admin 20%
Buildings	5	3	1	1
Plant	25	15	5	5
Total	30	18	6	6

3   Non-current assets: property, plant and equipment

	Land and Buildings £000	Plant and Machinery £000	Total £000
At Cost	210	125	335
Depreciation b/f	48	75	123
Charges this year	5	25	30
Total	53	100	153
Net book value	157	25	182

3.9   Task 1: Journal

	Debit £	Credit £
Interest – Income statement	10,000	
Accruals – Balance sheet		10,000
Payments in advance – Balance sheet	12,200	
Administrative expenses – Income statement		12,200
Distribution costs – Income statement	21,300	
Accruals – Balance sheet		21,300
Increase in provision for doubtful receivables – Income statement	2,400	
Provision for doubtful receivables – Balance sheet		2,400
Inventories – Balance sheet	340,600	
Inventories – Income statement		340,600
Tax – Income statement	45,000	
Tax payable– Balance sheet		45,000

Task 2: Grandware plc: Income statement for the year ended 31 December 20-2

Continuing Operations	£
Revenue	2,640,300
Cost of sales[1]	(2,067,500)
GROSS PROFIT	572,800
Distribution costs[2]	(237,620)
Administrative expenses[2]	(219,280)
PROFIT FROM OPERATIONS	115,900
Income from non-current asset investments	2,100
	118,000
Finance costs (10,000 +10,000)	(20,000)
PROFIT BEFORE TAX	98,000
Tax	(45,000)
PROFIT FOR THE YEAR	53,000

Statement of changes in equity (extract)

Retained earnings

Balance at 1 January 20-2	164,276
Profit for the year	53,000
	217,276
Dividends paid	(20,000)
Balance at 31 December 20-2	197,276

Grandware plc: Balance Sheet as at 31 December 20-2

	£	£
NON-CURRENT ASSETS		
Property, plant and equipment (110,060 + 235,000)		345,060
Investments		20,000
		365,060
CURRENT ASSETS		
Inventories	340,600	
Trade and other receivables[3]	415,526	
Cash and cash equivalents	20,640	
	776,766	
Total assets		**1,141,826**
CURRENT LIABILITIES		
Trade and other payables[4]	(459,550)	
Tax liabilities	(45,000)	
	(504,550)	
NET CURRENT ASSETS		272,216
		637,276
NON-CURRENT LIABILITIES		
10% Loan stock		(200,000)
Total liabilities		**704,550**
NET ASSETS		437,276
EQUITY		
Share capital		200,000
Share premium		40,000
Retained earnings		197,276
TOTAL EQUITY		437,276

Working notes

		£000
1	**Cost of sales**	
	Opening inventories	318,500
	Purchases	2,089,600
		2,408,100
	Closing inventories	(340,600)
		2,067,500
2	**Distribution costs**	
	Distribution costs	216,320
	Accruals	21,300
		237,620
	Administrative expenses	
	Administrative expenses	220,180
	Prepaid	(12,200)
	Bad debts	8,900
	Increase in provision for doubtful receivables	2,400
		219,280
3	**Trade and other receivables**	
	Trade receivables	415,800
	Provision for doubtful receivables	(12,474)
	Administrative expenses prepaid	12,200
		415,526
4	**Trade and other payables**	
	Trade payables	428,250
	Interest accrued	10,000
	Distribution costs accrued	21,300
		459,550

3.10   Task 1

			£000	£000
1	DR	Inventories – Balance sheet	7,878	
	CR	Inventories – Income statement		7,878
2	DR	Tax – Income statement	1,920	
	CR	Tax payable – Balance sheet		1,920
3	DR	Revenue – Income statement	204	
	CR	Trade receivables – Balance sheet		204
4	DR	Interest – Income statement	240	
	CR	Accruals – Balance sheet		240
5	DR	Land – Balance sheet	500	
	CR	Revaluation reserve – Balance sheet		500

Workings (£000):

Interest: £6,000 x 8% x $\frac{1}{2}$ = £240

Revaluation: £5,500 – £5,000 = £500

Task 2

Hightink Limited: Income statement for the year ended 31 March 20-2

Continuing Operations	£000
Revenue[1]	31,506
Cost of sales[2]	(14,178)
Gross profit	17,328
Distribution costs	(6,852)
Administrative expenses	(3,378)
PROFIT FROM OPERATIONS	7,098
Finance costs[3]	(480)
PROFIT BEFORE TAX	6,618
Tax	(1,920)
PROFIT FOR THE YEAR	4,698

Statement of changes in equity (extract)

Retained earnings

Balance at 1 April 20-1	6,217
Profit for the year	4,698
	10,915
Dividends paid	(400)
Balance at 31 March 20-2	10,515

Revaluation reserve

Revaluation of land	500

Working notes:

1	**Revenue**	£000
	Revenue per TB	31,710
	Credit sales in wrong period	(204)
		31,506
2	**Cost of sales**	
	Opening inventories	6,531
	Purchases	15,525
	Closing inventories	(7,878)
		14,178
3	**Finance costs**	
	Interest per TB	240
	Accrued interest	240
		480

Hightink Limited: Balance Sheet as at 31 March 20-2

	£000	£000
NON-CURRENT ASSETS[1]		14,105
CURRENT ASSETS		
Inventories	7,878	
Trade receivables[2]	5,251	
Cash and cash equivalents	304	
	13,433	
Total assets		**27,538**
CURRENT LIABILITIES		
Trade and other payables[3]	(2,603)	
Tax liabilities	(1,920)	
	(4,523)	
NET CURRENT ASSETS		8,910
		23,015
NON-CURRENT LIABILITIES		
Long-term loan		(6,000)
Total liabilities		**10,523**
NET ASSETS		17,015
EQUITY		
Share capital		4,000
Share premium		2,000
Revaluation reserve		500
Retained earnings		10,515
TOTAL EQUITY		17,015

Workings:
All figures in £000

1   **Non-current assets**

Property, plant and equipment	Cost	Accumulated Depreciation	Net Book Value
Land	5,500	–	*5,500
Buildings	3,832	564	3,268
Fixtures and fittings	2,057	726	1,331
Motor vehicles	3,524	1,283	2,241
Office equipment	2,228	463	1,765
	17,141	3,036	14,105

     * Land: 5,000 + 500 = £5,500

2   **Trade receivables**

Trade receivables	5,455
Credit sales in wrong period	(204)
	5,251

3   **Trade and other payables**

Trade payables	2,363
Interest accrued	240
	2,603

Task 3
Hightink Limited: note for published accounts

DIVIDENDS
(note for published accounts)

£000

Amounts recognised as distributions to equity holders
during the year:
- *Final dividend* for the year ended 31 March 20-1
  of 7.5p per share   300
- *Interim dividend* for the year ended 31 March 20-2
  of 2.5p per share   100
      400

Proposed final dividend for the year ended 31 March 20-2
of 10p per share   *400

The proposed final dividend is subject to approval by shareholders at the Annual
General Meeting and has not been included as a liability in these financial statements.

* working (£000): £4,000 x 10p = £400

3.11

WYVERN OFFICE PRODUCTS LIMITED
Income statement for the year ended 31 December 20-4

	£000
Continuing Operations	
Revenue[1]	10,576
Cost of sales[2]	(6,667)
Gross profit	3,909
Distribution costs	(1,700)
Administrative expenses	(1,411)
PROFIT FROM OPERATIONS	798
Finance costs[3]	(160)
PROFIT BEFORE TAX	638
Tax	(215)
PROFIT FOR THE YEAR	423

Statement of changes in equity (extract)

Balance at 1 January 20-4	571
Profit for the year	423
	994
Dividends paid	(120)
Balance at 31 December 20-4	874

Balance Sheet as at 31 December 20-4

	£000	£000
NON-CURRENT ASSETS		
Property, plant and equipment[4]		1,674
Investments		1,850
		3,524
CURRENT ASSETS		
Inventories	2,533	
Trade and other receivables[5]	1,536	
Cash and cash equivalents	44	
	4,113	
Total assets		**7,637**
CURRENT LIABILITIES		
Trade and other payables[6]	(2,198)	
Tax liabilities	(215)	
	(2,413)	
NET CURRENT ASSETS		1,700
		5,224
NON-CURRENT LIABILITIES		
10% Debentures		(1,600)
Total liabilities		**4,013**
NET ASSETS		3,624
EQUITY		
Share capital		2,000
Share premium		750
Retained earnings		874
TOTAL EQUITY		3,624

working notes (£000)

1 **Revenue** 10,641 less returns inwards 65 = 10,576

2 **Cost of sales**

Opening inventories	2,220
Purchases	7,028
Returns outwards	(48)
	9,200
Closing inventories	(2,533)
Cost of sales	6,667

3   Finance costs

80 + 80 (half-year's interest on 10% debentures accrued) = 160

4   Non-current assets

Property, plant and equipment	Cost	Accumulated depreciation	Net book value
Land	510	–	510
Buildings	1,490	705	785
Fixtures and fittings	275	197	78
Vehicles	316	172	144
Office equipment	294	137	157
	2,885	1,211	1,674

5   Trade and other receivables

Trade receivables	1,592
Provision for doubtful receivables	(80)
Prepayments	24
	1,536

6   Trade and other payables

Trade payables	2,051
Accruals from T/B	67
Interest accrued (see above)	80
	2,198

3.12   Teme plc: Income statement for the year ended 31 March 20-6

Continuing Operations	£000
Revenue	40,000
Cost of sales[1]	(29,000)
GROSS PROFIT	11,000
Distribution costs[2]	(5,710)
Administrative expenses[2]	(1,855)
PROFIT FROM OPERATIONS	3,435
Finance costs	(150)
PROFIT BEFORE TAX	3,285
Tax	(1,400)
PROFIT FOR THE YEAR	1,885

Statement of changes in equity (extract)

Retained earnings

Balance at 1 April 20-5	2,550
Profit for the year	1,885
	4,435
Dividends paid	(2,000)
Balance at 31 March 20-6	2,435

Working notes

1. **Cost of sales**

	£000
Opening inventories	6,000
Purchases	30,000
	36,000
Closing inventories	(7,000)
	29,000

2. **Operating Costs**

	Distribution £000	Administrative £000
Auditors' remuneration		25
Delivery expenses	2,160	
Office expenses		900
Office rent, rates, heat and light		400
Showroom costs	1,500	
Wages and Salaries		
Delivery staff	800	
Directors' salaries	90	310
Office staff		200
Showroom staff	500	
Depreciation		
Delivery vans	60	
Office cars		20
Showroom premises and equipment	600	
	5,710	1,855

CHAPTER 4: ACCOUNTING FOR ASSETS

4.1 (a)

4.2 (b)

4.3 1 (a) 2 (c)

4.4   (b)

4.5   (a)

4.6   (a)   IAS 38, *Intangible Assets*, states that development can only be recognised on the balance sheet when the entity can demonstrate all of the following:

- the technical feasibility of completing the intangible asset so that it will be available for use or sale

- its intention to complete the intangible asset and to use or sell it

- its ability to use or sell the intangible asset

- the way in which the intangible asset will generate probable future economic benefits

- the availability of resources to complete the development and to use or sell the intangible asset

- its ability to measure the development expenditure reliably

(b)   *Included*: direct costs (eg materials, labour, fees to register legal rights)

Excluded: general overheads (eg administrative expenses)

4.7   (a)   An impairment review is carried out in three steps:

STEP 1   The asset's carrying amount is ascertained

STEP 2   The asset's recoverable amount is ascertained

STEP 3   If recoverable amount is greater than carrying value, there is no impairment. If carrying value is greater than recoverable amount, then the asset is impaired and should be written down to its recoverable amount.

Terms used:

Carrying amount is the amount at which an asset is recognised after deducting any accumulated depreciation/amortisation and accumulated impairment losses.

Recoverable amount is the higher of the asset's fair value, less costs to sell, and its value in use.

Fair value, less costs to sell is the amount obtainable from the sale of an asset (or cash generating unit) in an arm's length transaction between knowledgeable, willing parties, less the costs of disposal.

Value in use is the present value of the future cash flows obtainable as a result of an asset's continued use, including cash from its ultimate disposal.

(b)   When an asset is impaired it should be written down to its recoverable amount in the balance sheet. The amount of the impairment loss is recognised as an expense in the income statement, unless it relates to a previously revalued asset, when it is debited to the revaluation reserve within equity (to the extent of the revaluation surplus for that particular asset).

4.8   (c)

4.9   *External sources of impairment*

- a significant fall in the asset's market value
- adverse effects on the entity caused by technology, markets, the economy, laws
- increases in interest rates
- the stock market value of the entity is less than the carrying amount of net assets

Internal sources of impairment

- obsolescence or physical damage to the asset
- adverse effects on the asset of a significant reorganisation within the entity
- the economic performance of the asset is worse than expected

4.10   A *finance lease* is usually a longer-term lease, under which substantially all the risks and rewards of ownership are transferred to the lessee.

An *operating lease* is usually a shorter-term lease, where there is no transfer of the risks and rewards of ownership to the lessee.

IAS 17, *Leases*, requires that a finance lease is initially recognised on the balance sheet of the lessee as both an asset and a liability. The amount shown will be the lower of the fair value of the asset and the present value of the minimum lease payments. Finance lease payments to the lessor are then apportioned between the finance charge – recognised as an expense in the income statement – and a reduction of the outstanding liability on the balance sheet. The leased asset is depreciated on the same basis as assets which are owned – the amount of depreciation being recognised as an expense in the income statement.

With an operating lease, the lessor recognises lease payments as an expense in the income statement – usually on a straight-line basis over the lease term.

4.11   *Owner-occupied property* is property being used in the ordinary course of business.

Investment property is property held to earn rent or for capital appreciation, but not being used in the ordinary course of business.

IAS 16, *Property, Plant and Equipment*, states that all tangible assets (except for land) have a limited useful life and are subject to depreciation. IAS 16 requires that all tangible assets should be measured initially at cost and then a systematic allocation of the depreciable amount is applied over the assets' useful lives. Alternatively, the revaluation model can be used provided that the revaluation policy is consistent – ie that if one asset is revalued, then all assets within that class should be revalued. Note that any increase in value is usually credited directly within equity to a revaluation surplus, while any reduction in value is usually recognised as an expense in the income statement (although a decrease which reverses part or all of a previous increase for the same asset is debited to the revaluation surplus).

If a property is deemed to be an investment property, then IAS 40, *Investment Property*, applies. Under this standard, the entity initially measures the property at cost. After that, the entity chooses as its accounting policy either the fair value model or the cost model, which is then applied to all its investment property. With the fair value method, the property is subsequently measured at fair value; any gain or loss arising from a change in the fair value is recognised in the income statement for the period to which it relates. With the cost model, the property is subsequently measured at cost less accumulated depreciation and impairment losses.

4.12   **Task 1**

Makeshift Enterprises plc

Balance sheet (extracts) as at 31 December

	20-0	20-1	20-2	20-3
	£000	£000	£000	£000
NON-CURRENT ASSETS				
Investment property	400	400	440	460
Gain/(loss) for year		40	20	(80)
	400	440	460	380

Income statement (extracts) for the year ended 31 December

	£000	£000
20-1		
Gain in value of investment property		40
20-2		
Gain in value of investment property		20
20-3		
Loss in value of investment property	80	

Note that, for investment property, all gains and losses arising from changes in the fair value are recognised in the income statement for the period to which they relate.

Task 2

Makeshift Enterprises plc

Balance sheet (extracts) as at 31 December

	20-0	20-1	20-2	20-3
	£000	£000	£000	£000
NON-CURRENT ASSETS				
Freehold property	400	400	440	460
Increase/(decrease) in valuation		40	20	(80)
	400	440	460	380
EQUITY				
Revaluation surplus	–	40	60	–

Income statement (extracts) for the year ended 31 December

	£000	£000
20-3		
Decrease in value of freehold property	20	

Note that, for property, plant and equipment, any increase in value is generally credited within equity to a revaluation surplus; any reduction in value is recognised as an expense in the income statement (although, in this example, the decrease of £80,000 in 20-3 reverses all of the previous increases totalling £60,000, leaving £20,000 to be recognised as an expense in the 20-3 income statement).

4.13 (a)   Project Xchem has all the attributes of being research expenditure, as set out in IAS 38, *Intangible Assets*. As a consequence, the costs incurred of £295,000 should be recognised as an expense in the income statement of the year in which it is incurred.

Chemco Company

Income statement (extract) for the year to 31 December 20-3

	£000
Expenses	
Research and development costs	295

(b)   Project Zchem appears to meet all the requirements of IAS 38 and therefore should be capitalised on this year's balance sheet as an intangible asset.

Chemco Company

Balance Sheet (extract) as at 30 December 20-3

	£000
Non-current Assets	
Intangible asset – development costs	435

IAS 38 states that intangible assets are to be recognised initially at cost. After acquisition an entity can choose either the cost model or the revaluation model. In view of the limited life of Project Zchem it would seem appropriate to use the cost model and to amortise the intangible asset over the five years (20-4 to 20-8) during which no competition can enter the market. This means that with the straight line method of amortisation, £87,000 (£435,000 ÷ 5) will be recognised in the income statement each year, until it is totally written off the balance sheet by the end of 20-8.

4.14 (a)   Development costs may be deferred to future periods if all of the following criteria given by IAS 38, *Intangible Assets*, can be demonstrated by Poussin Limited:
- the technical feasibility of completing the intangible asset so that it will be available for use or sale
- its intention to complete the intangible asset and to use or sell it
- its ability to use or sell the intangible asset
- the way in which the intangible asset will generate probable future economic benefits
- the availability of resources to complete the development and to use or sell the intangible asset
- its ability to measure the development expenditure reliably

It appears that the company has considered these criteria and that it can justify the deferral of the development costs. An intangible asset of £351,572 will be recognised on the balance sheet at cost. Poussin Limited must then choose either the cost model or the revaluation model as its accounting policy. Under the cost model, the intangible asset is carried at cost, will be amortised over the life of the project, and will be reviewed for indicators of impairment. Under the revaluation model, the intangible asset is carried at a revalued amount, being its fair value, less any subsequent amortisation and impairment losses.

(b)   The principle of inventory valuation, as set out in IAS 2, is that inventories should be valued *at the lower of cost and net realisable value*.

This valuation applies the prudence concept under which profits are not anticipated and should only be recognised when they can be reliably measured. Thus the auditors are correct in wishing to value the inventory at the net realisable value of £110,648.

4.15 **1** (a) IAS 16, *Property, Plant and Equipment*, permits use of the revaluation model after acquisition. The company will have to choose this model as the accounting policy and it will then have to be applied to the entire class of land and buildings.

(b) In the financial statements, the asset is carried in the balance sheet at the revalued amount, being the fair value less any subsequent depreciation and impairment losses. Revaluations must then be made regularly to ensure that the carrying amount does not differ materially from its fair value at the balance sheet date.

The increase in value of the land and buildings is generally credited directly within equity to a revaluation surplus. Any subsequent reduction in value is recognised as an expense in the income statement (although a decrease which reverses part or all of a previous increase for the same asset is debited to the revaluation surplus).

(c) Revaluation would improve gearing (see Chapter 7). The lower gearing would make the company look less risky from the point of view of the bank and thus it may be more willing to lend money to the company.

(d) Future results would be affected because depreciation on the buildings would be calculated on the revalued amount and not on the basis of the original cost.

2 The investment is a current asset, as it was purchased for resale, and, in accordance with the prudence concept, should be shown at the lower of purchase price and net realisable value. The prudence concept requires that financial statements should always, when there is any doubt, report a conservative figure for profit or the valuation of assets. As we can foresee a loss on the sale of this current asset investment, it should be shown at its net realisable value of £56,000.

3 IAS 2 states that inventories should be shown *at the lower of cost and net realisable value (NRV)*. NRV is the estimated selling price less the estimated costs of completion and the estimated costs necessary to make the sale. If NRV is lower than cost then, under the prudence concept, the inventories should be reduced to NRV. The comparison of cost and NRV should be carried out for separate items or groups of inventory and not on the total of all inventories. Applying this policy would lead us to value the undervalued items at cost of £340,000 and the overvalued items at the sales price of £15,000. The effect of this is to reduce the value of inventories overall from the £365,000 in the financial statements to £355,000.

CHAPTER 5: ACCOUNTING FOR LIABILITIES AND THE INCOME STATEMENT

5.1 (d)

5.2 (b)

5.3 (d)

5.4 (b)

5.5 (d)

5.6 (a)

5.7 (d)

5.8 (c)

5.9 Quite often there will be events occurring after the balance sheet date which will provide new evidence about the value of assets and liabilities at that time. Changes can be made to these valuations up until the time the financial statements are authorised for issue (usually by the board of directors). After this time it becomes impossible to alter them.

IAS 10, *Events after the Balance Sheet Date*, identifies adjusting and non-adjusting events.

Adjusting events provide evidence of conditions that existed at the balance sheet date. If material, changes should be made to the amounts shown in the financial statements. Examples of adjusting events include:

–   the settlement after the balance sheet date of a court case which confirms that a present obligation existed at the balance sheet date

–   non-current assets – where the purchase price, or sale price, of assets bought or sold before the year end is fixed after the year end

–   assets, where a subsequent valuation shows impairment

Non-adjusting events are indications of conditions that arose after the balance sheet date. No adjustment is made to the financial statements; instead, if material, they are disclosed by way of notes which explain the nature of the event and, where possible, give an estimate of its financial effect. Examples of non-adjusting events include:

–   business combinations (see Chapter 8)

–   discontinuing a significant part of the business

–   major share transactions

5.10 These are uncertainties that must be accounted for consistently in financial statements, if user groups are to achieve a full understanding. IAS 37, *Provisions, Contingent Liabilities and Contingent Assets*, aims to ensure that appropriate recognition criteria and measurement bases are applied to provisions, contingent liabilities and contingent assets, and that sufficient information is disclosed in the notes to the financial statements, to enable users to understand their nature, timing and amount.

IAS 37 states that a **provision** is to be recognised as a liability in the financial statements when:

• an entity has an obligation as a result of a past event
• it is probable (more then 50% likely) that an outflow of economic benefits will be required to settle the obligation (eg payment)
• a reliable estimate can be made of the obligation

The amount of a provision is recognised as an expense in the income statement, and a liability is shown on the balance sheet (under the heading of long-term provisions).

Disclosure in the notes to the financial statements requires:

• details of changes in the amount of provisions between the beginning and end of the year

• a description of the provision(s) and expected timings of any resulting transfers

• an indication of the uncertainties regarding the amount or timing of any resulting transfers

A **contingent liability** is a possible obligation, ie there less than 50% likelihood of its occurrence.

A contingent liability is not recognised in the financial statements but should be disclosed as a note which includes:

- a brief description of the nature of the contingent liability
- an estimate of its financial effect
- an indication of the uncertainties relating to the amount or timing of any outflow
- the possibility of any reimbursement

Thus in summary:

Provision = Probable = more than 50% likely, recognised in financial statements and disclosed in notes.

Contingent liability = Possible = less than 50% likely, not recognised in financial statements, but disclosed in notes.

5.11 (a) IAS 23, *Borrowing Costs*, sets out the 'benchmark' accounting treatment for borrowing costs as being recognised as an expense in the income statement of the period in which they are incurred.

  (b) The alternative treatment is that borrowing costs in relation to the acquisition, construction or production of a qualifying asset can be capitalised as part of the cost of the asset. A qualifying asset is defined by IAS 23 as an asset that 'takes a substantial period of time to get ready for its intended use or sale.'

5.12 **Task 1**

Basic earnings per share

profit for the year attributable to equity holders

$$\frac{\text{Profit after tax}}{\text{Number of issued ordinary shares}} = \frac{£330,000}{20,000,000} = 1.65\text{p per share}$$

profit for the year from continuing operations attributable to equity holders

$$\frac{\text{Profit after tax from continuing operations}}{\text{Number of issued ordinary shares}} = \frac{£390,000}{20,000,000} = 1.95\text{p per share}$$

Both of these EPS figures are to be presented on the face of the income statement.

Task 2

New issue of shares at full market value

EPS is calculated on the basis of the weighted number of shares in issue during the period. This would be:

20,000,000 + (5,000,000 ÷ 2 [half of a year, ie six months]) = 22,500,000

EPS calculation would be:

profit for the year attributable to equity holders

$$\frac{£330,000}{22,500,000} = 1.47\text{p per share}$$

profit for the year from continuing operations attributable to equity holders

$\dfrac{£390,000}{22,500,000}$ = 1.73p per share

5.13   IAS 14, *Segment Reporting*, requires that financial information relating to the various activities of a company should be given (segmented) in two main ways:

–   by type of product or service (eg hotels, pubs, clubs)

–   by geographical area (eg United Kingdom, European Union, North America)

Each segment may have different levels of profitability, growth or risk. Information about segments is therefore relevant to assessing the performance of an entity, but may not be available from the aggregated information given in the financial statements.

IAS 14 applies to all entities whose shares or debt are publicly traded; other companies can choose to disclose segment information voluntarily.

The two types of segment identified by IAS 14 are:

–   a business segment

–   a geographical segment

Both of these segments are defined on page 160. An entity has to decide which is the primary segment and which the secondary segment. The deciding factor will be the dominant source and nature of the entity's risks and returns.

Segment information must conform to the accounting policies used by the entity for preparing and presenting its financial statements.

5.14   (a)   Although the selling of the inventory is an event which happened after the year end, under IAS 10, *Events after the Balance Sheet Date*, this is an example of an adjusting event. Such events provide evidence of conditions that existed at the balance sheet date; if material, changes should be made to the amounts shown in the financial statements. The sale of inventory provides evidence as to the net realisable value of the inventory reported in the financial statements for the year under review. Under IAS 2, *Inventories*, inventories are to be valued at the lower of cost and net realisable value.

(b)   A dividend declared or proposed on ordinary shares after the balance sheet date is, under IAS 10, an example of a non-adjusting event. Such events are indicative of conditions that arose after the balance sheet date; no adjustment is made to the financial statements – if material, they are disclosed by way of notes which explain the nature of the event and, where possible, give an estimate of its financial effect. The proposed ordinary dividend cannot be recorded as a liability at 30 September 20-6 as it was not a present obligation of the company at the financial year end. The details of the proposed dividend will be given in the notes to the financial statements, including the amount of £75,000.

(c)   Under IAS 10, this is an example of a non-adjusting event after the balance sheet date. Although the employee was working for Gernroder Limited at the financial year end, the legal proceedings do not relate to conditions that existed at the balance sheet date. Instead, the legal proceedings are indicative of conditions that arose after the balance sheet date and no adjustment is to be made to the financial statements. The amount of £20,000, if material, is to be disclosed by way of a note which explains the nature of the event and the financial effect.

CHAPTER 6: CASH FLOW STATEMENTS

6.1   (d)

6.2   (b)

6.3   (a)

6.4   (d)

6.5   Advantages of producing a cash flow statement:

(a)   Cash is said to be the life blood of any business, and the survival of a company will depend on its ability to generate sufficient cash in order to fund its activities and meet its day-to-day obligations.

(b)   The level of cash is an important indicator of business performance.

(c)   Users of financial statements can easily identify with cash (often more so than profit) - for example, employees may look at the level of cash when negotiating the next pay award.

(d)   Cash flow accounting can be used to compare business performance against previous periods or against other companies. Cash flow forecasting can also assume a role in the budgeting process, by reviewing past performance and as a planning tool for future growth.

6.6

CASHEDIN LIMITED		
CASH FLOW STATEMENT FOR THE YEAR ENDED 30 SEPTEMBER 20-5		
Cash flows from operating activities	*£000*	*£000*
Profit from operations	24	
Adjustments for:		
Depreciation for year	318	
Increase in inventories	(251)	
Increase in trade receivables	(152)	
Increase in trade payables	165	
Cash (used in)/from operations	104	
Interest paid	(218)	
Income taxes paid	(75)	
Net cash (used in)/from operating activities		(189)
Cash flows from investing activities		
Purchase of non-current assets	(358)	
Proceeds from sale of non-current assets	132	
Net cash (used in)/from investing activities		(226)
Cash flows from financing activities		
Proceeds from issue of share capital	150	
Proceeds from long-term borrowings	200	
Dividends paid	(280)	
Net cash (used in)/from financing activities		70
Net increase/(decrease) in cash and cash equivalents		(345)
Cash and cash equivalents at beginning of year		395
Cash and cash equivalents at end of year		50

6.7

RADION PLC
CASH FLOW STATEMENT FOR THE YEAR ENDED 31 DECEMBER 20-3

Cash flows from operating activities	£000	£000
Profit from operations	104	
Adjustments for:		
Depreciation for year	30	
Increase in inventories (203–175)	(28)	
Increase in trade receivables (141–127)	(14)	
Increase in trade payables (142–118)	24	
Cash (used in)/from operations	116	
Interest paid	(5)	
Income taxes paid	(19)	
Net cash (used in)/from operating activities		92
Cash flows from investing activities		
Net cash (used in)/rom investing activities		–
Cash flows from financing activities		
Repayment of long-term borrowings	(50)	
Dividends paid	(20)	
Net cash (used in)/from financing activities		(70)
Net increase/(decrease) in cash and cash equivalents		22
Cash and cash equivalents at beginning of year		(16)
Cash and cash equivalents at end of year		6

6.8   Task 1

PRATT PLC
Reconciliation of profit from operations to net cash flow from operating activities

	£000
Profit from operations	2,520
Adjustments for:	
Depreciation for year[1]	318
Loss on sale of non-current assets[2]	3
Increase in inventories (84–69)	(15)
Decrease in trade receivables (270–255)	15
Increase in trade payables (108–81)	27
Cash (used in)/from operations	2,868
Interest paid	(168)
Income taxes paid[3]	(744)
Net cash (used in)/from operating activities	1,956

Task 2

PRATT PLC
CASH FLOW STATEMENT FOR THE YEAR ENDED 31 OCTOBER 20-3

	£000	£000
Net cash (used in)/from operating activities		1,956
Cash flows from investing activities		
Purchase of non-current assets[4]	(629)	
Proceeds from sale of non-current assets	8	
Net cash (used in)/from investing activities		(621)
Cash flows from financing activities		
Proceeds from issue of share capital[5]	627	
Repayment of long-term borrowings	(1,800)	
Dividends paid[6]	(144)	
Net cash (used in)/from financing activities		(1,317)
Net increase/(decrease) in cash and cash equivalents		18
Cash and cash equivalents at beginning of year		30
Cash and cash equivalents at end of year		48

Working notes

1

Accumulated Depreciation

20-3		£000	20-2		£000
Oct 31	Disposal	18	Nov 1	Balance b/d	1,500
Oct 31	Balance c/d	1,800	20-3		
			Oct 31	Income statement (bal fig)	318
		1,818			1,818
			20-3		
			Nov 1	Balance b/d	1,800

2

Non-current Asset disposals

20-3		£000	20-3		£000
Oct 31	At cost	29	Oct 31	Accum depreciation	18
			Oct 31	Sale proceeds	8
			Oct 31	Income statement (bal fig)	3*
		29			29

Denotes a loss on sale

3

Taxation

20-3		£000	20-2		£000
Oct 31	Paid (bal fig)	744	Nov 1	Balance b/d	285
Oct 31	Balance c/d	291	Oct 31	Income statement	750
		1,035			1,035
			20-3		
			Nov 1	Balance b/d	291

4

Non-current Assets

20-2		£000	20-3		£000
Nov 1	Balance b/d	8,400	Oct 31	Disposals	29
20-3					
Oct 31	Additions (bal fig)	629	Oct 31	Balance c/d	9,000
		9,029			9,029
20-3					
Nov 1	Balance b/d	9,000			

5

	£000
Issue of called up shares (3,000–2,550)	450
At a premium	177
Total proceeds from issue	627

6   From the information given, the amount of dividends paid in 20-3 is £144,000 (being the proposed dividend for 20-2). The proposed dividend for 20-3 of £225,000 will be shown in the cash flow statement for 20-4.

6.9

SADLER PLC

CASH FLOW STATEMENT FOR THE YEAR ENDED 30 JUNE 20-3

Cash flows from operating activities	£000	£000
Profit from operations	1,100	
Adjustments for:		
Depreciation for year[1]	1,900	
Gain on sale of non-current assets[2]	(200)	
Increase in inventories (340–300)	(40)	
Increase in trade receivables (1,300–1,200)	(100)	
Increase in trade payables (800–660)	140	
Decrease in prepayments (100–80)	20	
Increase in accruals (120–60)	60	
Cash (used in)/from operations	2,880	
Interest paid	(100)	
Income taxes paid[3]	(300)	
Net cash (used in)/from operating activities		2,480
Cash flows from investing activities		
Purchase of non-current assets[4]	(4,300)	
Proceeds from sale of non-current assets	1,400	
Net cash (used in)/from investing activities		(2,900)
Cash flows from financing activities		
Proceeds from long-term borrowings (debentures)	1,000	
Dividends paid[5]	(600)	
Net cash (used in)/from financing activities		400
Net increase/(decrease) in cash and cash equivalents		(20)
Cash and cash equivalents at beginning of year		40
Cash and cash equivalents at end of year		20

Working notes

1

Accumulated Depreciation

20-3		£000	20-2		£000
Jun 30	Disposal	400	Jul 1	Balance b/d	8,160
Jun 30	Balance c/d	9,660	20-3		
			Jun 30	Income statement (bal fig)	1,900
		10,060			10,060
			20-3		
			Jul 1	Balance b/d	9,660

2

Non-current Asset disposals

20-3		£000	20-3		£000
Jun 30	At cost	1,600	Jun 30	Accum depreciation	400
			Jun 30	Sale proceeds	1,400
Jun 30	Income statement (bal fig)*	200			
		1,800			1,800

* Denotes a gain on sale

3

Taxation

20-3		£000	20-2		£000
Jun 30	Paid (bal fig)	300	Jul 1	Balance b/d	300
			20-3		
Jun 30	Balance c/d	260	Jun 30	Income statement	200
		560			560
			20-3		
			Jul 1	Balance b/d	260

4

Non-current Assets

20-2		£000	20-3		£000
Jul 1	Balance b/d	13,600	Jun 30	Disposals	1,600
20-3					
Jun 30	Additions (bal fig)	4,300	Jun 30	Balance c/d	16,300
		17,900			17,900
20-3					
Jul 1	Balance b/d	16,300			

5   From the information given, the amount of dividends paid in 20-3 is £600,000 (being the proposed dividend for 20-2). The proposed dividends for 20-3 of £500,000 will be shown in the cash flow statement for 20-4.

6.10 Task 1

GEORGE LIMITED	
Reconciliation of profit from operations to net cash flow from operating activities	
	£000
Profit from operations	237
Adjustments for:	
Depreciation for year	275
Gain on sale of non-current assets	(2)
Increase in inventories (210–200)	(10)
Increase in trade receivables (390–250)	(140)
Decrease in trade payables (150–160)	(10)
Cash generated from operations	350
Interest paid	(20)
Income taxes paid	(21)
Net cash (used in)/from operating activities	309

Task 2

GEORGE LIMITED		
CASH FLOW STATEMENT FOR THE YEAR ENDED 31 MARCH 20-5		
	£000	*£000*
Net cash (used in)/from operating activities		309
Cash flows from investing activities		
Purchase of non-current assets	(110)	
Proceeds from sale of non-current assets[1]	7	
Net cash (used in)/from investing activities		(103)
Cash flows from financing activities		
Proceeds from issue of share capital (40–25)	15	
Proceeds from long-term borrowings (200-100)	100	
Repayment of debentures	(500)	
Dividends paid	(30)	
Net cash (used in)/from financing activities		(415)
Net increase/(decrease) in cash and cash equivalents		(209)
Cash and cash equivalents at beginning of year		10
Cash and cash equivalents at end of year		(199)

Working note

1 **Proceeds from sale of non-current assets**

Non-current Assets

	£		£
Non-current assets (cost)	10,000	Accumulated depreciation	5,000
Gain on sale	2,000	Proceeds (bal fig)	7,000
	12,000		12,000

CHAPTER 7: INTERPRETATION OF FINANCIAL STATEMENTS

7.1 (d)

7.2 (c)

7.3 (d)

7.4 (a)

7.5 1 (b)
       2 (d)
       3 (b)
       4 (a)
       5 (c)

7.6 **Task 1**

		Hanadi PLC	Abeer PLC
(a)	Gross profit %		
	$\dfrac{\text{Gross profit} \times 100}{\text{Revenue}}$	$\dfrac{250 \times 100}{350} = 71\%$	$\dfrac{200 \times 100}{300} = 67\%$
(b)	Net profit %		
	$\dfrac{\text{Profit from operations} \times 100}{\text{Revenue}}$	$\dfrac{150 \times 100}{350} = 43\%$	$\dfrac{150 \times 100}{300} = 50\%$
(c)	ROCE		
	$\dfrac{\text{Profit from operations} \times 100}{\text{Capital employed}}$	$\dfrac{150 \times 100}{470} = 32\%$	$\dfrac{150 \times 100}{350} = 43\%$
(d)	Current ratio		
	$\dfrac{\text{Current assets}}{\text{Current liabilities}}$	$\dfrac{220}{215} = 1{:}1$	$\dfrac{160}{135} = 1.2{:}1$
(e)	Acid test ratio		
	$\dfrac{\text{Current assets} - \text{inventories}}{\text{Current liabilities}}$	$\dfrac{220 - 110}{215} = 0.5{:}1$	$\dfrac{160 - 70}{135} = 0.7{:}1$

Task 2

	Hanadi plc	**Abeer plc**
Gross profit	Better performance	
	More revenue at a higher margin	
Net profit		Better performance
		More control over costs and expenses
ROCE		Both results are good but Abeer has a higher return; it is utilising its capital far more effectively than Hanadi.
Current ratio		Both are on the low side but Abeer has a better margin from which to pay off debt.
Acid test ratio		Again both are on the low side but Abeer has more cash in the business to pay off short-term debt whereas Hanadi appears to have too much cash tied up in inventories.

Conclusion: Abeer plc is more attractive than Hanadi plc from an investment point of view.

7.7 Accounting ratios need to be analysed and interpreted and not just listed as sets of numbers. Ideally they need to be compared with the previous year's figures and wherever possible, with similar companies to evaluate and highlight trends.

But there are dangers in relying on the numbers without first looking behind the figures:

1 Financial statements present only an overall picture of the company, and the balance sheet is only a snapshot of the company at a particular moment in time. The balance sheet may not actually be representative of the company as a whole, eg the accounting year-end of a business with seasonal trade is typically timed for when the business is least busy.

2 The problem with accounting policy is no more evident than with ratio analysis. Depreciation and inventory valuation, for example, involve different methods of valuation and the choice of method can lead to distortion in comparative figures.

3 Larger businesses frequently aggregate operations and this can make comparison of individual areas of activity difficult.

4 Comparisons can be difficult between a company which finances non-current assets by renting them (thus showing the rental as an expense with no asset on the balance sheet) and a company which purchases its assets outright and then depreciates them over the anticipated working life.

5 Ratios should be open to interpretation, as what is good for one company may not be suitable for another. For example it is generally accepted than the ideal current ratio is 2:1. However retailers such as supermarkets can in fact work on a much lower margin because of rapid inventory turnover and their predominantly cash revenues (ie few receivables).

6   Whilst in principle inter-firm comparisons are very worthwhile, there may be considerable differences between companies in the same industry. They may, for example, vary in size and in application of accounting policies.

In conclusion, ratios are a very useful way of investigating the performance of a company over a number of years or comparing one company with a similar one. However ratios cannot be relied upon as the absolute answer and should not be used as absolute standards of performance. Care and consideration needs to be given to points 1-6 above.

7.8

REPORT

To: Jake Matease

From: A Student

Subject: Interpretation of financial statements

Date: December 20-1

This report has been prepared to assist in the interpretation of the financial statements of Fauve Limited. It considers the profitability and return on capital of the business for 20-0 and 20-1.

(a)   Calculation of the ratios

	20-1	20-0
Return on capital employed	$\dfrac{1,251}{8,430} = 14.8\%$	$\dfrac{624}{5,405} = 11.5\%$
Net profit percentage	$\dfrac{1,251}{4,315} = 29\%$	$\dfrac{624}{2,973} = 21\%$
Gross profit percentage	$\dfrac{2,805}{4,315} = 65\%$	$\dfrac{1,784}{2,973} = 60\%$
Asset turnover	$\dfrac{4,315}{8,430} = 0.51$	$\dfrac{2,973}{5,405} = 0.55$

(b)   Explanation and comment

Return on capital employed

- This ratio shows in percentage terms how much profit is being generated by the capital employed in the company.
- The company is showing a higher return on capital employed in 20-1 compared to 20-0 and hence is generating more profit per £ of capital employed in the company.

Net profit percentage

- This ratio shows in percentage terms how much profit from operations is being generated from revenue.
- The ratio has increased over the two years.
- This could be explained either by an increase in the gross profit margin or by a decrease in expenses, or both.

- It is also the case that the percentage of expenses to revenue has decreased from 39% in 20-0 to 36% in 20-1.

Gross profit ratio

- This ratio shows in percentage terms how much gross profit is being generated by the revenue of the company and thus indicates the gross profit margin on revenue.
- The ratio has improved over the two years with an increase in the percentage from 60% to 65%.
- The company is increasing its revenue without significantly cutting its margins.
- This may be due to increasing its selling price or reducing the cost of sales or both.

Asset turnover

- This ratio shows how efficient the company is in generating revenue from the available capital employed/net assets.
- The ratio has deteriorated between the two years – less revenue is being generated from the available capital employed/net assets in 20-1 than in 20-0.
- Considerable new investment has been made in non-current assets and current assets in 20-1 and it may be that the investment has yet to yield the expected results.

(c)   Overall

The ratios show that the return on capital employed has improved in 20-1 and that the company is generating more profit from the capital employed/net assets. This is due to increased margins and to greater control over expenses, perhaps brought about by economies of scale. However, the efficiency in the use of assets has deteriorated in 20-1 and this has reduced the increase in return on capital employed. It may be that the increased investment in assets that has taken place in 20-1 has yet to yield benefits in terms of a proportionate increase in revenue and that the situation will improve when the assets are used to their full potential.

The dividends for 20-1 are more than those for 20-0; nevertheless, the dividends are well covered by profits – there may well be scope for increased dividends in the future.

Regards,

AAT Student

7.9

	Company A		Company B	
Return on capital employed	$\dfrac{200}{1,000}$	= 20%	$\dfrac{420}{2,800}$	= 15%
Net profit margin	$\dfrac{200}{800}$	= 25%	$\dfrac{420}{2,100}$	= 20%
Asset turnover	$\dfrac{800}{1,000}$	= 0.8:1	$\dfrac{2,100}{2,800}$	= 0.75:1

Other possible ratios:

Gross profit margin	$\dfrac{360}{800}$ = 45%		$\dfrac{1,050}{2,100}$ = 50%	
Expenses: revenue	$\dfrac{160}{800}$ = 20%		$\dfrac{630}{2,100}$ = 30%	

From the calculations we can see that Company A has both the highest return on capital employed and also the highest profit margin and asset turnover. It would, therefore, be the better company to target for takeover. However, the gross profit margin for Company B is, in fact, higher suggesting that the underlying business is more profitable. It is only because of the expenses of Company B in relation to revenue that it has a lower net profit margin. If Company B could be made more efficient in terms of expenses and utilisation of assets by the introduction of a new management team on takeover, then, given the more profitably underlying business, it might be worth considering as a target for takeover.

7.10

REPORT

To: **Finance Director, Rowan Healthcare plc**
From: **AAT Student**
Date: **3 December 20-8**
Re·   **Analysis of Patch Ltd's financial statements**

Introduction
The purpose of the report is to analyse the financial statements of Patch Ltd for 20-8 and 20-7 to determine whether to use the company as a supplier.

Calculation of Ratios
The following ratios for the company have been computed:

	20-8	Industry Average 20-8	20-7	Industry Average 20-7
Return on capital employed	$\dfrac{552}{5,334}$ = 10.3%	9.6%	$\dfrac{462}{5,790}$ = 8.0%	9.4%
Net profit percentage	$\dfrac{552}{2,300}$ = 24%	21.4%	$\dfrac{462}{2,100}$ = 22%	21.3%
Quick ratio/acid test	$\dfrac{523}{475}$ = 1.1:1	1.0:1	$\dfrac{418}{465}$ = 0.9:1	0.9:1
Gearing: Debt/Capital employed	$\dfrac{1,654}{5,334}$ = 31%	36%	$\dfrac{2,490}{5,790}$ = 43%	37%
or Debt/Equity	$\dfrac{1,654}{3,680}$ = 45%		$\dfrac{2,490}{3,300}$ = 75%	

Comment and Analysis

The overall profitability of the company has improved from 20-7 to 20-8. The return on capital employed has increased from 8% in 20-7 to 10.3% in 20-8. This means that the company is generating more profit from the available capital employed in 20-8 as compared with 20-7. The company was below average for the industry in 20-7, but has performed better than the average in 20-8. The net profit percentage has also improved. It increased from 22% in 20-7 to 24% in 20-8. This means that the company is generating more profit from revenue in 20-8 than in the previous year. In both years the company had a higher than average net profit percentage when compared against the industry average. From these ratios it would seem that the company is relatively more profitable in 20-8 as compared with 20-7 and that it now performs better than the average of the industry. This suggests that its long-term prospects for success are higher than the average of the industry.

The liquidity of the company has also improved in the year. The quick ratio shows how many current assets, excluding inventories, there are to meet the current liabilities and is often thought of as a better indicator of liquidity than the current ratio. The quick ratio in Patch Ltd has improved from 20-7 to 20-8. It has gone up from 0.9:1 to 1.1:1. This means that in 20-8 there were more than enough quick assets to meet current liabilities. Again, the quick ratio of Patch Ltd is better than the industry average in 20-8, and matched it in 20-7. We can conclude that Patch Ltd is more liquid than the average of the industry in 20–8.

There has been a considerable decline in the gearing of the company in 20-8 as compared with 20-7. In 20-7 the gearing ratio was 43% and this has fallen to 31% in 20-8. This means that the percentage of debt funding to equity funding has declined between the two years. High gearing ratios are often thought of as increasing the risk of the company in that, in times of profit decline, it becomes increasingly difficult for highly geared companies to meet the finance costs of debt, and in extreme cases the company could be forced into liquidation. The gearing ratio of Patch Ltd was above the industry average in 20-7, making it relatively more risky, in this respect, than the average of companies in the industry. However, the ratio in 20-8 is considerably less than the industry average and hence may now be considered less risky than the average. There is thus less of a risk from gearing in doing business with the company than the average of companies in the sector.

Conclusions

Overall, based solely on the information provided in the financial statements of the company, it is recommended that Rowan Healthcare should use Patch Ltd as a supplier. The company has increasing profitability and liquidity and a lower level of gearing in 20-8 than in 20-7. It also compares favourably with other companies in the same industry and seems to present a lower risk than the average of the sector.

CHAPTER 8: CONSOLIDATED ACCOUNTS

8.1 (b) 40% x £10,000

8.2 (c) 80% x £300,000 = £240,000; cost of investment £305,000

8.3 (a) 25% x £220,000

8.4 (b) 20% x £200,000 (profit after tax)

8.5 (b)

8.6 (d) £85,000 + (£40,000 − £10,000)

8.7   IFRS 3, *Business Combinations*, states that an acquirer is assumed to have control over another company when it owns more than 50 per cent of the voting shares of the acquiree.

Where there is less than 50 per cent ownership of voting shares, control can still be obtained if the acquirer has:

- power over more than 50 per cent of the voting rights of the other company as a result of an agreement with other investors.

- power to govern the financial and operating policies of the other company as a result of legislation or an agreement.

- power to appoint or remove the directors of the other company.

- power to cast the majority of votes at a board meeting of the other company.

8.8   **Phantom plc**

Calculation for Goodwill	*Equity £000*
Share capital	800
Share premium account	200
Revaluation reserve	700
Retained earnings	1,750
	3,450
Group share 80% x £3,450	2,760
Cost of acquisition	2,900
Goodwill on acquisition	140
Minority interest 20% x £3,450	690

8.9   **Ringer plc**

Consolidated Balance Sheet as at 30 April 20-3.

Non-current Assets	£000	£000
Goodwill	620	
Tangibles (6,000 + 1,900)	7,900	
		8,520
Current Assets		
Inventories (1,900 + 800)	2,700	
Trade receivables (1,500 + 500)	2,000	
Cash and cash equivalents (600 + 100)	700	
	5,400	

Equity

Called up share capital	2,000
Share premium account	1,000
Retained earnings	4,100
	7,100
Minority interest (40% x 2,300)	920
	8,020

Working notes

Ringer holding in Sterling	=	$\frac{600,000}{1,000,000}$	x 100	=	60%
Minority interest	=	$\frac{400,000}{1,000,000}$	x 100	=	40%

Revaluation	Debit Non-current Assets	£300,000
	Credit Revaluation reserve	£300,000

Goodwill

	Equity *100%* *£000*	*Group* *60%* *£000*	*Minority* *40%* *£000*
Share capital	1,000	600	400
Share premium	500	300	200
Revaluation	300	180	120
Retained earnings	500	300	200
Total	2,300	1,380	920
Price paid by Ringer		2,000	
Goodwill		620	

8.10   Consolidated Income Statement

	£000
Profit before taxation (25% x £420K)	105
Tax (25% x £120K)	(30)
Share of post-acquisition profits (25% x £300K)	75

Consolidated Balance Sheet

Goodwill	145
Share of net assets of trade investment (25% x £1,000K)	250
	395

Working Note: Goodwill on acquisition

	£000
Share of net assets at acquisition (£1,000K − £300K = £700K x 25%)	175
Cost of investment	320
Goodwill	145

8.11 Winston plc

Consolidated Balance Sheet as at 30 November 20-3

	£000	£000
Non-current Assets		
Goodwill (495 − 99)	396	
Tangibles (5,000 + 600)	5,600	
		5,996
Current Assets		
Inventories (150 + 30 − 5 unrealised profit)	175	
Trade receivables (80 + 35 − 10)	105	
Cash and cash equivalents (10 + 5)	15	
	295	
Current Liabilities		
Trade payables (160 + 120 − 10)	(270)	
Net Current Assets		25
		6,021
Equity		
Called up share capital		4,000
Retained earnings (1,980 + 90 − 5 − 99)		1,966
		5,966
Minority interest (10% x 550)		55
		6,021

Working notes:

■ Winston **holding** in Churchill = $\dfrac{360,000 \times 100}{400,000}$ = 90%

■ **Minority interest**   = $\dfrac{40,000 \times 100}{400,000}$ = 10%

■ **Goodwill**

	Equity 100% £000	Group 90% £000	Minority 10% £000
Share capital	400	360	40
Retained earnings	50	45	5
Total	450	405	45
Price paid by Winston		900	
Goodwill		495	

Impairment loss (2 years at 10% per year):

£495,000 x 10% x 2 years = £99,000 impairment loss debited to income statement

- **Consolidated retained earnings**

Holding Co retained earnings	1,980	
Post-acquisition profit	90	(£150,000 – £50,000 x 90%)
Unrealised profit on inventories	(5)	(£20,000 x 25% profit margin*)
Impairment loss on goodwill	(99)	
	1,966	

*Note: a profit mark-up of 33.3% is a profit margin of 25%

- **Minority Interest**

Share capital	40	(£400,000 x 10%)
Retained earnings	15	(£150,000 x 10%)
	55	

8.12   **TOM LIMITED AND SUBSIDIARIES**

Consolidated Income Statement for the year ended 31 December 20-2

Continuing Operations		£000
Revenue	800 + 400 + 300 – 20 – 80	1,400
Cost of sales*		(890)
Gross profit		510
Distribution costs	80 + 50 + 20	(150)
Administrative expenses	100 + 30 + 20	(150)
Profit from operations		210
Finance costs		–
Profit before tax		210
Tax		(68)
Profit for the year		142

8.13

PERRAN PLC

Consolidated Income Statement for the year ended 31 March 2006

Continuing Operations	£000
Revenue	45,900
Cost of sales	(23,090)
Gross profit	22,810
Distribution costs	(6,945)
Administrative expenses	(4,745)
Profit from operations	11,120
Finance costs	(2,020)
Profit before tax	9,100
Tax	(2,480)
Profit for the year	6,620
Attributable to:	
Equity holders of the parent	6,100
Minority interest	520
	6,620

Workings

All figures £000

- Revenue: £
  - Perran 36,450
  - Porth 10,200
  - Inter-company sale (750)
  - 45,900

- Cost of sales:
  - Perran cost of sales 18,210

Appendix:
photocopiable resources

These pages may be photocopied for student use. It is recommended that they are enlarged to A4 size.

These pages are also available for download from the Resources Section of www.osbornebooks.co.uk

The forms and formats include:

JOURNAL			
Date	Details	Debit £	Credit £

COMPANY INCOME STATEMENT

FOR THE YEAR ENDED ....

£000

Continuing Operations

Revenue

Cost of sales

Gross profit

Distribution costs

Administrative expenses

Profit/(loss) from operations

Finance costs

Profit/(loss) before tax

Tax

Profit/(loss) for the year from continuing operations

Discontinued Operations

Profit/(loss) for the year from discontinued operations

Profit for the year attributable to equity holders

STATEMENT OF RECOGNISED INCOME AND EXPENSE

FOR THE YEAR ENDED ....

£000

Gains/(losses) on revaluation of properties

Tax on items taken directly to equity

Net income recognised directly in equity

Transfers

Profit/(loss) for the year

Total recognised income and expense for the year

COMPANY BALANCE SHEET AS AT ....

£000

Non-current assets
Goodwill
Other intangible assets
Property, plant and equipment
Investments in subsidiaries
Investments in associates
_____
_____

Current assets
Inventories
Trade and other receivables
Cash and cash equivalents
_____
_____

Total assets
_____

Current liabilities
Trade and other payables
Tax liabilities
Bank overdrafts and loans
_____
_____

Net current assets
_____

Non-current liabilities
Bank loans
Long-term provisions
_____
_____

Total liabilities
_____

Net assets
_____

EQUITY
Share capital
Share premium account
Revaluation reserves
Retained earnings

Total equity
_____
_____

COMPANY CASH FLOW STATEMENT

FOR THE YEAR ENDED ....

	£000
NET CASH (USED IN)/FROM OPERATING ACTIVITIES	
INVESTING ACTIVITIES	
NET CASH (USED IN)/FROM INVESTING ACTIVITIES	———
FINANCING ACTIVITIES	
NET CASH (USED IN)/FROM FINANCING ACTIVITIES	———
NET INCREASE/(DECREASE) IN CASH AND CASH EQUIVALENTS	
CASH AND CASH EQUIVALENTS AT BEGINNING OF YEAR	
CASH AND CASH EQUIVALENTS AT END OF YEAR	———

CONSOLIDATED INCOME STATEMENT
FOR THE YEAR ENDED ....

£000

Continuing Operations

Revenue

Cost of sales

Gross profit

Distribution costs

Administrative expenses

Profit/(loss) from operations

Finance costs

Profit/(loss) before tax

Tax

Profit/(loss) for the year from continuing operations

Discontinued Operations

Profit/(loss) for the year from discontinued operations

Profit/(loss) for the year

Attributable to:

Equity holders of the parent

Minority interest

CONSOLIDATED STATEMENT OF RECOGNISED INCOME AND EXPENSE

FOR THE YEAR ENDED ....

£000

Gains/(losses) on revaluation of properties

Tax on items taken directly to equity

Net income recognised directly in equity

Transfers

Profit/(loss) for the year

Total recognised income and expense for the year

Attributable to:

Equity holders of the parent

Minority interest

CONSOLIDATED BALANCE SHEET AS AT ....

£000

Non-current assets
Goodwill
Other intangible assets
Property, plant and equipment
Investments in subsidiaries
Investments in associates
⎯⎯⎯
⎯⎯⎯

Current assets
Inventories
Trade and other receivables
Cash and cash equivalents
⎯⎯⎯

Non-current assets as held for sale
⎯⎯⎯
Total assets
⎯⎯⎯

Current liabilities
Trade and other payables
Tax liabilities
Bank overdrafts and loans
⎯⎯⎯
⎯⎯⎯

Net current assets
⎯⎯⎯

Non-current liabilities
Bank loans
Long-term provisions
⎯⎯⎯
⎯⎯⎯

Total liabilities
⎯⎯⎯

Net assets
⎯⎯⎯
▬▬▬

EQUITY
Share capital
Share premium account
Revaluation reserves
Retained earnings
⎯⎯⎯
Equity attributable to equity holders of the parent

Minority interest
⎯⎯⎯
Total equity
▬▬▬

REPORT
To: From: Subject: Date:

if required, continue on a separate sheet

Index of international accounting standards

International Financial Reporting Standards (IFRSs)

International Accounting Standards (IASs)

Note: gaps in the numbers represent standards that have been withdrawn.

Text index

for your notes

for your notes

for your notes

for your notes

for your notes

for your notes

for your notes